D1104671

# 100
## GREATEST
# AFRICAN AMERICANS

# 100
## GREATEST
## AFRICAN AMERICANS

**A BIOGRAPHICAL ENCYCLOPEDIA**

## MOLEFI KETE ASANTE

**Prometheus Books**

59 John Glenn Drive
Amherst, New York 14228-2197

Photo credits. With the exception of the photographs listed below, all photographs are used with the permission of Temple University's Urban Archives. Photographs of Crispus Attucks, Gwendolyn Brooks, John Henrik Clarke, Marcus Garvey, John H. Johnson, Dorie Miller, Garrett Morgan, Elijah Muhammad, and Madame C. J. Walker are used with the permission of the Association of Nubian Kemetic Heritage. Ralph Bunche's photograph is used with the permission of William Greaves Associates. Lorraine Hansberry's photograph is used with the permission of United Press International (UPI). Charles Houston's photograph is used with the permission of the Moorland-Spingarn Research Center at Howard University. Maulana Karenga's photograph is used with the permission of Tiamoyo Karenga. Toni Morrison's photograph is used with the permission of WNET/13. The painting of Harriet Tubman is used with the permission of the U.S. Postal Service. August Wilson's photograph is used with the permission of August Wilson. Oprah Winfrey's photograph is used with the permission of Harpo Productions, Inc. Tiger Woods's photograph is used with the permission of Allsport. The photographs/drawings of Guion Bluford, Mae Jemison, Colin Powell, Sojourner Truth, and Phillis Wheatley are in the public domain.

The drawings of Hank Aaron, Ira Aldridge, Muhammad Ali, Romare Bearden, Mary McLeod Bethune, Arna Bontemps, Blance K. Bruce, George Washington Carver, Kenneth B. Clark, John Coltrane, Bill Cosby, Alexander Crummell, Countee Cullen, Martin R. Delany, Paul Laurence Dunbar, Katherine Dunham, James Forten, Henry Highland Garnet, Prince Hall, Fannie Lou Hamer, Jack Johnson, Ernest Just, Martin Luther King Jr., Edmonia Lewis, Alain Locke, Elijah McCoy, Claude McKay, Oscar Micheaux, Rosa Parks, Hiram Revels, John Russwurm, Arturo Schomburg, Benjamin "Pop" Singleton, William Trotter, Kwame Ture, Henry McNeal Turner, Nat Turner, David Walker, and Daniel Hale Williams are the original renderings of artist Eric Rivers, and are used with his permission.

Margaret Jerrido of Temple University's Urban Archives went to great lengths to assist me in finding photographs. I am grateful to her and to the staff of the Urban Archives for their assistance.

Published 2002 by Prometheus Books

Inquiries should be addressed to
Prometheus Books, 59 John Glenn Drive, Amherst, New York 14228–2197
VOICE: 716–691–0133, ext. 207, FAX: 716–564–2711
WWW.PROMETHEUSBOOKS.COM

06 05 04 03 02    5 4 3 2 1

Library of Congress Cataloging-in-Publication Data

Asante, Molefi K., 1942–
    100 greatest African Americans : a biographical encyclopedia / Molefi Kete Asante.
        p. cm.
    Includes bibliographical references and index.
    ISBN 1-57392-963-8 (alk. paper)
    1. African Americans—Biography—Encyclopedias. I. Title: One hundred greatest African Americans. II. Title.
E185.96 .A83 2002
920'.009296073—dc21

                                                                                    2002018993

Printed in Canada on acid-free paper

For

**MOLEFI KHUMALO ASANTE**

# CONTENTS

# ACKNOWLEDGMENTS

A book such as this is meant to provide the reader with access to information about the greatest men and women who have helped to make African American history. Of course, no work like this is a product of one mind; this book derives its strength from a collective effort and I am pleased that others have aided me in data collection, research, and editing.

I owe a special thanks to several people who assisted me in producing this book. I am grateful to Nzingha Gaffin, Suzuko Morikawa, and Mario Root for the research they did for this book. I could not have achieved the purpose of this volume without their willingness to help. It is impossible to forget the enthusiasm with which my project was greeted by the staff of Temple University's Urban Archives. I particularly want to thank the director, Margaret Jerrido, and Evan Towle of the photographic department for their assistance. Eric Rivers produced the exceptional illustrations. I remain grateful for his prodigious work.

Good books are most often due to great editors. Therefore, I also want to personally thank Linda Regan, my editor, who has guided me through the completion of this volume. She has been wise, judicious, diligent, and consistent as an editor. It is rare to find a brilliant editor; she has been tough but encouraging. Her faith in my ability to pull this off has given me inspiration along the way. I only hope that I have satisfied her high goals for this book.

My agent, Jay Acton of Spartan Literary Agency, must be credited with urging me to undertake this work in the midst of many other obligations. I am pleased that he understood as much as he did about the need for such a book. I appreciate his advice and counsel. As most readers will appreciate, while others have assisted me in this work, they bear no responsibility for its shortcomings. I have, with the only skills I possess, attempted to carry out my objectives with the best intentions. Finally, I want to give my warmest thanks to Ana Yenenga, whose patience, constructive criticism, and organizational ability are without peer. She has granted me the benefit of her generous gifts.

# INTRODUCTION

In *100 Greatest African Americans* I am attempting to make accessible the history of some of the most important American personalities. To write a complete history of African Americans, something I have previously done, is a major undertaking, but to distill the greatest people in African American history to a finite number is an even more difficult task. To limit the number to one hundred, a reasonable number, is quite challenging. However, few people have ever been blessed with so many wonderful possibilities for greatness as African Americans.

In 1619, when Africans first came ashore in the swampy Chesapeake region of Virginia, the conditions they confronted created the opportunity for individuals to distinguish themselves. Staying alive and sane in a society that increasingly saw Africans as inferior to whites was itself a monumental undertaking. Whether seeking to raise a family, to build a farm, to escape bondage, to fight against injustice, or to demonstrate intelligence and knowledge, the African people faced the future with courage, conviction, determination, and, most of all, optimism. These have remained the qualities of a people bent on greatness.

Often we are exposed to the most popular or the most famous African Americans, and on occasion there is a book about influential African Americans. In all of these cases we are dealing with criteria quite different from those governing *100 Greatest African Americans*. This book is not about the African Americans who have the largest popular following or the ones who sell the most CDs or who establish the best records in athletics. To do this would cause me to rely too heavily on contemporary individuals whose reputations and popularity, because of the role of the media, might be far more extensive than someone who lived during the eighteenth century. The power of the media to make some people household names should not be mistaken for great-

ness. I have relied upon neither prominence, political office, organizational leadership, wealth, nor "firsts" to create this list. Yet
it is true that many of the greatest have often been the most
prominent—political office holders, organizational or business
leaders, or the first to achieve a certain status. I have developed
criteria that will allow the reader to understand how I came to
include the individuals on my list.

## A POINT OF HISTORICAL REFERENCE

When Carter G. Woodson and Charles Wesley wrote their
famous book *The Negro in Our History* in the 1940s, it was easy
to think of the African's presence in the United States as merely
an insertion into the European story in America. According to
this view, the colonial period, the Manifest Destiny, the westward expansion, the Civil War, and other themes and events
determined not just the story of white Americans but of blacks
as well. Fitting Africans into the grand American story was considered writing "African American history." However, it has
become clearer to historians over the years that Africans were
creating their own stories in America. Consequently, the same
individuals who may have been important to whites may not
have been considered significant by African people who did not
become American citizens—hence, African Americans—until
after the Civil War.

The route of the African to American citizenship began deep in
the continent of Africa. When European slave ships came to the
coast of Africa and began the infamous capture and imprisonment
of Africans for the eventual voyage to America, they interrupted the
natural developments of ancient civilizations. Millions of Africans
were uprooted and transported across the ocean to the Americas,
North and South, and the pain, suffering, misery, sadness, and
agony caused by such disruption of society created a bitter cleavage
in the histories of Africans and Europeans in the Americas. Such
was the origin of African American history in North America.

The Dutch ship that brought twenty Africans to Jamestown, Virginia, in 1619 became a fixture in African history in the Americas because it was the first time that Africans were introduced into the English colonies. The Spaniards and the Portuguese had for one hundred years used African labor in their colonies by the time Africans entered Virginia. But from this isolated and lonely beginning on the James River a nation of Africans grew.

Initially Africans were indentured servants, as were many of the whites, but within a generation whites, fearing competition, had passed laws that made the indenture of Africans permanent and also forbade the enslavement of whites. Subsequent laws curtailed all the freedoms that Africans had enjoyed up to this point in time and made it impossible for Africans to ever consider liberation from enslavement in their lifetimes.

The sting of enslavement, with its many indecencies and violences, would not end until after the Civil War. More than 186,000 Africans, men and women, fought in the Civil War. They were eager to see the victory of the Union because that meant they would see freedom. Africans fought for their liberation. Out of a population of little more than 3 million, the fighting men and women gave good account of themselves.

When General Lee surrendered to General Grant at Appomattox on April 8, 1865, it meant the end of the enslavement. The Thirteenth Amendment legally freed Africans—but little did they know that they would still have a long struggle ahead of them. Proposals had been made to give each freed family "forty acres and a mule" in order to assure African loyalty to the new country. However, instead of giving Africans land, the Union land policy allowed Northern whites to lease Southern plantations under the guise of providing support for federal troops stationed in the South. These Northern adventurers would then require the freed Africans to sign labor agreements that amounted to a new form of slavery. When Andrew Johnson became president, Africans lost all hope that they would receive land. The aim of the Johnson presidency was to restore white plantation owners to their lands as fast as he could in order to

remain on peaceful terms with the South. Although our African
ancestors were granted citizenship by the Fourteenth Amendment to the Constitution of the United States, it was a citizenship
that proved to be second-class. Segregation ruled the land and
discrimination was pervasive. When the Fifteenth Amendment
was approved, allowing African men to vote, the anger of the
white racists reached a boiling point and the aftermath of
African Americans voting during the Reconstruction (1865–
1877) was a white backlash that produced the Ku Klux Klan and
other white supremacy groups.

The entire history of the twentieth century was one of
protests and demonstrations. Those who became great in the
minds of the African American community were those who best
exemplified the characteristics of intrepidity, dignity, creativity,
determination, and pride in the face of the most intransigent
hatred of the African people. They were our heroes. Of course,
the twentieth-century heroes are modeled after those in every
other century of American history. Each century, from the sev-
enteenth to the twenty-first, would require certain attributes and
traits that reflected on the best interests of the African people at
a particular moment in history.

The litany of African American achievements could extend ad
infinitum. Suffice it to say that a people who had experienced the
longest and most cruel treatment under an oppressor in history
made major contributions to science, art, literature, military sciences and martial arts, dance, music, education, business, theology,
oratory, poetry, sports, entertainment, engineering, construction,
and religion. Canvassing the history of a people with such a wide
range of contributions and achievements means that one must
examine character as well as activities in order to gain a true picture of the magnitude of the personalities considered the greatest.

# SELECTING THE 100
# GREATEST AFRICAN AMERICANS

It is rare in history for any individual, out of the relative obscurity of his or her birth, to carve out a persona that transcends his own life. It is rarer still for an individual to be considered among the greatest within a community comprised of thousands of active and creative personalities. I have used five overarching criteria to develop my list of the 100 greatest African Americans. They include: (1) significance in the general movement of the African American people toward full equality in the American social and political system; (2) self-sacrifice and the undertaking of risk for the collective good; (3) unusual will and determination in face of the greatest danger and against the most stubborn odds; (4) a consistent posture toward the social, cultural, and economic uplifting of African American people; and (5) personal achievement that calls attention to the capability and genius of the African American people. Using these criteria allowed me to choose individuals who crossed various disciplines and communities of interest. Furthermore, the criteria were meant to provide a more balanced array of requirements for the people chosen, rather than, say, criteria that included only popularity, media attention, or public presence. Of course, I recognize that different observers might find some entries debatable, but I believe that the criteria I have outlined will hold in nearly all cases.

There are certainly other approaches to such a book, but I developed my criteria against the long backdrop of the historic efforts of African Americans to discover zones of liberation, equality, freedom, fairness, justice, and honor within the American society. This means that I was particularly interested in those individuals who are considered "the greatest" by the general will of the African American people, and these tended to be those persons who have achieved in light of the criteria outlined above. By employing these criteria, my list relies on my interpretation of the general will of the African American people as represented in the literature and reflected by the informed judgment of scholars. For this reason I have included an extensive bibliography at the end of the book. Since the community is quite diverse and complex, different criteria would have rendered some other type of list of individuals. Had I been interested only in the 100 greatest intellectuals, I might have added contemporaries such as Charles Ogletree, Cornel West, Asa Hilliard, St. Clair Drake, Houston Baker, Manning Marable, Henry Louis Gates, or Darlene Hines. Had I wanted to name the 100 greatest administrators of higher-educational institutions, I might have included H. Patrick Swygert or Ruth Simmons. One could think of preachers such as Jeremiah Wright, Gardner Taylor, Frank Reed, George Stallings, or T. D. Jakes, with charisma far greater than ordinary individuals, as among the greatest African Americans. Certainly, Bobby Seale, Fred Gray, Cecil B. Moore, and Ella Baker could be on a list for courage and organizational genius. A list of the 100 greatest athletes would have yielded Bill Russell, Oscar Robertson, Venus Williams, Julius Erving, Michael Jordan, Jackie Joyner-Kersee, Allen Iverson, and Jim Brown. One could identify a list of the 100 greatest scientists that would include Benjamin Carson or Linda Jackson. And, of course, a list of 100 richest African Americans would have yielded individuals such as Robert Johnson, founder of BET, or Eileen Norton, founder of Norton Utilities. But the pursuit of money alone has never constituted greatness in the African American experience; it has been more what people do in terms of the broad struggles for justice and equality that matters to us. Therefore, one will discover on the list of the 100 greatest many individuals who are wealthy, but their wealth is only secondary to their other achievements.

It is useful to remember that all such books are the subjective opinions of their authors. I have tried to provide the kind of criteria that will allow the reader to make a personal judgment about the individuals chosen. As the creator of the first doctorate program in African American Studies, I have had the unique advantage of calling upon a few of my former graduate students for their assessments. They are now all professors in their own right at various universities and colleges around the world, and my poll of them, using the above criteria, has helped me to isolate my list of the 100 greatest African Americans.

Let me briefly discuss the pitfalls of such a book. It is easy to fall into the trap of writing about twentieth-century individuals because their biographies are easily acquired. The American society produces an enormous amount of information about entertainers, musicians, and athletes, and one could quite simply fall into the cult of the recently exposed. This would mean that the 100 greatest African Americans would be the 100 most popular African Americans in history. We are fortunate to have the long window of history from which we can peer into the past while standing here in the present and speculating about the future.

This list of the 100 greatest African Americans is not ranked. There is almost no way that such a list could be adequately and scientifically ranked for greatness, so I have listed them in alphabetical order. What one comes to understand is that greatness is inherent in the quality of the lives lived, in the nature of the challenges faced, and the length of the memory of those still alive. Some may have been considered great while they lived, but when their age passed, they were forgotten by succeeding generations. Some may have been great for a season, but in the weeding-out of men and women that always occurs at the hands of historians, they were left behind. Others may blossom like flowers in some far-off corner in some insignificant town and yet in time become the greatest individual among a people. So it is not possible to rank these individuals. How does one rank a Harriet Tubman, a Marcus Garvey, a Martin Luther King Jr., a Frederick Douglass, a Booker T. Washington, or a Fannie Lou Hamer? You don't, because you cannot. They are certainly, one could say, in the pantheon of the greatest—but so are all of the individuals that I have included in this book.

# THE 100 GREATEST IN
## ALPHABETICAL ORDER

# HANK
# AARON

1934–

**H**ank Aaron's greatness rests on his using his home-run record to advance the cause of equality for African Americans. It was not simply the fact of his immense talent to hit home runs that gave him a place in the panoply of great African Americans, it was his insistence that racism had to be conquered that made him a hero to many people. Henry Louis Aaron was born in 1934 in Mobile, Alabama, the third of eight children of Herbert and Estella Aaron. As a young African American in Alabama, Aaron had the opportunity to see the famous teams and players of the old Negro League. He was very impressed as a young man when he watched the Mobile Black Bears, his hometown team, play against other outstanding teams. As a youngster Aaron wished to be out in center field with the fans shouting out his name, or at home plate preparing to knock the ball out of the field. The old Negro Baseball League teams inspired thousands of young men like Hank Aaron. It did not take Aaron long, however, to become one of those players. He played with the Pritchett Athletics, the Mobile Black Bears, and the Indianapolis Clowns. In 1952 Aaron was drafted to the major leagues to play shortstop in the Milwaukee Braves' farm system at Eau Claire, Wisconsin. He then played in Jacksonville, Florida. Two years after being drafted Aaron made it to the main team, the Milwaukee Braves. The Milwaukee Braves became the Atlanta Braves, and when Aaron retired he was given a front-office position with the Braves.

There are probably only two or three players in the history

of baseball in Aaron's league as a player. Aaron broke more batting records than any other player in baseball history during his twenty-three-year career. The records Aaron holds includes runs batted in (RBIs), 2,297; and he was a three-time Gold Glove winner in 1958, 1959, and 1960. However, Aaron's most historic accomplishment came on April 8, 1974. At the age of forty, he hit a 385-foot home run against the Los Angeles Dodgers, surpassing Babe Ruth's record of 714 career home runs. He ended his career with 755 home runs. This historical achievement was not universally praised. The most telling evidence of white racism came when Aaron received hundreds of letters and telegrams with racist messages. He was stunned and became a spokesman against racism. In retirement, Aaron has been very busy first as an Atlanta Braves vice president for player development; then, in 1989, as senior vice president. He has also served as corporate vice president of community relations for Turner Broadcasting Systems, Inc. (TBS), and as a member of the Sterling Committee of Morehouse College. To his credit, he has been actively involved in the African American and general community, founding the Hank Aaron Rookie League program. Hank Aaron was inducted into the National Baseball Hall of Fame in 1982.

# IRA
# ALDRIDGE
## 1805–1867

**M**ost authorities agree that Ira Aldridge was born in Belaire, Maryland, but the precise date is uncertain. Whatever the condition and place of his birth, he soon found his way to New York City, where he became one of the greatest Shakespearean actors of all time. An artist of genius is always a unique creature: He believes his place is in the vanguard and he believes in his ability to transform the historical consciousness of his audience through his artistic ability. Aldridge was such an artist.

Ira Aldridge earned international recognition as one of the nineteenth century's finest actors for his moving theatrical performances throughout England, Scotland, Ireland, Europe, and the United States. Aldridge saw limited theatrical opportunities in the United States and, after training at the African Free School in New York City, left the United States for Europe in 1824. Intent on pursuing an acting career, he studied drama at the University of Glasgow in Scotland for more than a year.

Aldridge's debut was on the London stage of the Royal Coburg Theater in 1825. He was an immediate success, winning praise as a Shakespearean actor, particularly in the role of Othello. He was the defining actor in that role for many years. Indeed, the actors who came after him declared him to have set the standard for acting that challenging role. He acted in many Shakespearean dramas during his life, but the London debut of Othello established his trademark role. He performed in the Theatre Royal in Brighton, England, and then went on to tour Eng-

25

land, Scotland, and Ireland for the next six years. Aldridge mastered various characters throughout his dramatic career and was cited by critics for his genius. His best-known roles were title roles in Thomas Southerne's *Oroonoko* and Thomas Norton's *The Slave*, and characters in Matthew Gregory Lewis's *The Castle Spectre*, Isaac Bickerstaff's *The Padlock*, and Edward Young's *The Revenge*.

Some authors have claimed that Ira Aldridge was the greatest actor of his time. He had an indefatigable love for the theater and believed that he could bring any audience to laughter or tears. His demonstration of the variety of human emotions on the stage led to his celebrity in England, and his fame spread across the British Isles and into Europe.

Aldridge later toured Germany and France performing Shakespearean tragedies, and was so successful during the 1852 tour that he was invited to play Othello at the prestigious Lyceum Theatre in London. He was offered the same role by the Haymarket Theatre in 1865.

Aldridge died of a respiratory illness while on tour in Poland in 1867. But Aldridge had done more than any other African American to establish a distinctive tradition in the theater by the time of his death. His great booming voice, charisma, personality, and style made him the darling of British theater and the most important African American stage performer in Britain until the rise of Paul Robeson in the twentieth century.

# MUHAMMAD
# ALI
1942–

**P**rizefighting is considered by some to be the greatest test of manly skills. Perhaps the most exciting fighter of the twentieth century was born in Louisville, Kentucky, on July 17, 1942, as Cassius Marcellus Clay Jr. He was the son of a sign painter and a domestic, Marcellus Clay and Odessa Grady Clay. They knew that their son would become a good boxer because when he was twelve he expressed a desire to "whup someone" who had stolen his new bicycle. Steering Clay's anger at the loss of his bicycle into the gymnasium, Joe Martin, a Louisville policeman, directed him toward boxing. The young Muhammad Ali was a dedicated amateur boxer, appearing in 108 bouts in just five years, from 1955 to 1960. Along the way he won six Kentucky Golden Gloves titles, two national Amateur Athletic Union (AAU) championships, and two National Golden Gloves crowns. Finally, in the 1960 Summer Olympic Games in Rome, Italy, he won the gold medal in the light heavyweight division. By the time he was twenty-one years of age he was the world's heavyweight champion and one of the most famous people in the world. His career was explosive and stunning. His fights were international events infused with the magnetism of his personality. He won fight after fight, almost as if it was his will to win at any time. During his early years in the boxing ring he compiled a glorious record that would endear him to his fans and engender fear in his opponents. However, nothing would erase the bitterness he felt after returning to Louisville—having won the gold medal for the United States in the Olympic

Games—and a restaurant refused to serve him when he entered wearing the gold medal. He threw the medal in the Ohio River as an indication of his disgust with segregation and racism. He would later change his name to Muhammad Ali and make that name even more popular than Cassius Clay.

It might be said that the 1960s and 1970s, the era of Black Power and Black is Beautiful, could not have been complete without a Muhammad Ali. He came to symbolize so many of the attributes that African Americans considered necessary for the new era. He was self-motivated, brilliant at his game, outspoken, disciplined, and reliable. He won an Olympic gold medal in boxing and went on to capture the world heavyweight championship three different times. Ali also successfully defended his championship belts on nineteen occasions. As the dominant practitioner of the sport of boxing, he had no competition in skill and promotion during the height of his reign. He was the "greatest."

Perhaps the most dramatic event in boxing during his era was his match with the "invincible" Sonny Liston. On February 25, 1964, in Miami Beach, Florida, Ali challenged Liston for the heavyweight championship in a match many boxing experts believed Liston would easily win. History would prove otherwise. The confident and talkative young twenty-two-year-old from Louisville spent weeks building up the fight by telling reporters that he would win the contest. When Liston was unable to answer the bell in the seventh round of the bout, boxing had changed course and the reigning champion would go on to a coronation in the hearts of the people.

Ali defended his heavyweight championship nine times in two years, proving himself to be an active champion. In 1967 his title was revoked when he refused to serve in the United States military, citing his Islamic beliefs. He was given a five-year sentence, but was eventually released on appeal.

In the boxing ring, Ali brought his personality to bear on the sport. He was expressive, talkative, dramatic, and skillful. His style of boxing changed the game forever, making him a legend in his own time. Ali was an athlete who would become a celebrity.

It was his assertion that he would not hide or conceal his racial pride, his religious beliefs, or his confidence in his boxing skill that made him a hero among African Americans—and many others who admired his sense of identity and dignity. But the same assertion caused others to hate him and to deride him for interjecting his personality into the "business" of boxing. Ali set the standard for boxers and other athletes because he refused to allow his celebrity to interfere with his love of his culture and his people. Indeed, every opportunity he got he celebrated the culture, becoming one of the icons in the halls of African American greatness. He converted to Islam when it was less popular among the masses of American people but when the power of the Muslims, in the tradition of Elijah Muhammad and Malcolm X, was at its most intense. Ali became, along with Malcolm X, the most significant follower of the Honorable Elijah Muhammad. This alienated some blacks and whites who felt that he should not be so outspoken about his religion. His reply was that he had no difficulty expressing his faith in a black man as his spiritual leader. Furthermore, he opposed the Vietnam War (1959–1975), claiming that "no Vietnamese has ever called me a nigger." Muhammad Ali was described in the 1970s as "the most recognizable human being on earth." By the time of his retirement in 1981, Ali was already a legend.

Great historical protagonists often have great opponents. Ali's career in the ring could not have been as majestic as it was without his grand battles with Joe Frazier, who handed Ali his first loss on March 8, 1971, but who lost the fifteen-round decision at the "Thrilla in Manila" in the Philippines on October 1, 1975. Nor could he have been considered great as a fighter if he had not fought against other giants of his time, such as George Foreman, who lost to Ali in Kinshasa, Congo, on October 30, 1974; or Larry Holmes, who punished Ali in a bruising fight before knocking him out in the eleventh round on October 2, 1980. The following year, the "greatest" retired from the ring. Muhammad Ali's prowess as a boxer was comprised of his quickness; knowledge of the ring; rapid use of his left jab to confuse an opponent; a sharp right-hand cross; rhythm in the ring, especially as he danced in and away from his opponents; the ability to take a punch; and cleverness and feigning hurt in order to wear down an opponent and then to pounce on him with lightning speed.

However, his greatness as a person was in his ability to rally the audiences to his cause, whether in or out of the ring. Recognition of his greatness has come from all corners of the world. He has been featured on postage stamps in Africa and celebrated by African Americans, Egyptians, Chinese, Brazilians, French, and English audiences. *Sports Illustrated* magazine ranked Ali first on its "Forty for the Ages" list. In 1987, the *Ring* magazine called him the greatest heavyweight champion of all time. Ali was inducted into the International Boxing Hall of Fame in 1990 and into the U.S. Olympic Hall of Fame in 1983. In 1995 the beautiful Muhammad Ali Museum opened in Louisville, Kentucky, and a hero was finally honored again in his hometown.

# RICHARD
# ALLEN
## 1760–1831

**C**hallenges are sometimes unexpected, and how one manages to confront them has tremendous repercussions in history. Sixteen years before the Declaration of Independence, Richard Allen was born in Philadelphia as an enslaved person. His challenges would not overwhelm him, but would propel him into the center of African American history as one of the greatest individuals to live among us.

Richard Allen's birth in 1760 was not auspicious. He grew up working for others but his intention was never to be enslaved in perpetuity, though he recognized that to be the plight of virtually every African in the country. When his Philadelphia slave owner, lawyer Benjamin Chew, sold Allen, his parents, and his three siblings to Stokeley Stugis, a plantation owner in Delaware, Richard Allen, not more than twenty years old, vowed to gain his freedom. He committed himself to the constant search for freedom, and when Sturgis agreed to free him if he could raise the equivalent of $2,000—in today's sum about $50,000—Allen leaped at the chance, not knowing how difficult it would be. Allen started in earnest to perform little jobs that would increase his savings, working long hours into the night, assisting whoever needed someone to work, thus demonstrating a desire for freedom. There was nothing in his early life as a wagon maker and woodcutter to commend him as one of the greatest African Americans. Perhaps the driving force in his life was persistence and a deep resentment of the superiority that whites reserved for themselves in colonial society. He did not like being a slave and

realized quite early that the only way he could overcome the barriers placed in his way was through his individual efforts. Soon
he was able to secure enough funds, keeping his wages secret and
away from his slave master, to purchase his and his brother's
freedom. Allen was quite aware of the precarious situation of an
enslaved person: literally everything that the person earned
belonged to the slave master. In finding Sturgis willing to allow
him to work for his freedom and that of his brother, Allen was
fortunate. When an African found a slave owner who was
willing to allow the slave to purchase himself, he was quite
pleased. Some slave masters would take the slave's money and
still not release him. Allen's freedom was purchased in 1786,
about six years after his agreement with Sturgis, and he immediately threw himself into the activities of Philadelphia as a free
man. Already he had begun to attend Methodist meetings and to
engage in the public debates around religion, and now he joined
more fully into those activities. By the time he purchased himself
he had already learned how to read and write by studying the
Bible. His piety brought him great attention, since many blacks
and whites believed that he was "called to preach" and this
inspired him to take leadership in the African American community. When he died in 1831, the same year of the Nat Turner
rebellion, he had written by his life's achievements a dramatic
episode in the history of African Americans.

When he converted to Methodism, one of the leading religious movements of the day, he took it on as a passionate believer
and began to teach his community the values of sobriety and
moral living. There was a strong charismatic magic in his presence. After all, he had been born into slavery and yet had lifted
himself from it by the power of his own work. Surely, in the
minds of black Philadelphians, Allen was an example of what
one could achieve by industry and steadfastness.

In 1787 Richard Allen was invited to preach at the large
Saint George's Methodist Episcopal Church in Philadelphia. This
was a white congregation that allowed some Africans to attend.
Soon, however, Allen's preaching and passion attracted great

numbers of African people, which alarmed the white member-ship. When the whites installed a balcony in the church to accommodate the Africans, Allen and Absalom Jones founded the Free African Society, a mutual aid organization. Allen remained a member of the Saint George's Methodist Episcopal church for a while longer, learning all he could about the Chris-tian religion. Soon an event would happen that changed forever the history of Africans in America.

In 1792 Absalom Jones came to the church and, along with some other members, chose to sit in the main sanctuary rather than the balcony. Several white trustees, after a big commotion, pushed and shoved Jones and the others out to the curb of the street. A walkout followed of all the black members seated in the balcony. It became increasingly clear that Africans would have to start their own church. In 1794 the Bethel African Church was founded in Philadelphia. The members of the Free African Society consecrated the church as a part of the Episcopal Church because of the Methodists' treatment of Africans, although Allen and Jones were committed to the doctrine of Methodism. Both Richard Allen and Absalom Jones were leaders in the church. Jones was the first priest and Allen was ordained the church's first deacon. Bethel African Church opened on April 9, 1794, in a renovated blacksmith's shop on land purchased by Richard Allen. In 1816 the various African churches united under the umbrella of the convention of African Methodists and named their organization the African Methodist Episcopal Church. Allen was elected bishop and remained the major leader of the church until his death in 1831. When visiting Mother Bethel Church in Philadelphia, one can sense the history that was made by Richard Allen. His tomb in the basement of the church reminds the visitors of the esteem in which he has been held by African Americans through the centuries.

# MARIAN
# ANDERSON
## 1897–1993

**M**arian Anderson was born in Philadelphia, Pennsylvania, in 1897. Her parents had two other daughters after Marian. Both John Berkeley Anderson and his wife, Anna D. Anderson, worked to make a good life for their children. John Berkeley was a vendor of coal and ice, selling coal in the winter and ice during the summer months. His wife was a teacher and a launderer. She took in laundry to help the family meet its expenses. Although the family was on the verge of poverty, Marian's family was well fed and cared for during the life of her father. Unfortunately, when she was twelve years old, her father was injured on the job and died.

Marian was clearly talented as a child. She was singing in her father's church, Union Baptist, when she was six years old, and soon the church members dubbed her the "Baby Contralto." She taught herself to play the piano, and by the time she was thirteen she could accompany herself in concerts. She also joined the senior choir of the church. To earn money for the fatherless family, she began to sing professionally in high school and toured churches to sing. Graduating from South Philadelphia School for Girls in 1921, she earned enough to help her family purchase a house. But by 1924 she had experienced bitter criticism. She performed in a concert at Town Hall in New York City, and the poor reviews of her singing caused her such great anguish she stopped singing for several months. Resuming her career in 1925, she won the opportunity to appear at Lewisohn Stadium with the New York Philharmonic Orchestra. The next ten years saw her travel to Europe for study and tours. She increased the songs in her repertoire to more than one hundred. Increasing her diversity as well as the range of her voice, she was able to make an astounding impact on her audiences.

One of the great performing halls in 1939 was the Daughters of the American Revolution's (DAR) Constitution Hall in Washington, D.C. Most performers would have given their last drop of blood to perform there. The DAR came straight out and said that they were denying Marian Anderson the right to sing at Constitution Hall because she was an African American. Eleanor Roosevelt, wife of President Franklin D. Roosevelt and a devoted admirer of the singing of Marian Anderson, resigned from the DAR in protest.

Secretary of the Interior Harold Ickes, angered over the actions of the DAR in denying Anderson the right to sing, arranged an open-air concert at the Lincoln Memorial on Easter Sunday. Seventy-five thousand people attended the performance. Having reached international stature as one of the greatest voices of her times, Marian Anderson was invited to perform at the Metropolitan Opera House in New York. In 1955 Anderson became the first African American to perform at the famous hall, singing the role of Ulrica in the composition of Italian operatic composer Giuseppe Verde's *Un Ballo in Maschera* (A Masked Ball).

In 1958, President Dwight D. Eisenhower appointed Marian Anderson to the United States delegation to the United Nations, where she spoke on behalf of African independence. Given the opportunity to state the case of African people, she eloquently spoke on behalf of the liberation of the continent of her cultural origin. She retired in 1965 and spent the rest of her time on her farm in Danbury, Connecticut, which she and her husband, Orpheus Hodge Fisher, purchased after their marriage in 1943. Credited with bringing fame to African American music, Anderson received numerous awards, including the Spingarn Medal in 1939, the highest award given by the National Association for the Advancement of Colored People (NAACP), for her contribution to African American freedom and transracial cooperation. She was honored and feted at numerous gatherings of performers, artists, and scholars. She sang at the inauguration of Eisenhower and, in a poignant counterpoint to 1939, Anderson performed once more from the Lincoln Memorial, as part of the March on Washington in 1963. By 1977 she was such a venerable star of the American performing stage that President Jimmy Carter presented her with a congressional gold medal bearing her profile.

# MAYA
# ANGELOU

1928–

Commitment to the authentic artistic traditions of one's people is one of the more serious elements of greatness. Maya Angelou was born Marguerite Johnson in St. Louis, Missouri, on April 4, 1928. She has become an internationally acclaimed writer, actor, and poet. Her poem "On the Pulse of the Morning," read by herself, was the featured work at the 1993 inauguration of President William Jefferson Clinton. Her name is a combination of her childhood nickname, "Maya," and "Angelos," the name of her first husband.

Soon after her birth her family moved to California, and when she was three years old her parents divorced and she was sent to live with her paternal grandmother in Stamps, Arkansas. She returned to California when she was a teenager and finished high school in San Francisco. Always a lover of drama and dance, she found time to take courses in the arts.

While still in high school, she became San Francisco's first female streetcar conductor. According to her autobiography, she gave birth to her only child, Guy Johnson, when she was sixteen years of age. She soon found herself scrambling to support her son, taking on a variety of jobs, including serving as a madam for two prostitutes.

Maya Angelou became a professional dancer in her twenties and made a tour of Europe and Africa in *Porgy and Bess* in 1954. She worked for the Southern Christian Leadership Conference from 1960 to 1961 as the coordinator of activities in the north. Her civil rights credentials were based on a strong devotion to the African American quest for liberation and freedom. She moved to Africa in 1961 and spent five years working in Ghana and Egypt as a journalist and university professor teaching dance and journalism. When she arrived in the United States in 1966, she joined the Harlem Writers Guild and was soon asked by a Random House editor to write her life story. In 1970 this story became the best-seller *I Know Why the Caged Bird Sings*.

Maya Angelou's published works have included poetry, autobiographical essays, and screenplays, but she is best known for her autobiographical works, which have made her a major literary figure in the African American community. In 1971 Angelou's first published book of poetry, *Just Give Me a Cool Drink of Water 'fore I Diiie*, was nominated for a Pulitzer prize. Five additional volumes of poetry have been published by Angelou. The prose autobiographical works are *Gather Together in My Name* (1974), *Singin' and Swingin' and Gettin' Merry Like Christmas* (1976), *The Heart of a Woman* (1981), and *All God's Children Need Traveling Shoes* (1986). She published *Wouldn't Take Nothing for My Journey Now*, a collection of essays, and "On the Pulse of Morning," the poem she read at President Clinton's inauguration.

Angelou has had a distinguished career in film and television as well. The 1971 *Georgia, Georgia* was the first motion picture screenplay by a black woman ever to be made into a film. She was nominated for a Tony Award in 1973 for her performance in *Look Away*. In 1977 she was nominated for an Emmy Award for her performance in *Roots*. Angelou is Reynolds Professor of American Studies at Wake Forest University in Winston-Salem, North Carolina. She has had a powerful love for the African American culture and often speaks of herself as a pathfinder and road builder for those who will come after her, because she has benefited from those who came before her. Angelou's greatness resides in her humility and willingness to share what she has learned and what talents she has been given.

# ARTHUR
# ASHE

1943–1993

**A**rthur Robert Ashe Jr. was born on July 10, 1943, in Richmond, Virginia. He would use his athletic prowess to gain access to a public voice in order to speak out against injustices in society. Like Jackie Robinson, Jesse Owens, Muhammad Ali, and Hank Aaron, Ashe believed that he should use his celebrity to call attention to the discrimination against African Americans. Ashe rose to become the top-ranked tennis player in the world in 1975. He became a vocal critic of racial bigotry, and later wrote a book on African American sports.

Arthur Ashe's parents, Mattie and Arthur Robert Ashe Sr., started him playing tennis under the guidance of the legendary African American Dr. Walter Johnson, at the young age of ten. Under Johnson's tutelage, he captured three American Tennis Association (ATA) boys' championships. He became the first African American junior to be ranked by the United States Lawn Tennis Association (USLTA).

His life was one of mission. He sought to be the best tennis player he could be, and in three years, 1960 to 1963, he won three ATA men's singles titles, was selected as the first African American to serve on the U.S. Junior Davis Cup team, and became the first African American to win a USLTA national title in the south. Ashe's achievements were phenomenal at the time and earned him a full scholarship to the University of California at Los Angeles, which he attended from 1961 to 1966, earning a bachelor's degree in business administration. At UCLA, Ashe won the U.S. intercollegiate singles championship, which catapulted UCLA through his leadership into winning the National Collegiate Athletic Association (NCAA) team championship.

After Ashe left UCLA he played in the Davis Cup, losing both of his matches, and sustained defeat as part of the U.S. national team against Spain, Brazil, and Ecuador. This was a great disappointment for the competitive Ashe. He recommitted himself to his training regimen, recovered his will to win, and in 1968 he won the U.S. Open during the first year that it was opened to amateurs. He quickly turned professional in 1969.

During an eleven-year career, Arthur Ashe played in more than three hundred tournaments. He won fifty-one tournaments, including victories in the 1970 Australian Open and the 1975 Wimbledon. By 1975 he was ranked the top player in the world.

Arthur Ashe met with several crises in his life. A life-threatening heart condition forced him to retire in 1980. Although he continued to serve as the nonplaying captain of that year's U.S. Davis Cup team, his career was effectively over. However, in 1985 he became the second African American, after Althea Gibson in 1971, to be inducted into the International Tennis Hall of Fame.

An intellectual as well as an athlete, Arthur Ashe wrote a three-volume study entitled *A Hard Road to Glory: A History of the African-American Athlete* (1988). He gave lectures against racism in the United States and South Africa, championing the rights of the oppressed, and especially encouraging African American youth to enter tennis, a sport that was virtually all white.

Ashe's announcement in 1992 that he had contracted the human immunodeficiency virus (HIV), from a blood transfusion during one of his two heart bypass operations, came as tragic news. He became an active and aggressive campaigner to get increased funding to study the disease. On February 6, 1993, Arthur Robert Ashe Jr., experiencing complications from AIDS, died in New York. Yet the legacy of this incredibly gifted individual transcended his death, and the numerous tennis clubs and competitions named for him suggest that his work as a campaigner against all forms of discrimination, and his talent as an athlete, will live for generations to come.

# CRISPUS
# ATTUCKS
1723–1770

**C**anonization demands, it would appear, sacrifice, intelligence, will, courage, and a national spirit. Crispus Attucks, a seaman—strong, courageous, and forceful—met his death on the evening of March 5, 1770, never knowing that he would set in motion the events leading to the Declaration of Independence on July 4, 1776. He had been born into slavery in 1723 in Framingham, Massachusetts, and was probably owned by one Deacon William Brown. One of the characteristics of greatness in the African population of America has been the utter hatred of bondage, the passionate love of liberty, and the determination to see fairness in human relations. Attucks had these feelings, and when he was nearly thirty years of age he escaped from his slave master and went to work as a dockworker and seaman at the busy Boston Harbor. Having found his own liberty precious, he would come to symbolize the meaning of freedom.

Attucks becomes one of the greatest African Americans by virtue of the fact that a little over one hundred years after Africans landed in Jamestown, Virginia, as the first group of black indentured servants in the English colonies, he took upon his own shoulders the weight of defying the British troops in Boston. He was not alone, but he was to be the first to die in a hail of bullets on that fateful March day. His martyrdom forever placed before the American nation the irony of an African dying for a liberty that would be denied for another ninety-five years to Africans, while whites in the society would gain their independence from Britain in a mere six years.

The elevation of Attucks to a place of national significance was swift to come. President John Adams, himself from Massachusetts, declared of the resistance and assault on Boston Common, "On that night the foundation of American independence was laid." At the very base of the foundation was the solid rock of Crispus Attucks.

During the late 1760s and into 1770, Boston had become a cauldron of resentment against the British, who were seen more and more as an occupying army rather than the legitimate government of the colonies. There were rumors everywhere. Verbal assaults on the governor were increasingly strident. Demonstrators took to the streets to defy the bayonet-carrying British soldiers. King George III had become the bitter enemy of the leading opinion makers in the American colonies, and people like Thomas Paine and Samuel Adams and the Liberty Boys kept the community informed and emotionally engaged through their pamphlets and articles in the radical *Boston Gazette*.

Events reached a fever pitch when, on the night of March 5, a group of about forty colonists led by Crispus Attucks, carrying torches for light, clubs, and bats, met seven British sentries with bayonets fixed on their way to Boston Common. There was a tense standoff, with insults thrown from both sides. At length, Attucks is said to have shouted to the colonists, "Attack the main guard and the rest will give way." With this shout, the colonists threw stones, sticks, and torches toward the startled soldiers. The word went out: "Do not be afraid, they dare not shoot!" But shoot the British did.

Crispus Attucks was the first to be shot and killed. He fell, and near him fell four others who died on Boston Common. In addition to the marking of Crispus Attucks Day in Boston from 1858 to 1870, Attucks's name was mentioned by every major African American orator who defended liberty and sought the freedom of those still enslaved. Only with the rise of the celebration of July 4, 1776, did March 5, 1770, lose its place as the day to be honored in celebrated struggle against England. Even so, neither the substitution of the Day of Independence nor the abolition of the enslavement could minimize the role of Attucks in history. Clearly, he established a pattern of sacrifice and courage to stand for justice and right in African American history that would be emulated from generation to generation.

# JAMES
# BALDWIN

1924–1987

**J**ames Baldwin was one of America's best essayists during the turbulent 1960s, and perhaps the best essayist in African American history. He knew fundamentally what it was that African Americans wanted, and he saw his mission clearly as articulating that objective. He was born on August 2, 1924, in Harlem, New York, and died on December 1, 1987, in St.-Paul-de-Vence, France.

The intellectual and artistic force in Baldwin's writing came from a deeply religious undertone. He could see the hypocrisy in the church, the society, and the government and felt that he had to speak out against all forms of injustice. Feeling that it was his duty and, indeed, the duty of others who had similar moral and ethical commitments to truth, honesty, and justice to speak out, he was moved to write with such force that those who read his works understood and were motivated by them. He could say in the essay *No Name in the Street*, "We are responsible for the world in which we find ourselves, if only because we are the only sentient force which can change it"—and then he could go out and participate in all types of political and social actions to bring about the change that was necessary. He was a writer, not principally an activist, although he did not shy away from debating the leading reactionaries and conservatives of his day. He was an artist, although he could and did march in demonstrations against prejudice and racism. His greatness lay in his close association with the African American community.

James Baldwin's mother gave birth to him out of wedlock, but was soon married to David Baldwin, an industrial worker and a Sanctified Church preacher. He was raised with seven half-siblings in a strict, disciplined, and sometimes abusive environment. This difficult upbringing marked and shaped much of Baldwin's writings. Seeing reading as a way to escape and to travel to distant centuries and far-off places, he immersed himself in historical and literary works. When he entered Frederick Douglass Junior High School, he became the editor of the school's literary paper and was briefly under the tutelage of Countee Cullen, the paper's literary adviser.

With his extraordinary gift for words, he turned to preaching at the age of fourteen. He had absorbed much of his father's teachings and knew the Scriptures so well that the church believed that he was called to the ministry. People began speaking of him as a "prophet" who was sent to call the people to repentance. But the period of his religious prophecy would not last long, and by the time he was eighteen, he had left the church and Christianity. When he graduated from high school in 1942, he moved to New Jersey and worked many odd jobs. His father's death and the Harlem uprising of 1943, coming within a day of each other, was, to him, a sign to return to New York. He settled in Greenwich Village and began to write for magazines. He would become a prophet with the bolder and more immediate message that if the conditions of segregation and racism in America did not change, there would be urban conflagrations. His book *The Fire Next Time*, published in 1963, was a powerful prophecy of the urban uprisings of the late 1960s and early 1970s. Drawing upon his religious and cultural background, Baldwin took the title of the book from a spiritual: "God gave Noah the rainbow sign/No more water, the fire next time."

In 1944 Richard Wright, who was the reigning African American novelist, encouraged Baldwin to apply for the Eugene Saxton Fellowship, with his recommendation. Baldwin won the award in 1945. He published his first essay in the *Nation* in 1946 and was on the way to fame as an essayist. He wrote for the *New Leader*, *Commentary*, and *Partisan Review*. One of the decisive moments in Baldwin's life came after he was awarded the 1948 Rosenwald Fellowship. It enabled him to buy a one-way ticket to Paris, and he left the United States on November 11, 1948. It was his intention, following Richard Wright, to spend his time in the more liberal air of Paris, writing about the conditions of African Americans. He would periodically return to America, but by the early 1950s he was an expatriate writer par excellence. Baldwin's devotion to the causes of racial and personal freedom set him apart from many writers of his day. He knew that while his subjects were American and his interests the liberation of the minds and bodies of African people, he could not truly be the international writer he desired if he remained fixed in New York.

The earlier relationship between Baldwin and Wright, who was in many ways Baldwin's mentor, was shattered by the publication of Baldwin's 1949 essay "Everybody's Protest Novel." In this essay Baldwin criticized Richard Wright's character Bigger Thomas, from the acclaimed novel *Native Son*, saying, "Below the surface of this novel there lies, it seems to me, a continuation, a complement of that monstrous legend it was written to destroy. Bigger is Uncle Tom's descendant, flesh of his flesh. . . ." Two years later, just to drive home his point, Baldwin wrote another essay, "Many Thousands Gone," that was critical of Wright's works, saying that one gets the impression from protest novels that "in Negro life there exists no tradition, no field of manners, no possibility of ritual or intercourse, such as may, for example, sustain the Jew even after he has left his father's house."

Baldwin's best novel, *Go Tell It on the Mountain,* was published in 1953. Subsequently he wrote two novels that described gay relationships, *Giovanni's Room* (1956) and *Another Country* (1962). Both novels established a new frontier in literature, because Baldwin used both his blackness and his homosexuality to expose the hypocrisy that existed in society. He also published the collections of essays *Notes of a Native Son* (1955), and *Nobody Knows My Name* (1961).

In the 1960s he was one of the most visible intellectuals in the civil rights movement. His friends included Lorraine Hansberry,

Harry Belafonte, Lena Horne, and Martin Luther King Jr. Along with the literary establishment, King recognized James Baldwin as one of the major interpreters of the struggle for justice.

James Baldwin's play *The Amen Corner* was published in 1955 and became an immediate success on Broadway. The 1964 play *The Blues for Mr. Charlie* became his second play on Broadway. Among his other works during the 1960s were *Going to Meet the Man* (1965), a collection of short stories, and the novel *Tell Me How Long the Train's Been Gone* (1968). He published several other novels, collections of essays, and short essays.

In 1986 Baldwin came to Philadelphia to attend the opening of *Amen Corner* at the University of Pennsylvania. He was invited, along with Gwendolyn Brooks and Houston Baker, by Rowena Stewart, director of the Afro-American Museum in Philadelphia, to a small dinner party at her home in Society Hill. Baldwin spoke passionately about how America mistreated those who spoke truth to it. He never received a major American literary prize, although the French gave him the Croix de Guerre in 1986 and other nations had officially recognized him. Those in attendance assured him that his name would be honored among the greatest of our writers. He died of cancer on December 1, 1987. He was still working at the time of his death. His memorial service at the Cathedral of Saint John the Divine in New York City drew thousands of admirers, including Maya Angelou, Toni Morrison, and Amiri Baraka. Nothing could be said of James Baldwin more than what was said by his literary agent, Jay Acton, that "he was consciously aware of his surroundings at all times."

# BENJAMIN
# BANNEKER
1731–1806

**B**enjamim Banneker was born in Baltimore County, Maryland, in 1731, one of several children born to Robert and Mary Banneker. Robert was born on the Guinea coast of Africa, possibly Ghana, and Mary was the daughter of Molly Welsh, who had come from England as an indentured servant. Benjamim and his sisters were born free and were raised on a farm where the family grew tobacco. He received the equivalent of an eighth-grade education and showed an early inclination for mathematics. He was interested in solving math quizzes and puzzles and spent lots of time with numbers. After his father's death in 1759, he took over the farm and became a successful farmer. While managing his farm, he learned to read the stars and taught himself astronomy. From his knowledge of mathematics and astronomy, it was only logical that he would be interested in time. One of the crowning achievements of his life was the construction of a mechanical clock made of mostly wood components. In addition to making the clock, Banneker planned the survey for Washington, D.C., after the abandonment of the project by Pierre-Charles L'Enfant, and published his own almanacs.

Banneker was only twenty-two when he made his clock out of wood, after investigating the workings of a watch owned by a friend. Since watches were made by skilled craftsmen, the idea that an African farmer could make a reliable time instrument out of wood was astonishing to many of Banneker's neighbors. Proving himself quite a sculptor, Banneker used his knife to carve the components of the clock, and after two years he had an instrument that kept accurate time for the rest of his life.

He was fifty-nine when he quit farming and started to study astronomy full-time, devoting his life to science and experimentation. He observed nature closely and was able to successfully publish almanacs that assisted planters. He had become friends with George Ellicott, another amateur astronomer and a surveyor, and Ellicott loaned his books to Banneker. He was so knowledgeable in mathematics and astronomy that when President George Washington, in February 1791, commissioned Ellicott and the French engineer L'Enfant to help plan the construction of the nation's capital on an area of land twenty-five sq km (ten sq mi) in Virginia and Maryland, Ellicott asked Banneker to assist him. Soon thereafter the Frenchman abandoned the project over a dispute with some Americans. L'Enfant refused to leave his plans with the surveying team, but because Banneker had paid close attention to the mathematical details he was able to reproduce most of the plans and ideas from memory. For this reason, some refer to Washington, D.C., as Banneker's Town.

When the Washington project was completed, Banneker returned to his farm where he continued to write, issuing ten almanacs that were sold in England and the United States. He used his genius to chart the stars and predict solar eclipses and rains. His information was so dependable that many navigators and farmers found his conversion charts, maps, and discussions of the heavenly bodies and their impact on the land to be indispensable.

Thomas Jefferson received a copy of Banneker's almanac in August 1791, while serving as secretary of state under President George Washington. Jefferson had written that blacks were inferior to whites, and Banneker's work was one of the first attempts by an African to demonstrate that he was as intelligent as any white in the society. Jefferson congratulated Banneker on his publication and expressed a desire to see more proof "that nature has given to our [black] brethren talents equal to that of other colors of men." Furthermore, it is believed that Jefferson forwarded a copy of Banneker's almanac to the Academy of Sciences in Paris, France. Jefferson apparently thought so much of Banneker's work that he felt it should be shared with one of the great centers of science in the world at that time. When Banneker died in 1806, he had left behind a legacy of accomplishment that would sustain the dreams and hopes of African Americans for many centuries. Even today, one can drive from Ellicott City to Washington, D.C., by way of Columbia, Maryland, and sense the presence of Banneker throughout the area. Had he lived in another century, perhaps, there would have been a real Banneker City right next to Ellicott City in Maryland, because he is equally important in the history of that state and the United States of America.

# AMIRI
# BARAKA
1934–

**A**miri Baraka was born Everett Leroy Jones in Newark, New Jersey, to Coyette Leroy Jones, a postal supervisor, and Anna Lois Russ Jones, a social worker. He later changed his first name to LeRoi and finally, during the 1960s, Imam Hajj Heeshaam Jaaber named him Ameer Barakat. Baraka later bantuized the Arabic name to "Amiri Baraka." He was also called Imamu by the African American philosopher Maulana Karenga.

Baraka attended Newark public schools and majored in chemistry at Howard University in Washington, D.C., before choosing to study literature.

Financial difficulties forced him to leave Howard University to join the U.S. Air Force in 1954. Baraka studied poetry by reading and reciting the works of outstanding American poets. He was mainly influenced by the works of the American poet Ezra Pound and the Irish novelist James Joyce. The influences of these writers would reassert themselves throughout his career. However, Baraka was impressed by the struggles for equality and integration during the 1950s, and this changed his direction toward dealing with more socially relevant literature.

When Baraka was discharged from the air force in 1957 for possessing communist literary journals, he joined the Greenwich Village literary community. He was one of the leading black writers of the Beat Generation, interacting with the avant-garde writers of the period and discovering his own voice in the meantime. In 1961 he published an outstanding book of poetry, *Preface to a Twenty Volume Suicide Note*. He participated in various literary movements, editing and coediting journals.

The influence of Maulana Karenga, the civil rights movement, and the revolutionary work of the Cuban people had a profound impact on Baraka. He soon left the Bohemian lifestyle of Greenwich Village, becoming more political in his writings. He was now committed to the African American struggle in a determined manner. Although he started as a poet, it was his plays, particularly *Dutchman* and *The Slave* (both 1964), that asserted his new literary militancy. He also published a collection of poems called *The Dead Lecturer* (1964) that had the same militancy.

Finding Malcolm X and the jazz musicians John Coltrane, Cecil Taylor, Sun Ra, Ornette Coleman, and Charlie Parker as his new mentors, Baraka discovered a way to produce art that was founded upon African American cultural roots. In 1996 he met Maulana Karenga at Spirit House, which had been founded in Newark, New Jersey, after the close of the Harlem Repertory Theater, and began a collaboration that lasted until 1972. Baraka moved vigorously to expand Spirit House as a part of the Black United Front. He demonstrated in several books that he was as adept at social criticism as he was at the creative arts.

After the death of Malcolm X, Baraka moved from Greenwich Village to Harlem, where he worked to create a black aesthetic. This was his mission as he saw it. Thus, he worked with the Black Arts Repertory Theatre, whose aim was a major transformation of the black aesthetic mission, and indeed, put his theory to a practical test in the work of Spirit House.

Along with the writer Larry Neal, Baraka is credited with founding the Black Arts Movement, as seen in their work *Black Fire* (1968), a collection of the revolutionary voices of young black poets of the 1960s.

Amiri Baraka's activism during the 1972 Gary, Indiana, Black Political Convention, and his participation in local Newark, New Jersey, politics, thrust him in the forefront of community politics during the 1970s. He advocated self-determination, self-reliance, and self-help. The story of the Gary Convention was the emergence of Amiri Bakara as a major intellectual force in the African American community.

Although he was attracted to Marxism-Leninism during the late 1990s, he never gave up the name that he had taken during his earlier cultural nationalist days. His works *The Motion of History* (1978), *Reggae or Not!* (1981), *Daggers and Javelins* (1984), and *The Autobiography of LeRoi Jones* (1984) came as a result of his new orientation. While Baraka has reinvented himself on numerous occasions, he has maintained a consistently high regard for social and political criticism. As a professor of African American Studies at the State University of New York at Stony Brook, Baraka has created a persona of brilliant antiracist, anticolonialist, and antipaternalist activism.

# ROMARE
# BEARDEN
1912–1988

**R**omare Bearden was born in Charlotte, North Carolina, and grew up in Pittsburgh, Pennsylvania. It was in New York City, however, where he developed into one of the master artists of his century. Bearden's contributions to art are immense, and his reputation as an artist is among the greatest of any African American artist. He was influenced by images and experiences of the African American struggle for freedom. In fact, the civil rights movement may have been Bearden's greatest intellectual inspiration. Yet Bearden was impressed by what he saw in the art of Pablo Picasso, Henri Matisse, and other modern European artists, who had drawn on traditional African forms for much of their inspiration. When he brought African American artists together in the 1960s to celebrate the civil rights movement, he was projected as the leader of a new group. This was short-lived, however, when the artists rejected the idea that the official medium be collage, a medium that Bearden had perfected but that other artists believed limited their expressive range. What is important here is that Bearden was committed and devoted to demonstrating that artists had a role to play in the civil rights movement.

Bearden's own collages made him famous. He was able to combine acrylic and oil paints in innovative ways that resembled the narratives of photographs and newspapers. His works, in the tradition of functionality, told a story or gave one an idea. One could not come away from a Bearden work without being touched by the power of his art. All of his collages show African

Americans involved in the ordinary experiences of living, mostly in urban environments.

Like many artists of his generation, Bearden drew upon the African origins of African Americans to sharpen his art. For example, as an authority on African art, he would sometimes use an African mask to highlight a particular African American situation. There was a grammar of African structure in his work, since he was interested always in a multiplicity of textures in his art. All great artists must rely upon their cultural roots; Bearden used his roots infinitely. He employed scenes from the night-clubs, jazz music, dances in Harlem, and social and political protest as elements in his work.

It is believed by many critics that Bearden's art was a plastic form of jazz. What is meant by this is that Bearden took the key constructive elements of the jazz form and brought it to the canvass, much like some have claimed Kwame Toure did on the rhetorical platform. The jazz motif is highly prized in the African American tradition, and its classical nature carries an artist's work right to the heart of the audience. So Bearden's creations were images of juxtapositions and improvisation that found their own rhythms in his constructions. Thus, one sees all the contradictions of form, the brevity of segments, the piercing color of a small piece of painted paper, the paradoxes of shapes upon shapes, and the skidding of one distortion after another until the artist lands upon a clear vision of a project. Indeed, Bearden's work could be surreal, but most of the time it simply gave the impression of the surreal until one examined it closely.

Bearden started his career in art as a cartoonist. By the time he was studying at New York University, 1931 to 1935, he had already created cartoons for the school's humorous newspaper, the *Medley*. But he also sent submissions to other papers, such as the *Chicago Defender, Pittsburgh Courier, Philadelphia Tribune, Baltimore Afro-American, Collier's*, and the *Saturday Evening Post*. Soon thereafter he began to create paintings in the genre of social realism, and worked with the German social artist George Grosz, who encouraged him to do more politically conscious art.

In the late 1930s Bearden attempted his first paintings, genre scenes of black city life executed in the then-popular style of social realism. His travels in Europe were evident in his multi-faceted artistic career. He served in the United States Army and gained a wider appreciation of the history of art in the Western world. Finding an opportunity to learn from the creativity and techniques of others, he sought out the best examples and models of contemporary art. He was inspired by Picasso's cubism, studied at the Sorbonne in Paris, and wrote a few songs in order to earn a living while living in Europe after the army, but in the end he returned to the love of African American culture with its richness, energy, and style as his principal mode of translating his passion and, as he would say, dispassion about living.

# MARY McLEOD
# BETHUNE

## 1875–1955

**C**onsidered by those who knew her the most dominant figure in African American politics during the New Deal, Mary McLeod Bethune became a legendary educator and political power broker.

Mary McLeod Bethune was born in the country near Mayesville, South Carolina, in 1875. When she was ten years old she enrolled at Trinity Presbyterian Mission School. She was considered such a good student that one of the teachers, Emma Jane Wilson, encouraged and assisted her to move to Scotia Seminary in Concord, North Carolina, in 1888. She attended Scotia as a boarding student, since it was a missionary school and a great distance from her home in Mayesville. She received a good, solid education, based on the idea that black children should learn to fit into the postslavery economy. She was instructed in vocational activities such as home economics and religion. From Scotia, she went to the Moody Bible Institute where she was sure she would be trained to be a missionary to Africa. From everything she had learned in school, she believed that Africa needed the Christian religion. But after studying at Moody for one year, her application to serve the Lord in the continent of her people's origin was rejected because it was the policy of Moody not to permit African Americans to serve in Africa. That was a consciousness-raising moment for Bethune, because she was made to wonder what the white missionaries could be telling the Africans that they did not want African Americans to know, or why whites were considered good enough to go to Africa while blacks were not.

This rejection did not keep Bethune from teaching. The end of the century and the beginning of the new century inspired thousands of African Americans to create schools and institutes or to enter the profession of teaching. Bethune got a job in 1896 at Haines Institute in Augusta, Georgia, and a year later moved to the Presbyterians' Kendall Institute in Sumter, North Carolina. She was always looking for the best situation to teach African American students. Most of the schools did not allow her the freedom to teach as she wanted to, and she became disillusioned. She soon left Kendall, and in 1900 moved to Palatka, Florida, where she established two schools. After four years in Palatka, Bethune moved to Daytona, Florida, and founded the Daytona Educational and Industrial Training School for Negro Girls. Bethune started the school with five students in a small rented house. Within a few years Bethune's school had expanded to include a high school, a farm, and a nursing school. In 1929, during the Great Depression, Bethune's Daytona Institute merged with Cookman Institute, becoming coeducational, and the resulting institution was renamed Bethune-Cookman College. The institution was fully accredited in 1943.

Mary McLeod Bethune was on her way to becoming one of the greatest women in America when she was named the winner of the Spingarn Award from the National Association for the Advancement of Colored People (NAACP) for founding the Daytona Institute, and became the president of the Bethune-Cookman College. She became an ardent student of American politics at the local and national levels, demonstrating in the arena of fund-raising that she knew how to raise money for a poor African American college. In the process, she entered the offices of the wealthiest people in America and met all types of politicians. Her quest for the education of her people was always foremost in her mind. It was not just her presidency that captivated the masses, it was also her willingness to risk her position to speak the truth to white politicians.

She founded several black women's organizations, which culminated in the 1935 establishment of the National Council of

Negro Women (NCNW). Had the American society not been seg-regated, there is no question that Bethune would have been one of the first women leaders in the nation. As it was—and she was cer-tainly secure in her role—she became the most famous black woman of her time. By the time she relinquished the reins of the NCNW, she had established it as a strong and powerful organiza-tion. The sponsorship of numerous African American women's seminars, planning workshops, and political organizations made the NCNW the leading voice for social justice for black families.

No one who knew what was going on in the African Amer-ican community during the 1930s and 1940s could disregard Bethune. In one sense, Bethune replaced Booker T. Washington, who had died in 1915. When Franklin Delano Roosevelt became president, he moved quickly to develop political muscle among blacks who had not voted for him. But when he tapped Bethune as one of his informal advisers, it almost ensured that he would be the choice of the African American community for the next two presidential elections.

From 1936 to 1945 Bethune was the administration's "senior black representative," and she participated in the organization of the Federal Council on Negro Affairs as one of Roosevelt's "Black Cabinet" members. Bethune became the director of Negro affairs for the National Youth Administration in 1939 and kept the post until 1943. In this post she fought for racial justice, defended African Americans against the worst forms of discrimination in the federal government, and sought to distribute funds and posi-tions in the federal government to qualified African Americans.

A tireless worker for humanity, Bethune advocated interna-tionalism and the commonality of all humans. It is this legacy, along with her commitment to education and national equality, that marks her as one of the greatest African Americans. During the years of the Red scare in the early 1940s in American poli-tics, she was labeled a communist by the House Committee on Un-American Activities. This did not stop or scare Bethune, whose campaign for civil rights never wavered. She was one of the black leaders who joined A. Philip Randolph in the March on

Washington in 1941, a threat that forced the United States to end segregation and discrimination in the federal workplace. She died in 1955, leaving her Last Will and Testament to her people to seek self-determination.

# GUION
# BLUFORD
1942–

**G**uion Bluford was born on November 22, 1942, in Philadelphia, Pennsylvania. He attended the public schools of Philadelphia, graduating from Overbrook High School. After attending college, he entered the air force and became a pilot. He flew over 4,800 hours on several different jets. Bluford also trained as an aerospace engineer.

Bluford became an astronaut in 1979. He has made three space flights and has spent more than 688 hours in space.

In 1983 Gluford became the first African American to go into space aboard STS-8. This mission made the first nighttime launch and landing of the space shuttle. In 1985 he flew aboard a Spacelab mission. In 1991 and 1992 Bluford flew on two Department of Defense missions. He subsequently retired from the astronaut program and became a private businessperson. In the face of numerous obstacles, Bluford set out to achieve on his own merit at the highest level of national service in the military, and he succeeded, by virtue of his intrepidity and determination, in becoming a heroic African American.

# ARNA
# BONTEMPS
## 1902–1973

rna Bontemps was born in Alexandria, Louisiana, in 1902. His parents moved to Los Angeles when he was still young. After his mother's death, Arna Bontemps, without siblings, was raised alone by an austere father who wanted his son to join him as a brick mason. A very strict man, his father sent him to the Seventh-day Adventist schools for elementary and secondary education. After leaving high school, he entered Pacific Union College, from which he graduated in 1923. His life was to change dramatically, however, when he took a teaching job at the Harlem Academy in New York City.

New York City inspired his social, cultural, and political consciousness and he discovered his own creativity very soon after arriving in New York. He began writing poetry and sending it to journals. He was published in 1926 in the *Crisis*, a publication of the National Association for the Advancement of Colored People, and the National Urban League's *Opportunity*. Bontemps's poetry won the poetry award for the *Crisis* and for *Opportunity* in 1926 and 1927. He was considered one of the Harlem Renaissance's bright stars, alongside Zora Neale Hurston, Langston Hughes, Countee Cullen, and Claude McKay.

Bontemps got a job offer at a junior college in Alabama and reluctantly left Harlem in 1931. His first novel was published the same year. The novel, *God Sends Sunday*, was the story of Little Augie, a fun-loving jockey of the 1890s in St. Louis, Missouri. He used this story as a basis for *St. Louis Woman*, a play written in 1937 with Countee Cullen. The play ran successfully on Broadway in 1946.

Long before most writers of the Harlem Renaissance, Bontemps saw the need to write books for children. This was a direct result of his experience in Alabama, where he observed that black children did not have books depicting African Americans. He wrote the children's book *Popo and Fifina* in 1932, in collaboration with Langston Hughes. He then turned his full attention to children's books and completed fifteen other books for children and young adults, dealing with African American heroes such as Booker T. Washington and Frederick Douglass.

The historical novel *Black Thunder*, written in 1936, brought Bontemps a great deal of of literary attention. He was securely ensconced in the panoply of great black writers.

Bontemps earned a degree in library science and, in 1943, he became a librarian at Fisk University, with the task of preserving the papers of his fellow Harlem Renaissance figures, particularly Langston Hughes, James Weldon Johnson, Jean Toomer, and Countee Cullen. He edited some significant volumes of African American literature while at Fisk. As a young college student in Oklahoma I heard of Bontemps and traveled to Nashville to give him a copy of my first book of poetry, *The Break of Dawn*, published in 1964. He was gracious in receiving me in 1965 when I took the small book to him. Having met him, I was deeply impressed by his sincerity and willingness to assist young poets. He retired a year after I met him and was visiting professor at several institutions, including University of Illinois, Chicago Circle, and Yale University. Bontemps died in 1973.

# EDWARD W.
# BROOKE

1919–

**E**dward W. Brooke III was the first African American elected to the U.S. Senate since Reconstruction. He was born in 1919, the only son of Helen Seldon and Edward W. Brooke, a lawyer, in Washington, D.C. He attended school in Washington and graduated from Howard University in 1941 with a bachelor's degree in chemistry. He soon entered the army and became a United States Army captain. Brooke fought in Italy during World War II (1939–1945) and was granted the Bronze Star for combat. When the war was over, he entered Boston University's School of Law, where he became editor of the *Law Review*.

In 1950 Brooke's political career began with an unsuccessful run for the Massachusetts House of Representatives. Republican governor John Volpe appointed Brooke chairman of the Boston Finance Commission in 1961. Brooke held that position until he resigned in 1963, when he was sworn in as Massachusetts attorney general after winning the Republican nomination and election in 1962.

The election of Brooke to the United States Senate as a Republican in 1966 was a milestone for black politicians, but because he was known for his role as an aggressive prosecutor many black Americans viewed him as someone who would not speak up against racism. His reputation among African Americans suffered because of this—and because he was a Republican during the 1960s. In the Senate he was appointed to the Banking and Currency Committee and to the Aeronautical and Space Sciences Committee. He held his Republican seat for two terms until his defeat in 1978. In establishing himself as a competent, skillful senator, Brooke made history and in the process etched for himself a persona that has resonated with those who argue for many roads to justice.

Brooke published *The Challenge of Change* in 1966 and was the 1967 recipient of the Spingarn Medal, given by the National Association for the Advancement of Colored People (NAACP).

# GWENDOLYN
# BROOKS
1917–2000

**W**hen Gwendolyn Brooks died in December 2000, she had established herself next to Langston Hughes as the best loved of African American poets. Her poetry connected her to the ordinary lives of the masses of people in ways that made her a legend in her own time.

Gwendolyn Brooks was born in Topeka, Kansas, the daughter of David and Keziah Wims Brooks. They moved to the South Side of Chicago when she was an infant, and Brooks became identified with Chicago for the rest of her life. She was educated in the Chicago public schools and at Wilson Junior College.

When Brooks was in elementary school, her mother encouraged her to perform dramatic readings, believing that the child showed unusual promise as a performer. By the time she was thirteen she had met the leading African American writers of the day, including Langston Hughes and James Weldon Johnson, two of the most important poets of the era. Both Hughes and Johnson had shown a strong inclination to write poetry that was suited to performance, and this influenced the young Brooks. She published poetry in the famous *Chicago Defender*, the leading African American newspaper of that time, by the time she was sixteen.

Chicago was becoming a major capital of the black literary movement during the 1940s and 1950s, with the constant presence of writers such as Margaret Walker, Arna Bontemps, James Weldon Johnson, Frank Marshall Davis, Theodore Ward, and Richard Wright. Gwendolyn Brooks did not rest on her innate genius: she studied writing, especially poetry at the Inez Cunningham Stark poetry workshop at the South Side Community Art Center. Encouraged by her teachers and colleagues to send her poems to journals and magazines, Brooks was pleased to see that her work was accepted in major anthologies.

Gwendolyn Brooks was a proud African American writer and she believed that her skills and talents would propel her to greatness as a poet. She applied for numerous awards and prizes, winning many fellowships, awards, and prizes for her literary prowess. Her success in attracting critical attention landed her two Guggenheim Fellowships. Two books of poetry were published in the 1940s: *A Street in Bronzeville*, in 1945, and *Annie Allen*, in 1949. In 1950 Brooks won the Pulitzer prize for poetry, becoming the first African American to win the award.

The greatness of Brooks's poetry resides in her ability to assert the African American spirit in ways that literary critics considered modernist, but which were in reality the combination of the rhythms and voices heard and felt in the intricate spaces of black life in urban America. If her works were modernist, they were so because of the strong African content and element. The major influence on the construction of her sonnet was T. S. Eliot, and the major influence on her lyricism was Langston Hughes. However, neither Eliot nor Hughes wrote on as many aspects of identity, art, technology, gender, education, lifestyle, and race as Brooks. She was unique in her artistic style and gave powerful testimony to the inherent genius in the African American cultural experience. She would create not just art but a situation for art, meaning that she would pose a problem in her lectures about life and society and then introduce a poem that resolved the issue. She wrote a novel, *Maud Martha* (1953), a poetic portrait of the life of a young Chicago woman.

Brooks was in the forefront of the civil rights movement with her art. She wrote a collection of poetry, *The Bean Eaters*, that graphically portrayed the brutality of lynching in the American South and the story of fourteen-year-old Emmett Till's murder in Mississippi. Signaling her intention to remain in the vanguard of artistic representation of the concerns of the African American community, Brooks attended the Black Writers Conference at Fisk University in 1967 and immediately saw the potential of the new energy brought to the art world by young writers such as Amiri Baraka and Haki Madhubuti. She was identified with the black arts movement after this time and became the patron of many of the young writers. She published the 1968 collection *In the Mecca*, with poems dedicated to the activities of the young, politically active African Americans who struggled against racist oppression, poverty, and injustice. During her last years she published most of her works with Third World Press, maintaining a sense of connection to the 1960s.

In 1972 Brooks came to Los Angeles to speak and I was her designated driver. I remember asking her, "How would you compare the Harlem Renaissance era with the black arts movement?" She responded that "the Renaissance was not a revolution, this is a revolution. Any time you have poets on the streets, in the barber shops, and on the campus in such a profound way, something dramatic and real is going on in the soul of the people." Brooks wrote two autobiographical works, *Report from Part One* (1972) and *Report from Part Two* (1997). Unquestionably one of the greatest poets in the history of America, Brooks was a dominant poet who inspired millions.

# BLANCHE K. BRUCE

## 1841–1898

**B**lanche K. Bruce was the first person of African descent elected to a full term in the United States Senate. He was born in 1841 in Farmville, Virginia, and died a relatively young man in 1898. But between the year of his birth and the year of his death he achieved more than most men who live to much older ages.

Bruce was born into slavery, but his owner, Pettus Perkinson, seemed to regard him as different from the other enslaved Africans. In fact, it was as if Perkinson saw the young Bruce as a son. He was a playmate of the Perkinsons' son and was educated by the same tutor who taught the slave master's son. Bruce made the best of this situation, learning all he could and hating the institution of slavery for placing a ceiling on his possibilities. During the outbreak of the Civil War (1861–1865) he was living in Missouri, and when he saw the opportunity he escaped to Lawrence, Kansas. Although Bruce tried to enlist, the Union Army was not accepting Africans into its ranks. So he turned his attention to education and founded two schools for free blacks, one in Kansas and the other in Missouri. In 1866, when the war was over, he entered Oberlin College.

He moved south to maximize his chances for economic and political advancement that became available to African Americans. He chose Bolivar County in the Mississippi Delta as the place to settle. Bruce believed that Reconstruction policies had created a good climate for blacks interested in politics. He was clearly bent on helping African Americans develop economically and educationally. He purchased land and started his own cotton farm. Local Republicans, because theirs was the progressive party of the times, recommended him for public-speaking functions, and even appointed him to offices such as voter registrar for Tallahatchie County and tax assessor for Bolivar County in 1869. By 1871 Bruce had been appointed county sheriff of Bolivar County's political leader, a Republican, Bruce H. T. Florey.

To a large degree, Bruce appealed to the white Republican leadership class as much as to his black constituency. In 1871 he was made superintendent of education for Bolivar County and during his tenure, which lasted all of one year, he created twenty-one public schools without raising taxes. He resigned the post in 1872. But he was not out of politics at all; he was merely sizing up his chances to take an even larger share of the political power in the South.

Bruce had climbed to the top of the political heap in Bolivar County by 1874, during which time the Mississippi legislature elected him to the U.S. Senate. When he went to Washington, Bruce was a protégée to New York senator Roscoe Conkling, who appointed him to three committees: the Pensions, Manufactures, and Education and Labor Committees. Bruce was not the silent type, though his policies were moderate. He criticized the Republican Party for not supporting the Mississippi Republicans during the elections of 1875. He urged, to no avail, his Republican colleagues to seat P. B. S. Pinchback, an African American from Louisiana whose seat was contested by white southerners.

The record Bruce left is mixed. His political philosophy might be considered cautious. He opposed emigration to Africa as well as the Exodusters, who left the south for Kansas believing that life could be better for blacks in the South. He chided the Senate for not supporting the poorest people who felt they had to emigrate in order to escape slavery. He argued against the Chinese Exclusion Act and for more humane treatment of Native Americans. Bruce's most powerful position was as chairman of the Select Committee to Investigate the Freedmen's Savings and Trust Company, a company in which many former slaves lost money. Although the committee's report exposed corruption and incompetence on the part of its white directors, Bruce was unsuccessful in getting African Americans their lost money.

By January 1880 the Democratic Party had regained power in Mississippi, and the state legislature replaced Bruce. Living in Washington, he saw the resegregation of the city. He cultivated relationships with Washington blacks. He was named as a candidate for the vice presidential nomination at the Republican National Conventions in 1880 and 1888. He was twice appointed registrar of the Treasury, serving from 1881 to 1885 and from 1897 to 1898. He was a successful lecturer and a member of the boards of the Washington, D.C., public schools and Howard University. He died of complications from diabetes in Washington, D.C., in 1898.

# RALPH
# BUNCHE
## 1904–1971

**R**alph Johnson Bunche was born in Detroit, Michigan, in 1904 and spent his early life in the Motor City. After a few years he moved with his family to Albuquerque, New Mexico. Though he was orphaned at the age of thirteen, Bunche nevertheless rose to great heights. Bunche's role as the architect of the United Nations (UN) peacekeeping operations between Israel and the Arabs in the late 1940s and early 1950s established him as one of the leading African American diplomats. He was the first black American to receive the Nobel peace prize.

Ralph Bunche was always eager to attribute his achievements to the influence of his maternal grandmother, Lucy Johnson, with whom he lived in Los Angeles, California. His maternal grandmother pushed him to excel in school, which he did; he became the valedictorian of his high school class. It was through Johnson that Bunche learned pride in his race and the value of education. He was convinced from the time he was in high school that he had to go to college in order to contribute to the rise of African American people.

Ralph Bunche enrolled at the University of California at Los Angeles, where there is now a building named after him. He graduated summa cum laude in 1927 and entered graduate school at Harvard University. He was the first black American to earn a Ph.D. in political science from an American university. In 1934 Ralph Bunche was honored for writing the outstanding doctoral thesis, *The French Administration in Togoland and Dahomey*, in the social sciences. His research at Northwestern University, the London

School of Economics in England, and the University of Cape Town, South Africa, examined the African colonial political structures. In South Africa he had to defy the South African government's racist policies to conduct his research. Never one to back down from a challenge, Bunche succeeded in getting the information he needed to write a dissertation on the colonial control of Africa.

He joined the faculty of Howard University in 1928 and founded and chaired the Department of Political Science. He became an activist for integration and expressed a commitment to an open, fair, and equitable society. His emphasis on economic improvement in the African American community allowed him to organize committees to study black self-improvement. By 1936 he was able to help establish the National Negro Congress, a forum for political, social, and economic discussion. From 1938 to 1940 Bunche participated in the study of Swedish sociologist Gunnar Myrdal on American race relations. Myrdal's book was called *An American Dilemma: The Negro Problem and Modern Democracy* (1944).

Ralph Bunche served in World War II (1939–1945). He left his position at Howard University in 1941 and joined the Office of Strategic Services (OSS)—the predecessor of the Central Intelligence Agency (CIA)—where he specialized in African affairs. Bunche moved to the State Department in 1944, where, as the first African American to run a departmental division of the federal government, he worked on African issues.

In 1944 Bunche participated in the Dumbarton Oaks Conference, which laid the groundwork for the UN Charter that was signed a year later in San Francisco, California. In 1946 Bunche went to work full-time for the UN at the request of the organization's first secretary-general, Trygve Lie. He served as the principal director of the Department of Trusteeship and Information from Non-Self-Governing Territories from 1947 to 1954.

Ralph Bunche's greatest fame came as a peacemaker in 1949, when he defied all predictions and negotiated the truce that ended the first Arab-Israeli War. Dispatched to Jerusalem in 1948 as the assistant to UN mediator Count Folke Bernadotte, Bunche stepped in when Bernadotte was assassinated that same year. He worked almost single-handedly to bring Israel and the Arab states to an agreement. Bunche was awarded the Nobel Peace Prize in 1950.

Bunche's career at the United Nations was legendary. In 1955 he was appointed undersecretary for special political affairs. This meant that he supervised UN peacekeeping operations in some of the most heated conflicts around the world. As director of UN activities in the Middle East during and after the Suez Crisis of 1956, Bunche broadened the organization's peace-keeping role with the creation of the United Nations Emergency Force. Bunche has been described as "the principal architect" of the concept of international peacekeeping. Bunche changed the history of peacekeeping. Before him there was no international body willing to place its funds at the disposal of peacekeepers. He developed and implemented the first principles of international mediation used by the United Nations

Ralph Bunche was a committed advocate of international peace. He gave numerous speeches and participated as a visiting professor and lecturer at many universities. His contributions as a scholar were recognized in 1953, when he was elected the first black president of the American Political Science Association. Bunche won the Spingarn Medal in 1949. Bunche acted as an unofficial adviser to several civil rights organizations and joined Martin Luther King Jr. in the 1965 Selma-to-Montgomery Voting Rights March. President John F. Kennedy awarded Bunche the nation's highest civilian honor, the Medal of Freedom, in 1963. He retired from the United Nations in 1969 and died the following year in New York.

# GEORGE WASHINGTON
# CARVER
## 1864–1943

Science is an area of endeavor that creates an opportunity for greatness. George Washington Carver's record in the field of science remains one of the glowing achievements of African American brilliance. The fact that he was a genius would have made him successful in any era, but the record of his sacrifice for the sake of teaching made him great.

In 1864 Carver was born of enslaved parents in Diamond, Missouri. From an early age, he was eager to learn about the nature of plants in the rural area around Diamond. He collected plants and wildflowers from the forest and planted them in gardens close to his home so that he could examine them. When he was ten years of age, he left home to attend a nearby black school in Neosho, Missouri. In Neosho he performed chores for a black family in exchange for food and lodging. While he attended school he kept collecting plants, and when he finished school in Neosho, he put himself through high school in Minneapolis, Kansas, and began to draw pictures of the plants and flowers he had collected. He spent one year at Simpson College in Iowa and then enrolled in Iowa State College of Agricultural and Mechanic Arts in 1891. At college he sought to focus his study on plants and flowers. He graduated with a B.S. degree in botany and agriculture in 1894. He obtained a master's degree in 1896 in the same field of study. Carver was able to afford his education by teaching undergraduates and supervising the college's greenhouse.

Booker T. Washington heard about Carver's work and was so impressed that in 1896 Washington invited Carver to head the

Tuskegee Institute's agricultural department. For half a century George Washington Carver dedicated himself to the study of agriculture and the teaching of botany at Tuskegee. He raised the teaching of agriculture to a science and made his own meaningful discoveries available to other scientists and the ordinary public through constant research and experimentation. It is common knowledge that he discovered hundreds of uses for common plants and crops and improved the production of farms in the South.

Tuskegee's laboratory was created by Carver from pots, pans, tubes, wires, and even tires, as he collected the materials necessary for experimentation. Developing an appreciation for agriculture was the second task that Carver had to confront, given the fact that so many of his students came from backgrounds of poverty and sharecropping and had little interest in the field. He achieved his goal of creating an atmosphere for agriculture to be studied as a high science and art by demonstrating what could be developed from experimentation. He linked botany and chemistry with farming, creating the new field of scientific agriculture.

Carver also worked to change the farming methods in the South. He observed that the soil was lacking nitrogen because it had been farmed over and over again with the same crop. He taught farmers how to rotate crops and gain productivity. He traveled to all parts of the state of Alabama with an outreach program to teach farmers how to use his methods.

Carver worked hard on the creation of new products from the peanut, because the price of the crop had deteriorated since farmers were doing so well in cultivating it. He developed more than three hundred uses for the peanut and then, in 1921, helped the United Peanuts Growers Association influence Congress to pass a bill calling for a protective tariff on imported peanuts.

More than anything, Carver showed that common foods such as peanuts and tomatoes could be used to improve the nutrition of the African Americans in the South. He taught them how to use peanuts for protein and to eat tomatoes, once thought to be poisonous by African Americans. He worked with the pecan and the sweet potato as well, demonstrating more than one hundred uses for these products.

Carver was sought after by large corporations—even the Soviet Union wanted him as czar of agriculture—but he refused and remained at Tuskegee, believing his mission was more important than money. His desire to remain rooted to the development of the African American showed an enormous commitment to the elevation of his people.

Only three of Carver's nearly six hundred agriculture-based discoveries were patented. He did not believe that he should sell gifts with which he was born. He donated most of his salary to a fund for research and lived frugally at Tuskegee. By 1916 he had been appointed to the Royal Society of Arts in London, England. He received the Spingarn Award in 1923. The Memorial Museum at Tuskegee contains many of his inventions and creations. This great man went on teaching and inspiring until his death in 1943.

# SHIRLEY
# CHISHOLM
1924–

**S**hirley Anita St. Hill Chisholm was born in Brooklyn, New York, in 1924. She became the first African American woman elected to Congress and the first to campaign for the presidency. Shirley Chisholm was one of four girls born to an immigrant Barbadian family. Her mother and father worked as domestics and housecleaners, barely subsisting on the low wages they earned in Brooklyn. When Chisholm was three years old, her parents took her and her sisters to Barbados to be raised by their maternal grandmother. Island life was a joy for Chisholm, and she blossomed in the peace and happiness of Barbadian society. She was an outstanding student and received a solid education. When she was ten years old she returned to Brooklyn and continued to strive for excellence. She completed her education at the public schools of New York and entered Brooklyn College. She majored in sociology, participating in the debating society and becoming known as an incisive debater. She gave time to volunteer work, serving as a worker for the Brooklyn chapter of the National Urban League and in the National Association for the Advancement of Colored People (NAACP).

She went to Columbia University in the evenings and earned a master's degree in early childhood education. She was so committed to teaching children that she taught at a Harlem nursery and became supervisor of a large nursery school that had many African American and Puerto Rican children. Chisholm used the job as supervisor to become astute at managing people and problems. She became adept at political infighting, and as a member of the 17th District Democratic Committee helped to maneuver the election of a black attorney to the municipal court of New York in 1953.

Shirley Chisholm has been called one of the best orators to enter the United States House of Representatives. She is literate, well-read, learned, and "unbought and unbossed." She was one of the first female politicians to challenge male dominance in the Congress. She would not allow men to control her thoughts or ideas. She spoke up for the rights of women and children and made the condition of poor children her principal issue. She was a thorn in the side of the status quo and the politics of the "good ol' boys," making them pay publicly for supporting spending more money on defense than they did on the care of children. She was one of the few members of Congress to speak for Native Americans and Spanish-speaking Americans as well as the African American constituency that elected her to Congress.

In 1964 Shirley Chisholm won by a landslide her first election to become a member of the New York State Assembly. While serving in the Assembly (1965–1968), she and Assemblyman Arthur O. Eve created the legislation that established SEEK (Search for Education, Elevation, and Knowledge), a program that provided college funding to disadvantaged youths, and successfully introduced a bill that secured unemployment insurance for domestic workers and day-care providers. She won her seat in the United States House of Representatives in 1968. In the Congress she served on Education and Labor committees, and she was a leading campaigner for a higher minimum wage and federal funding for day-care facilities. Shirley Chisholm became the first African American woman to campaign for the presidency in 1972. She would later write an autobiography, *The Good Fight* (1973), explaining that her campaign helped to pave the way for others to run for Congress. One did not have to be a "wealthy, good-looking white male" to run for the highest office in the land.

Chisholm retired from Congress in 1982. Her career did not end, however. She remained an active campaigner for women's rights, education, and children's rights, and continued to give lectures and addresses to audiences around the country. Her political analyses and social commentaries were sought after by numerous political and community groups. She was incredibly bright and insightful and could have made a good president. Chisholm created the National Political Congress of Black Women and served on the Advisory Council of the National Organization for Women.

# KENNETH B.
# CLARK

1914–

**K**enneth Bancroft Clark was born in the Panama Canal Zone in 1914. He was brought to New York by his mother at a very early age. Clark attended school in New York and included among his acquaintances Countee Cullen, who taught at his junior high school, and Arturo Schomburg, the black Puerto Rican bibliophile who was the curator of the 135th Street branch of the New York Public Library. Clark graduated from George Washington High School in 1931.

Leaving New York for Washington, D.C., Clark entered Howard University and distinguished himself as an undergraduate student. He was easily attracted to social activism, and while at Howard led demonstrations against segregated facilities. There he met Mamie Phipps, the woman who would become his wife and his collaborator in most of his experiments in psychology. After they married, the Clarks entered Columbia University in New York City to study psychology. Kenneth Clark became Columbia's first black recipient of a Ph.D. in psychology in 1941. He joined the faculty of City College in New York City in 1942, becoming that college's first black permanent professor. He remained at City College until his retirement in 1975, but he also served as a visiting professor at Columbia, Harvard University, and the University of California at Berkeley. Clark's career paralleled many of the legal successes of the civil rights era. He was not content to allow his credentials and skills to remain corralled by the walls of the university; he sought to make social science useful to the cause of racial equality and justice. Therefore he made his skills available to the National Association for the Advancement of Colored People (NAACP) and others who wanted to challenge the racial construction of superiority-inferiority in society. Clark knew that the struggle against segregation would not be won simply in the courthouse, but that it had to be won also on academic, experimental, societal, and scientific grounds. Thus, in the early 1950s, he was one of the few African American expert witnesses against segregation.

Kenneth Clark's greatest achievement was his research on the self-image of black children. In a landmark study, Clark investigated the responses of more than two hundred black children who were given a choice between white or brown dolls. The study showed that black children preferred the white dolls from as early as three years old. Clark concluded that racial segregation was psychologically damaging because it had a self-deprecating effect on black children. His conclusion played a key role in *Brown* v. *Board of Education*, the Supreme Court case that outlawed racially segregated education.

Clark continued to make his case that racial segregation was psychologically damaging to black children and in his book *Dark Ghetto: Dilemmas of Social Power* (1965), he went so far as to argue that the condition of African Americans was like that of colonized people. Clark wrote numerous articles and several additional books explaining his ideas and opinions. He wrote *Prejudice and Your Child* (1955) and *The Negro American* (1966), coedited with Talcott Parsons. Another book, *The Negro Protest* (1963), was published in 1963.

Clark was active in the social reconstruction of the black community in New York. He showed optimism in the ability of the community to help itself and demonstrated a commitment to self-determination that showed in his tendency toward black nationalist thinking. He was a leader in the establishment in 1962 of Harlem Youth Opportunities Unlimited, a program that influenced President Lyndon Johnson's War on Poverty program. He served on the New York Board of Regents and kept up his fight against racist education.

Clark won the NAACP's Spingarn Medal in 1961. When he retired from City College, he became a consultant dealing with racial policy in education and economics.

# JOHN HENRIK
# CLARKE
1915–1998

**B**orn in Union Springs, Alabama, on January 1, 1915, and raised in Columbus, Georgia, John Henry Clark ran away to Harlem, changed his name to John Henrik Clarke, and became one of the most significant intellectual activists of his time.

John Henrik Clarke was called "the dean of African American historians" and "the walking encyclopedia" for his unusual memory of facts and figures in African American history. He became a leading intellectual in African American nationalism because of his insistence that African Americans did not have a true understanding of the economic, political, and historical nature of white supremacy and its control of the lives of African people. He attracted widespread interest in his ideas and became the godfather of many younger intellectuals, who saw in his work the example they wanted to emulate. In the late 1960s he led a walkout of African and African American scholars from the African Studies Association at a convention in Montreal, Quebec, claiming that the organization was racist and set up to promote the European study of Africa. He later formed the African Heritage Studies Association devoted to the study of African history and politics from the vantage point of African interests. Barbara Adams, in her book *John Henrik Clarke: Master Teacher,* wrote, "There was never a question too complicated or too insignificant for him."

Clarke was a popular teacher and a great student of world history. Combining his interest in teaching with his devotion and dedication to history, Clarke taught the uses of history to bring about consciousness, often saying that "history is a clock, it allows one to tell time, to tell where you are on the clock of life."

As a youth in Georgia, he asked a white farmer to suggest some books on African American history so that he might learn about his own people. The white farmer looked at him and said, "Young man, I am sorry, there is no history of your people." Clarke says that from that day forward he vowed that he would look in every book, go to the ends of the earth, and discover in the remotest places all the information he could gather about his own people and their culture.

He took a freight train out of Georgia to New York. When he arrived, he went to Harlem and became an active participant in the literary and political life of the community in the 1930s. Clarke ventured, as a young man, to the offices of Arturo Schomburg, in his quest for information and knowledge about the African world. Clarke says that Schomburg received him and told him to go out and learn all he could about the enemies of the black man and he would have his information about black history.

Clarke became a writer, and sent his essays, poetry, and political opinions to a number of magazines. He was able to produce poetry, short stories (notably "The Boy Who Painted Christ Black" [1968]), and books on African history (*The Lives of Great African Chiefs* [1958]) and on Africans in the diaspora (*Harlem U.S.A.* [1971]) over a period of years that included the Black Power movement years. He was a friend and advisor to Malcolm X, an original member of the Harlem Writers Guild, and a founding editor of *Freedomways* magazine. He was the editor of William Styron's *Nat Turner: Ten Black Writers Respond*, a critique of Styron's fictionalized version of Turner's revolt, and author of the powerful critique *The African World Revolution*.

John Henrik Clarke served in the United States Air Force and attended New York University and the New School for Social Research. He was given numerous honorary doctorates. Beginning in 1964 he headed a federal antipoverty program. An active supporter of Pan-African political movements, he was on a first-name basis with many African leaders, and his Harlem home was a way station for visiting Africans. Clarke joined the faculty of Hunter College in 1969, establishing the black studies program there, and later assisted in setting up the African American Studies Department at Cornell University. He was president of the Sankofa University, an internet university, founded in 1995. Soon after his retirement, Clarke became professor emeritus at Hunter College and remained a highly sought-after speaker until his death at age eighty-three. The following statement from Clarke perhaps best summarizes his philosophy: "Wherever we are on the face of the earth, we are an African people."

Upon his death in 1998, there assembled in New York one of the greatest collections of African intellectuals in the history of the United States. More than two hundred scholars, teachers, and professors were among the more than fifteen hundred people who packed the Abyssinian Baptist Church to witness the funeral of John Henrik Clarke as an African king, in full regalia, with African drummers and dancers. Such was the life of Clarke that his legend was built each day he lived and walked the streets of Harlem.

# JOHN
# COLTRANE

1926–1967

J ohn William Coltrane, one of
the greatest American jazz
saxophonists, was a composer,
band leader, and compositional
innovator who led the free jazz
avant-garde movement of the 1960s.

Coltrane was born in Hamlet,
North Carolina, in 1926 and soon moved with his family to High
Point, North Carolina. John Coltrane's parents, John and Alice,
lived within an extended family headed by Reverend William
Blair, Coltrane's maternal grandfather. When Blair took a pas-
torate in High Point the entire family moved from Hamlet.

Coltrane's father was a lover of music but his real job was as
a tailor. He played the ukulele for his family's pleasure and created an atmosphere of music and rhythm in the household. Alice
Coltrane (not to be confused with the musician's second wife)
was a seamstress. She found her husband's music at home very
enjoyable and she would sing and play the piano at home and in
the gospel choir at church. Another couple lived in the household as well, that of Reverend Blair's daughter Betty, her husband, Goler, and their child, Mary. Cousin Mary, like John, was
an only child. They grew up like siblings in a relatively calm and
peaceful environment. While the family was not rich, it was not
destitute, as many families were.

Coltrane was a good student in the public schools, excelling
in history and making the honor roll on several occasions. He
soon discovered that his love for music was greater than his love
for studying history and geography. By the time he was sixteen,
four of the adults in the household had died. His father died in

1939 when John was thirteen years old. His grandfather died a few months later, and his uncle and aunt also died within three years. This shattered the family and changed the nature of the environment of Coltrane's adolescent years.

During this period Coltrane went more deeply into his study of music. He played in a community band, experimenting with the alto horn and the clarinet. He switched to the alto saxophone and remained attached to it for most of his apprentice period. He would later turn to the tenor saxophone. It is possible that this immersion in music was therapeutic because of the trauma he had experienced in his home. Nevertheless, we know for certain that he would practice from the afternoon until three or four in the morning.

When Coltrane completed high school in 1943 he headed north for Philadelphia. He was joined in the City of Brotherly Love by his mother, his cousin Mary, and another aunt, who had all gone to New Jersey to work in the wartime plants. Coltrane studied briefly at Granoff studios and then at the Ornstein Conservatory, where he studied saxophone technique and music theory, off and on, for eight years. He was an excellent student, his many years of practice in North Carolina coming into play. He loved his lessons, especially the advanced theoretical concepts taught by Dennis Sandole. However, he left music school in 1944 to join the United States Navy.

The two years he spent in the navy were good for Coltrane's musical experience. He played in several navy bands as a clarinetist, moonlighting as an alto saxophonist in a dance band in Hawaii. When Coltrane returned to Philadelphia, he would become an exceedingly competent musician. When he was nineteen years old, Coltrane was an acolyte of African American alto saxophonist Charlie Parker. Coltrane would later say that Parker came to him in a dream and encouraged him to study harmonics during his "sheets of sound" period. While the critics would call Coltrane antijazz, Parker would see the possibilities in the younger musician's work. Coltrane resumed his studies at the Ornstein Conservatory and practiced music with the local jazz brotherhood that included many who would eventually become jazz luminaries, including Jimmy Oliver, Benny Golson, Howard McGhee, "Philly" Jo Jones, Lee Morgan, Jimmy Heath, Bill Barron, and Cal Massey.

In the late 1940s, Coltrane switched from alto to tenor saxophone while working with Earl Bostic, who played the alto saxophone. On the alto saxophone, Coltrane was heavily influenced by the playing style of Parker. On the tenor saxophone, Coltrane relied on a variety of influences, including Dexter Gordon, Edward "Sonny" Stitt, and Theodore "Sonny" Rollins. He became the musician's musician, having a reputation among the best musicians long before he had a public following. By the early 1950s, he had played with many big-name rhythm and blues and jazz artists, including Big Maybelle, Daisie Mae and the Hep Cats, Charlie Parker, Earl Bostic, Eddie "Cleanhead" Vinson, Jimmy Smith, Johnny Hodges, and Dizzy Gillespie.

Music was not making him rich, and he hardly survived on the small stipends he received for playing with others. If not for his mother, he would have been living on the streets. He was underemployed and often forced to take behind-the-scenes jobs in theater that he felt were below the dignity of a serious musician.

Coltrane soon developed a heroin habit. This would have a major impact on his life, creating crises of one kind after another for him. He desperately tried to wean himself from the habit by drinking alcohol, only to discover that he had acquired two addictions. A chronic battle with weight loss and gain meant that he had to have two wardrobes, one for the times he was skinny and another for the times when he was larger.

Two events in 1955 had significance for Coltrane. He married Juanita Grubbs (Naima) in 1955 and joined the quintet of African American jazz trumpet player Miles Davis. With Davis he became one of the hard bop voices on alto saxophone, developing his style and creating a following. He was fired by Miles Davis in 1957 and traded places with Sonny Rollins. He joined the band of Thelonious Monk, while Rollins joined Miles Davis. He played the Five Spot Café engagement with Monk's band. In 1960 he founded his own band and played even more personal, perhaps haunting, sounds. He began to attract critical attention through recordings such as *'Round*

*About Midnight, Steamin', Relaxin', Cookin',* and *Workin'.* Coltrane thought of Monk as a musical architect of the highest order.

In 1957 Coltrane had an experience that caused him to tell his mother and his friend Eric Dolphy that he had "seen God." It was not clear what he meant, but the experience had a profound impact on his life. He wanted to dedicate his life and his music to spiritual awakening because he had finally found the strength to beat the heroin and alcohol addiction. He studied the religions and music of India and Africa and learned to experiment with improvisations utilizing a set of pitches, or modes, rather than functional harmony, as in bebop. He devised a set of harmonic formulas that musicians now call "Coltrane substitutions."

He was a creator without peer with the wind instruments. He reintroduced the soprano saxophone as a viable jazz instrument, coming forty years after African American clarinet and soprano saxophone player Sidney Bechet. He recorded *Blue Train* (1957), *Giant Steps* (1959), and his first hit record, *My Favorite Things* (1960), in this vein.

In 1961 Coltrane formed his classic quartet with himself on tenor and soprano saxophones, McCoy Tyner on piano, either Jimmy Garrison or Reggie Workman on bass, and Elvin Jones on drums.

Coltrane's classic quartet was his greatest gift to music. It toured the United States and Europe, and Coltrane won the *Down Beat* Poll in at least one category every year afterward. He was inducted into the *Down Beat* Hall of Fame in 1965 as Jazz Man of the Year, and his masterpiece, *A Love Supreme* (1964), was honored as record of the year. Some critics have said that his work with the classic quartet made him, after Parker, the most imitated saxophonist in jazz history. There was something spiritual about Coltrane's sojourn in music. He was admired not only for his musical genius but for his spirituality. In San Francisco, there is a church called after him, the Church of St. John Coltrane, where his most spiritual recordings—*Africa Brass* (1961), *Live at the Village Vanguard* (1961), *Crescent* (1964), *A Love Supreme* (1964), *First Meditations* (1965), and *Sun Ship* (1965)—are played regularly as part of the worship.

In 1966 Coltrane's second wife, Alice (née Alice McCleod), joined the band on piano, and Rashied Ali joined on drums. Pharoah Sanders (né Farrell Sanders) also joined the band on tenor and soprano saxophones. Coltrane explored all forms of sound, texture, composition, line, and rhythm, as well as group improvisation, stretching the parameters of music. Among the recordings of this period are *Live at the Village Vanguard, Again* (1966), *Live in Japan* (1966), *Stellar Regions* (1966), *Interstellar Space* (1967), and *Expression* (1967). Coltrane died at forty years of age in 1967. Hc was awarded the National Academy of Recording Arts and Sciences Grammy Award for Lifetime Achievement posthumously in 1991. In 2001 the city of Philadelphia, where he spent most of his professional life, created two huge murals in recognition of his artistic genius.

# BILL
# COSBY
1937–

**B**ill Cosby was born in Philadelphia, Pennsylvania, in 1937. He attended public schools and took courses at Temple University until a part-time job as a stand-up comedian became too demanding for him to continue his formal college education. By 1963 he had effectively established himself on the nightclub circuit in the northeastern United States. He auditioned to fill in for television talk show host Johnny Carson on the *Tonight* show. He was so successful, he became the first African American to regularly be called upon to host the show. Two years later, in 1965, Cosby starred in the television drama *I Spy* alongside Robert Culp, becoming the first African American to appear in a predominantly white drama on television. He was later compared to Jackie Robinson in baseball and Jack Johnson in boxing as an African American who had achieved in a new sector of the society. He won an Emmy for his acting on *I Spy* and became a celebrity with incredible audience appeal.

Cosby starred in his own show, *The Bill Cosby Show*, from 1969 to 1971, where he played high school basketball coach Chet Kincaid. With his career soaring and his reputation intact, Cosby picked up his undergraduate degree from Temple and entered the School of Education at the University of Massachusetts Amherst, where he earned a doctorate. A new show, *The New Bill Cosby Show*, featuring comedy and variety, aired in 1972 and 1973. The program *Cos* debuted in 1976.

When UCLA professor Gordon Berry, of the School of Education, led a team of advisors and soundboard crew for the animated Saturday morning feature *Fat Albert and the Cosby Kids* (1972–1977), there was a merger between current research and children programming. The idea behind the cadre's involvement was to advise Cosby and the script writers on the content impact of the messages on duty, discipline, veracity, and responsibility. Bill Cosby took the advisory team's suggestions seriously and showed a strong commitment to children, as seen in his cameo appearances in *Fat Albert* and *The Electric Company*.

*The Cosby Show* (1984–1992) ranked third in Nielsen ratings during its first season. It would win the title as the number-one ranked show in the Nielsen ratings for the next two years. In the *The Cosby Show*, Bill Cosby's depiction of Dr. Cliff Huxtable made him a household favorite. The Huxtable family included Cosby as Dr. Huxtable, his lovely and intelligent lawyer wife, and their five well-adjusted, beautiful, and successful children.

Bill Cosby did not shy away from fighting discrimination within the television industry. He learned how television worked, used his success to leverage more roles for African Americans, and demanded and got a larger role in the production of the show. Demonstrating his desire to make difference in Hollywood, he sought after and hired African American writers, directors, and dancers. In fact, he also brought in Dr. Alvin Pouissaint as an advisor and displayed the artwork of artist Varnette Honeywood on the set.

Cosby was already a star, but *The Cosby Show* made him a megastar, the biggest African American celebrity ever (until Oprah Winfrey) in terms of power and money. He was at the top of his career as a public figure. But Cosby did not slow down. He continued to appear on various television shows, perform live concerts, and produce comedy albums, and receive numerous Grammy awards. In addition, he wrote books, including the best-selling *Fatherhood* in 1986 and *Love and Marriage* in 1989. The Cosby family gave $20 million to Spelman College in 1989. Cosby's philanthropy has benefited many organizations, including the National Association for the Advancement of Colored People (NAACP), the United Negro College Fund, the National Sickle-Cell Foundation, and the National Council of Negro Women.

# ALEXANDER
# CRUMMELL
## 1819–1898

**A**lexander Crummell was the pioneer of those who loved African culture and African history without compromise. In his lifetime, he would become one of the greatest promoters of black culture the country had ever seen. Crummell was a dedicated and devoted prophetic voice of the African American people. He would become the vanguard intellectual of the black nationalist ideology.

Alexander Crummell was born in New York in 1819, the son of Boston Crummell, a prince of the Temne people of Sierra Leone. Crummell often said that his father had been stolen while playing on the beach in Africa. He attended school in New York and then transferred to a school in Canaan, New Hampshire, that accepted African children and taught them to read. However, this school was attacked and the building dragged into a pond by those who hated the fact that whites were teaching blacks how to read. Crummell and other students, including Henry Highland Garnett, took refuge in a barn. They were shot at, but Garnett returned fire and soon, in a truce, the African students were allowed to vacate the property. They left the area, but the incident had a lasting impact on the students. Crummell then attended school at the Oneida Institute in New York State.

After his training at Oneida, Crummell became a priest in the Episcopal Church and spent twenty years on the west coast of Africa as a missionary. He visited seventy different ethnic groups, mastering many of the languages and learning all he could about the history of the African people. When he returned to the United

States, he was rector of St. Philip's Church in New York for three years. After that, he was made rector of St. Luke's Church in Washington, D.C., where he remained for twenty-three years.

There was something missing in his soul that could not be filled by religion, so he spent the last days of his life publishing race tracts and establishing the American Negro Academy, the first body to bring African scholars from all over the world together in one place. He would often visit the seashore at Asbury Park and Point Pleasant, New Jersey, meditating on the condition of African people in a racist society. There in Point Pleasant, on the New Jersey shore, he died in 1898, in his eightieth year.

Crummell in many ways rivaled Frederick Douglass in charisma, but during the eventful years of 1850 to 1870, he was in Africa and so did not have the influence that Frederick Douglass claimed on American society. Crummell's power was unlike Douglass's: it was largely an influence and dynamism among the African people themselves, not necessarily an influence among the whites. He was quite accomplished as an orator, speaking in 1847 to the Colored Convention in Troy, New York, and then in 1848 to the Anti-Slavery Society in London. Crummell is said to have spoken with such power and passion that he won many converts to the cause of liberty. From London he visited Liverpool and preached at St. George's Church in Everton. Since the audience had never heard an African speak in public, Crummell's talk was to serve as a measuring rod of the African's intelligence and capability. He held the audience spellbound for an hour with his brilliance, his polished diction, his bearing in the pulpit, and his fire and force of utterance. Ferris maintained that Crummell's eulogy of Clarkson, delivered in 1846, was unsurpassed by any African speaker during the antebellum period.

Crummell's charisma attracted hundreds of blacks to his speeches, and his followers made his house a gathering and debating place. His dignity, knowledge, experience, and aristocratic bearing made him one of the most celebrated African Americans of his day. William Ferris is correct to say the historic Crummell was a "finished scholar, the magnetic preacher, the brave, uncompromising idealist, who was dreaded by imposters and fakirs and time-servers and flunkies."

Perhaps the ingredients that constituted his genius and his greatness were the venerable qualities of good manners, keen insight, repartee, humor, and wide knowledge that allowed him to become the magnet that he became. His "ineffable charm in conversation" made him the voice the African people needed in his time. One cannot help be impressed by W. E. B. Du Bois's richly textured essay, in his book, *Souls of Black Folk*, on the life of Alexander Crummell as one cannot help being moved by Crummell's chapter on Henry Highland Garnett in his publication for the American Negro Academy, all great African Americans.

Crummell's achievement was to see that education would play a major role in the liberation of the African. In 1897, at the nadir of African American history, when the Reconstruction had been turned back, lynchings had become endemic in the South, and the racist propagandists were having a field day attacking African capabilities, the aged Alexander Crummell found the energy and courage to organize the American Negro Academy in Washington, D.C., calling together the most distinguished individuals of the African American community. This organization had five objectives: (1) to defend the race against vicious assaults; (2) to publish scholarly work; (3) to foster higher education; (4) to formulate intellectual tastes; and (5) to promote literature, art, and science. Attending the first meeting on March 5, 1897, at the Lincoln Memorial Church were the young celebrities Paul Laurence Dunbar and W. E. B. Du Bois. When Crummell died the following year, Du Bois was elected president of the academy. It was Crummell's vision of a cadre of scholars who would advance the race that made the academy a significant institution at the beginning of the twentieth century.

# COUNTEE
# CULLEN

1903–1946

**C**ountee Cullen was the signature poet of the Harlem Renaissance. He was born in 1903 in Louisville, Kentucky, to Elizabeth Lucas, and raised in New York by Elizabeth Porter, who was probably his maternal grandmother. Cullen's early life was kept a mystery by Cullen himself and only recently has it become known what happened to him after he was adopted as a teenager. He was always reluctant to talk about his former family.

When Elizabeth Porter died around 1918, Countee Porter was taken in by the Reverend Frederick Cullen, pastor of Harlem's prominent Salem Methodist Episcopal Church, and his wife Carolyn. Countee considered the Cullens his parents and changed his name to Cullen out of respect for them.

He was sent to the predominantly white DeWitt Clinton High School, where he was an excellent student and editor of the school newspaper and literary magazine. At DeWitt Clinton, Cullen distinguished himself in literature and had a natural affection for reading novels and poetry. While still in high school, he won a citywide poetry contest. He had no difficulty in being admitted to New York University as an undergraduate. At NYU he composed scores of poems, many of which would find their way into his first two volumes of poetry. He graduated from New York University as a member of Phi Beta Kappa, a recognition of his intellectual prowess. He also published his first book, *Color*. Cullen left New York to enter Harvard and received a master's degree in English and French. Like many of the Harlem

Renaissance–era writers, Cullen sent his poetry to the *Crisis* and *Opportunity* for publication and award competitions. He was successful in winning prizes from both the Urban League's journal, *Opportunity*, and the National Association for the Advancement of Colored People's journal, the *Crisis*.

When Cullen graduated from Harvard in 1927, he knew that he wanted to write for a living. He became an assistant editor at *Opportunity*. He published two volumes of poetry in 1927, *Copper Sun* and *The Ballad of the Brown Girl: An Old Ballad Retold,* and he edited *Caroling Dusk: An Anthology of Verse by Negro Poets.*

Cullen's poetry was often characterized by the styles he acquired from studying European writers. He was seen by some of his peers as having an allegiance to the traditional forms of Europe rather than the experimental forms of the new literary renaissance. Nevertheless, Countee Cullen remained the most educated poet of his day and became more popular with black audiences when he wrote poems that spoke to the cultural experiences of the people. More poignant than most poets, he asked, and tried to explain, "What is Africa to me?"

Cullen received more literary prizes during the 1920s than any other Harlem writer. On April 9, 1928, his marriage to Yolande Du Bois, the only child of W. E. B. Du Bois, was the black social event of the year. In one act, the consolidation of the African American intelligentsia had occurred when the best-known African American poet married the daughter of one of the greatest intellectuals. The wedding attracted one thousand guests to the church led by Cullen's father.

The marriage did not last long, however, and by 1930 Cullen and Du Bois were divorced. He took a position as a French teacher at Frederick Douglass Junior High in Harlem, where James Baldwin was one of his students, and continued to write poetry. His book *The Black Christ and Other Poems,* published in 1929, received poor reviews, and Cullen's career as a writer began to wane. He wrote his only novel, *One Way to Heaven*, in 1934, two children's books, and *The Lost Zoo* and *My Lives and How I Lost Them* a couple years later. Countee Cullen became the first twentieth-century African American writer to publish a major translation of a Greek classical work with his translation of *Medea* in 1936.

Cullen remarried in 1940, and his second wife, Ida, attempted to keep his memory alive after his death in 1946. She was unable to keep Cullen's fame from being overshadowed by the rising star of Langston Hughes. Yet the indelible imprint of Countee Cullen on the Harlem Renaissance remains bold and impressive in the hearts of African Americans.

# BENJAMIN O.
# DAVIS JR.
## 1912–2002

**B**enjamin Oliver Davis Jr. was born in 1912. He was the son of Elnora and Benjamin Oliver Davis Sr., who became the first black general of the United States Army, himself a worthy candidate for greatness. The young Davis was a military child, living on a number of army bases with his parents. He attended high school in Cleveland, Ohio, where he excelled as a student and was elected president of his class. After high school, Davis attended Cleveland's Western Reserve University, now Case Western Reserve University. However, he transferred to the University of Chicago and spent time trying to enter the United States Military Academy at West Point. Although his father was a distinguished officer in the military and there had been other African Americans at the academy, it was still the practice of the military academy to discourage African Americans from applying. Chicago congressman Oscar DePriest, an active campaigner for black rights, finally got Davis an opportunity to take the entrance examination, and he was admitted to the academy in 1932.

Davis entered West Point in 1932 and recalled his time there as one of personal distress and abuse from his fellow students. He was isolated on campus when no one sat with him, shared a room with him, spoke with him unless giving an order, or otherwise recognized his presence. This treatment allowed Davis much time for reflection and study, thus he graduated from the United States Military Academy in the top 15 percent of his class, becoming the first African American graduate of West Point since Reconstruction.

Given his ranking he should have been able to select the branch of service he preferred to enter. This opportunity was denied him because the thinking of the day was that he had to work in a branch of the service where he could lead only black men, not white men. Although he asked for the United States Air Corps, then a part of the army, he was denied because there were no black squadrons. Recently married to Agatha Scott, he was assigned to Fort Benning, Georgia. The Georgia military base, like all others, was segregated, as was the law and the custom of the land during the late 1930s and early 1940s.

With the breakout of World War II, the administration of President Franklin Delano Roosevelt solidified its support among the African American population by making a number of key appointments, including promoting Benjamin Davis Sr. to the rank of general. But perhaps the most revolutionary action taken by Roosevelt was the creation of a training program for black pilots at the historically black Tuskegee Institute. Benjamin Davis Jr. was finally given a command that would establish him as one of the greatest African Americans. He went to Tuskegee to train black pilots during a time when the majority of whites in the country believed blacks to be incapable of flying. When the training was completed in 1942, Davis, because of the good job he had done in training the pilots, was given command of the 99th Pursuit Squadron, the first black air unit. By the middle of 1943, the 99th Pursuit Squadron was operating in Egypt and Libya.

Most of the missions flown by the 99th Pursuit Squadron did not involve fighting; they were routine supply missions. Whites were still concerned that blacks could not adequately fly military aircraft, so they denied the 99th Pursuit Squadron the opportunity to prove itself. Consequently, Davis's superior officers told the Pentagon that blacks were not capable combat pilots. Though this was a lie, without any substantiation, it was readily believed at the time.

A few months later, Benjamin Davis Jr. was ordered to command the 332nd Fighter Group. This group of black pilots was larger than the 99th Pursuit Squadron. Davis was elevated to the rank of lieutenant colonel and demanded that the Pentagon treat black pilots as it treated white pilots. He asked to be able to take his men into air combat with the enemy. Within a few months, in early 1944, the Pentagon agreed and assigned the 332nd to the Italian front. The fighting group was so effective that within six months the 332nd had shown that it was the equal of any air combat in southern Europe. Davis was given the Distinguished Flying Cross.

Davis became one of the most articulate spokespersons against racism in the armed services. He challenged the government to eliminate racism and discrimination against the African American fighting forces. President Harry S. Truman desegregated the armed forces in 1948. Soon thereafter Davis joined the air force, the newest branch of the services, and worked to end segregation in the air force. He was given command of a racially integrated flying unit during the Korean War and was afterward promoted to brigadier general. In 1965 he became the first African American in any military branch to reach the rank of lieutenant general. After commanding the Thirteenth Air Force in the Vietnam War, he retired in 1970 after a distinguished career of service.

Davis served as an assistant secretary at the Department of Transportation under President Richard M. Nixon after he left the armed forces. He worked for the development of airport security and highway safety and was among the chief proponents of the 55 MPH speed limit.

Benjamin O. Davis Jr. died on July 4, 2002, at the age of eighty-nine.

# MARTIN R.
# DELANY
## 1812–1885

**M**artin Robison Delany was born in 1812, the year of the second war between the United States and Great Britain. He would become a signif- icant defender of the African American people, a Civil War officer, and the leading black abolitionist of Pennsylvania. He was raised in Chambersburg, Pennsylvania. Early on, he attracted the attention of a wealthy mentor, John B. Vashon, who made it possible for him to obtain an education. Delany was one of the strongest supporters of African Americans being self-determining and self-defining. He was not a separatist, as some have claimed, but a realist. He came to believe, on the basis of his experience, that Africans would not receive equal treatment with whites in the American society and therefore Africans had to look out for themselves, even if that meant leaving America.

Delany came to these views gradually, but firmly. Delany risked his career and his life for his opinions and, in this respect, he was an early candidate for greatness. He was a leader of black nationalist thought, and in that regard an influence on every major African American leader since his time.

Delany was every bit as courageous and as intelligent as Fred- erick Douglass, and it is only because the masses of black people did not write the early histories of these two men that Douglass is considered the more significant person of that era. Both were considered defenders of African American liberties, both fought against racism and stood for human decency, but Delany always drove home his special belief that blacks had to do more for themselves. He did not want to be a part of any white organization where white leaders would act as paternal figures.

Because he wanted to demonstrate his own independence, Delany, as a black man in the mid-1840s, had to do many different jobs in order to make a living. He started practicing medicine in 1843. Later, he thought he would take some classes at Harvard Medical School, and during 1850 and 1851 he attended Harvard. Delany wrote a novel, *Blake, or the Huts of America*, which was published in segments over a period of several years from 1859 to 1862. He also bought and sold real estate in an effort to support himself. He served in the Union Army and was the most celebrated and the highest-ranking black officer in the Civil War.

In journalism he was well known in the Pittsburgh area for his publication of the *Mystery* (1843–1847), a black-owned newspaper. He served as a coeditor with Douglass from 1847 to 1849 of the *North Star*. But Delany's real interest was in writing antislavery pamphlets, so he devoted most of his time to writing and securing the protection of escaped slaves. He opposed the American Colonization Society's idea to resettle blacks in Africa as a form of forced exile. If blacks were to leave, they must be allowed to leave on their own, Delany believed. Thus, he could advocate emigration but only if it came from the minds of black people. For example, in *The Condition, Elevation, Emigration, and Destiny of the Colored People of the United States* (1852), he wrote the first book-length study of the status of African Americans. In 1856 Delany left the United States for Canada. He settled in Chatham, Ontario, and was the only prominent black leader at the meeting in Chatham where John Brown announced his intentions to form a rebel state in exile.

Delany played a role in the African American emigration conferences held in 1854, 1856, and 1858. In 1858 he set sail for West Africa, and in 1859, after visiting Alexander Crummell in Liberia, he journeyed to Nigeria to meet the Alake of Abeokuta, where he asked for the settlement of African Americans. The Civil War disrupted his plans and caused a concentration of local issues in North America.

As a recruiter for Massachusetts, Delany raised black troops for the Union Army. Many of the troops he recruited fought with the 54th of Massachusetts. When he was transferred to South Carolina and given a field command, it was the first time in the history of the United States that a black had been given such a command. When the war was over, he joined the Freedmen's Bureau in South Carolina. Delany believed that the South Carolina's Reconstruction government was corrupt because of the interference of white carpetbaggers. He criticized black and white members of the South Carolina assembly and eventually, in 1876, announced support for the Democratic candidate for governor, Wade Hampton III, who turned out to be one of the worst enemies of the Reconstruction. Later, Delany published *Principia of Ethnology: The Origin of Races with an Archaeological Compendium of Ethiopian and Egyptian Civilization* (1879) and was one of the movers behind the failed Liberian Exodus Joint-Stock Steamship Company. He died in 1885.

# FREDERICK
# DOUGLASS
## 1818–1895

**F**rederick Douglass was born in February 1818 in Talbot County, Maryland. He was the son of an enslaved woman named Harriet Bailey and an unknown father, though it was rumored that his slave owner was his father. He was called Frederick Bailey when he was first born. He would later change his name to Douglass after he escaped from bondage. When commenting on his birth and the uncertainty surrounding his early life, he spoke of this uncertainty as a part of the crime of slavery. Many Africans had the same uncertain origins as Douglass. He was raised by his grandparents, Betsy and Isaac Bailey, a free black man, who kept young Frederick away from the harsher realities of slavery at an early age. His grandmother was owned by the slave owner Aaron Anthony, who managed the plantation of the wealthier Col. Edward Lloyd. Betsy Bailey had the responsibility of taking care of young slave children so that their parents could work. Douglass did not know his own mother well.

At the age of six, Douglass was taken from his grandmother and brought to the plantation of Aaron Anthony. Douglass often recalled hearing the screams of Africans being whipped by Anthony. When Frederick was eight years old, he was sent to Baltimore, Maryland, to work for new slave masters, Hugh Auld and his wife, Sophia, who read to Frederick from the Bible and taught him biblical passages. But when Hugh Auld learned of Sophia's lessons he declared that Frederick "should know nothing but the will of his master and learn to obey it."

When he was twelve years of age, Frederick was able to acquire the book *The Columbian Orator*, and he learned to appreciate oratory from reading it. The Aulds soon sent Frederick to Hugh's brother Thomas, where the young Frederick was supposed to forget his exposure to literature. But this move back to the rural area only incited in Frederick the desire to escape slavery.

Frederick converted to Christianity, but even conversion did not soften the reality of the harshness of his slave owner. Frederick soon lost his faith in religion, since it did not seem to have any impact on the life of his slave owner. Auld hired Frederick out to Edward Covey, a brutal man who was known to injure Africans in order to keep them under control. At Covey's farm Frederick could see the beautiful Chesapeake Bay and, on the bay, the free sailing ships that seemed so carefree. This gave him a longing for his own freedom. He recalled thinking that he would run away and not stand for the brutality anymore.

There were several attempts to escape, particularly after he had struggled with Covey, but he was told by Auld that he would be free when he turned twenty-five years of age. In the meantime, Frederick was sent back to Baltimore. There he met and fell in love with a free black woman, Anna Murray, and the two decided to leave Maryland. Douglass posed as a seaman and made his way to the North through an informal network of free blacks and antislavery activists in 1838. He reached New York City and immediately abandoned the slave name of Bailey and became Frederick Johnson. Soon Anna Murray was able to join him and they were married. They settled in New Bedford and Lynn, Massachusetts, for several years. In New Bedford, Frederick discovered that the name Johnson was quite familiar, even being the names of his free African friends, Nathan and Mary Johnson. He therefore decided to choose a name from Walter Scott's *Lady of the Lake.* The name Frederick chose was Douglas, and he added an extra *s* to the name, spelling it "Douglass."

Douglass soon became, by virtue of his ability to interpret the needs of the African people, one of the great figures of the nineteenth century. During a century when European expansionism and white supremacy were at their heights, Douglass's lectures made him popular as a great abolitionist, reformer, author, and orator.

He had a major part in the nineteenth-century reform movements, not only through his abolitionism but through his support
for women's rights and black suffrage. He remained steadfast in
his search for the freedom of African people. Douglass knew that
if freedom came it would be necessary for Africans to demonstrate their own abilities, and he felt that one of the greatest
needs of the day was for Africans to take some responsibility for
overcoming slavery. To this end, he encouraged blacks to join
every effort to overturn slavery.

Douglas was gifted with the ability to write well. He excelled
at autobiography, and his three memoirs—*The Narrative of the
Life of Frederick Douglass* (1845), *My Bondage and My Freedom*
(1855), and *Life and Times of Frederick Douglass* (1881; revised,
1892)—told the story of enslavement—its brutality, pain, and
deprivation—as much as any work.

Douglass's rhetoric was eloquent. He had a definite sense of
style and cadence, a flair for drama, and the ability to provide his
audiences with a sense of the familiar.

Douglass found work on New Bedford's docks. His first
child, Rosetta, was born in 1839, followed by Lewis Henry, Frederick Jr., Charles Remond, and Annie during the next few years.
He was an inspiring speaker at the antislavery rallies and became
one of the great attractions to the meetings. When the abolitionist William Lloyd Garrison spoke in 1839, Douglass heard
him in New Bedford and decided that he wanted to do the same
thing. It was a turning point in his life.

In 1841 William C. Coffin, a New Bedford Quaker, invited
Douglass to an antislavery gathering on Nantucket that included
prominent abolitionists such as Garrison, Wendell Phillips, and
Parker Pillsbury. When Douglass spoke, people felt they had
heard the voice that could tell the Africans' story better than any
other. He was an immediate star. The Massachusetts Anti-
Slavery Society offered him a job for life.

He became an instant celebrity on the platform because of his
charisma, sincerity, and passion. But he did not find antislavery
an easy job. In Pendleton, Indiana, he was angrily attacked by a

mob throwing stones, sticks, and rotten eggs. In the melee his hand was broken and he barely escaped with his life. He was literally thrown out of railroad cars when he sat among the white passengers. So he was aware of northern prejudice as well as southern slavery and spoke out against both of them.

Douglass went to England to speak against slavery, and when he returned to the United States his fame was phenomenal. He had won over a large following in Britain, and in the United States he was now considered the "national spokesperson for the African American community." It is no wonder that at the 1848 women's rights convention in Seneca Falls, New York, Douglass was the only male supporter of woman suffrage invited to speak. He had demonstrated his outrage at the lack of women's voting rights as well as the lack of freedom for Africans.

In 1847 Douglass went to live in Rochester, New York, where he started a newspaper to support the antislavery cause. He would edit several papers, including *North Star* (1847–1851), *Frederick Douglass' Paper* (1851–1860), *Douglass' Monthly* (1859–1863), and the *New National Era* (1870–1874). After living in Rochester for twenty-five years, he moved to Washington in 1872.

Frederick Douglass did not back away from tough decisions, and during the early 1850s he started moving ideologically away from the position of William Lloyd Garrison and the pacifists. By 1859 Douglass had met in secret with white abolitionist John Brown to hear about the planned raid on Harpers Ferry, Virginia.

When the Civil War broke out Douglass hoped that Lincoln would recruit blacks to fight in the conflict. He tried hard to define the struggle as a fight against the evils of slavery. As the first African American to speak with a United States president, Frederick Douglass convinced President Lincoln to recruit black soldiers for the Union Army. Soon Lincoln was able to translate the war into a battle not just to preserve the Union but also, if necessary, to end slavery. The government was determined to fight against slavery and asked for black volunteers. The African Americans who fought in the war did so in segregated units, but they contributed greatly to the victory of the North over the South. There was never in confusion in the minds of the African American soldiers about the objectives of their fighting. Douglass had made it clear that black people were fighting to end slavery regardless of what others might have thought.

After the death of his wife, Douglass married Helen Pitts, a white woman, in 1882. Spending the remaining years of his life in the service to the United States government, he held several posts such as United States marshal for the District of Columbia (1877–1881), recorder of deeds for the District of Columbia (1881–1886), and chargé d'affaires for Santo Domingo, capital of the Dominican Republic, and minister to Haiti (1889–1891).

The passionate antilynching rhetoric of African American journalist and political activist Ida B. Wells convinced Douglass to join the national antilynching movement. Douglass wrote an essay, "Lynch Law in the South," that appeared in the *North American Review* in 1892. To add further to Ida B. Wells's campaign against lynching, as commissioner for the Republic of Haiti's exhibit at the 1893 World's Columbian Exhibition in Chicago, Douglass allowed Wells to distribute thousands of antilynching pamphlets from the Haitian pavilion. On the day of his death, Frederick Douglass attended a meeting of the National Council of Women.

# CHARLES
# DREW
1904–1950

**C**harles Richard Drew was born in Washington, D.C., in 1904. He attended the public schools of that city, becoming a well-known athlete and scholar during his high school years. His extraordinary achievements in basketball, baseball, football, and track at Dunbar High School earned him the recognition of many colleges; he eventually accepted a full-tuition scholarship to attend Amherst College in Massachusetts. While at Amherst College, Drew continued his achievements in athletics and scholarship, earning the distinction as the best all-around athlete at Amherst. When he graduated in 1926, he did so with the highest academic honors the school could give. He coached football, served as the athletic director, and, from 1926 to 1928, taught biology and chemistry at Morgan College, later Morgan State University, in Baltimore.

Drew applied to and was accepted into McGill University Medical School in Montreal in 1928. He began his studies to become a surgeon at the Canadian institution because he found it less difficult for an African American to be admitted to medical school in Canada than in the United States. At the time, neither Johns Hopkins University nor the University of Maryland accepted African American students for medical school. Drew excelled in sports at McGill, as he had done at Dunbar High and Amherst. Because of his equal gifts as a scholar, Drew was admitted to the medical honorary society of McGill University and awarded a Julius Rosenwald Fellowship. He was able to receive his M.D. and Master of Surgery degree from McGill University in 1933. After interning for two years in Canadian hospitals he returned to the United States in 1935 to take a teaching post at Howard University. Later he received a fellowship from the Rockefeller Foundation that enabled him to conduct the experiments that led to his most famous studies on blood. While at McGill he had become interested in determining how to preserve blood, a scientific puzzle that had not been resolved during the time of his study. He went to Columbia University to obtain a doctorate and discovered, while interning at Presbyterian Hospital in New York, that blood plasma, the liquid part of the blood without cells, could be preserved for long periods of time. This was something that could not be done with whole blood; it degraded after a few days in storage. Drew further discovered that blood plasma could be substituted for whole blood in transfusions. These were powerful breakthroughs in science and medicine.

Charles Drew followed his work by setting up an experimental blood bank at Presbyterian Hospital. Soon thereafter he completed his doctoral dissertation, entitled *Banked Blood: A Study in Blood Preservation*, and earned his Doctor of Science in Medicine degree from Columbia University in 1940.

Blood became more available for people in need of transfusions. This was particularly useful at the time of World War II, when there was a desperate need for blood on the battlefields of Europe. By 1940 the British, in immediate need of assistance in this area, asked the United States for help, and the Blood Transfusion Association of America selected Drew as the medical supervisor of the Blood for Britain program. Almost immediately in 1940, Drew arranged for large amounts of plasma to be flown to England and set up several blood banks there.

The effectiveness of Drew's efforts did not go unobserved or unremarked upon by the American scientific and health-care community. The American Red Cross asked Drew to establish a blood bank program in the United States in 1941. The irony of this request for Drew to lead the blood bank program was that the U.S. War Department had declared "it is not advisable to collect and mix Caucasian and Negro blood indiscriminately for later administration to members of the military forces." Drew called this "ignorant and unscientific" and vigorously protested the segregation of blood. He declared he would stand by his scientific principles and research that there was no racial difference in blood. For taking such a strong ethical and scientific stand he was fired as the director of the Red Cross Blood Bank Program in 1944. His position was that "the blood of individual human beings may differ by blood groupings, but there is absolutely no scientific basis to indicate any differences according to race." It would be the end of the decade, in 1949, before the U.S. military would stop segregating banked blood. Drew was already a renowned hematologist.

After the war Drew returned to Howard University and practiced surgery until a tragic automobile accident ended his life in 1950 at the age of forty-six. Six years earlier the National Association for the Advancement of Colored People (NAACP) had awarded Drew the prestigious Spingarn Medal.

# W. E. B.
# DU BOIS
1868–1963

illiam Edward Burghardt Du Bois was born in Great Barrington, Massachusetts, on February 23, 1868, three years after the end of the Civil War. He attended school in Great Barrington, one of the best students and the only African American student in his classes, and graduated with aspiration to seek higher education. He left home for Nashville, Tennessee, to attend Fisk University. He took with him a commitment to excellence and a passion for intellectual competition.

After completing his undergraduate work at Fisk University and being immersed in the African American culture in the southern United States, Du Bois returned to Massachusetts to attend Harvard University. Among his professors were George Santayana, William James, and Josiah Royce. He completed his doctorate at Harvard in 1895, writing his dissertation, *The Suppression of the African Slave Trade 1638–1870*. This manuscript became the basis for his first book and one of the major research pieces done on the slave trade in the nineteenth century. It was the first in a series of studies called the Harvard Historical Series. He was able to attend classes and lectures at the University of Berlin, then called Humboldt, from 1892 to 1894, and acquire a full understanding of the nature of European philosophical and historical thought. Du Bois always spoke of his German experience as significant to his intellectual development.

Du Bois took a job at Wilberforce, a small African American college in Ohio. He went to Wilberforce immediately after Harvard and left a year later, having married Nina Gomer, one of his former students. They moved to Philadelphia, Pennsylvania, where Du Bois was invited to work on a sociological study under the direction of the University of Pennsylvania. The project was to make an assessment and survey of the condition of Africans in the city of Philadelphia. This work led to the publication of *The Philadelphia Negro*, which provided the model for numerous sociological studies of urban communities. Du Bois took this model with him to Atlanta University in 1897, where he became a professor in the department of history and economics. Du Bois remained at Atlanta University for ten years.

The publication of *The Souls of Black Folk* in 1903 became the signature for Du Bois's response to the racial climate in America. He identified the color line as the problem of the twentieth century, spoke of double consciousness on the part of African Americans, and proposed the idea of the Talented Tenth, an idea he later abandoned because of its elitism. At the time, Du Bois had hoped that ten percent of the African American community, those skilled and talented, would lead the race up from segregation and discrimination. It was in *The Souls of Black Folk* that Du Bois turned up the political and critical heat on Booker T. Washington's ideas about black development. Du Bois saw Washington's efforts at securing for the white community a cadre of black workers as a betrayal of the people's right to political and educational equality. He did not want anything less than full political rights.

Du Bois was one of the founders of the National Association for the Advancement of Colored People (NAACP). It was a successor to the Niagara Movement, an organization that had proposed a national assault against racism and segregation. The NAACP sought to insert legal remedies into the arsenal of the social activists. The leadership of the NAACP was largely white at the beginning. Du Bois was the director of publication and research and editor of the *Crisis*, but he was the only black person in the top leadership of the organization at its inception.

One of the major instruments for the writers of the Harlem Renaissance was the *Crisis*. Du Bois used the magazine to publish Langston Hughes, Countee Cullen, and other Harlem

Renaissance figures. But the most important publications were always those coming from the mind of Du Bois himself. His far-reaching opinions had an impact on the nation as a whole because he defended African Americans from every form of racist argument. Finding his genius in polemics, Du Bois discovered the source of his greatness in using his logical and narrative gifts to advance the cause of justice.

Du Bois served as editor until 1934, when he resigned after a conflict with Walter White, secretary to the NAACP. But his publication program did not cease, nor did his involvement in organizations end. He had always been involved in publishing as well as the international sphere of human rights. For example, he had written *The Negro*, a sociological examination of the African diaspora, in 1915, and just a few years later he had helped to organize the First Pan African Congress in 1919 in Paris. He was deeply committed to the rise of Africa and African people and felt that he had to involve himself in every aspect of the intellectual life of Africa.

He published more books when he returned to Atlanta. Books such as *Black Reconstruction in America* (1934), *Black Folk: Then and Now* (1939), and *Dusk of Dawn: An Autobiography of a Concept of Race* (1940) showed that Du Bois was serious about making his influence felt on the question of the African in America. He founded the scholarly journal *Phylon* in 1939. He was forced to resign from Atlanta University in 1944, which some people believe happened because the administration felt he was too radical. Du Bois was seventy-six when he resigned from Atlanta University, but he rejoined the NAACP staff.

He soon turned his attention to fighting against international imperialism. He saw the Pan African Congress movement as an attack on colonization and settling of Africa by Europeans. He was made the international president of the Pan African Congress in 1945. He continued to publish, issuing *Color and Democracy: Colonies and Peace* (1945), and *The World and Africa* (1947). His criticism of the American government and its international policies caused the NAACP to dismiss him in 1948, and for the second time Du Bois was out of the NAACP.

Isolated by members of the civil rights establishment for speaking out so strongly against imperialism, Du Bois was an easy target for the reactionary elements in the government. He was indicted in 1950 under the Foreign Agents Registration Act of 1938, and was acquitted. Then the Department of State refused to issue Du Bois a passport in 1952, barring him from foreign travel until 1958. As soon as the travel ban was lifted, Du Bois and his wife, writer Shirley Graham Du Bois, traveled extensively, visiting England, France, Belgium, and Holland, as well as China, the USSR, and much of the Eastern bloc.

The Soviet Union awarded him its highest honor on May 1, 1959, when it gave him the Lenin Peace Prize in Moscow. In 1961 Du Bois moved to Ghana and, under the auspices of Kwame Nkrumah, began the development of the *Encyclopedia Africana*. In 1963 Du Bois died at the age of ninety-four, soon after becoming a citizen of Ghana. He is buried in Accra, Ghana, and his tomb is an international shrine of Pan-Africanism.

# PAUL LAURENCE
# DUNBAR

1872–1906

**T**he greatest user of the language of African Americans during the nineteenth century was Paul Laurence Dunbar. He was a poet par excellence. No poet before or after him captured the essence of the African American cadence and rhythm with as sharp an ear to the melody of ordinary folk. Dunbar was born in Dayton, Ohio, in 1872. His parents had been enslaved on Kentucky plantations and it was during their lifetimes that he heard the stories that formed the bulk of his poetic memory. Dunbar attended school in Dayton and completed school at Dayton High School, where, as the only black student, he was class president, editor of the school paper, president of the literary society, and class poet. Although he had been an exceptional student, when he graduated he could not find a job and had to take a position as an elevator operator in 1891.

Dunbar was the most famous African American poet of his day and one of the most respected American poets. His career brought him international fame, and he was, by any measure, a tremendous success. Dunbar was celebrated for his ability to use the language of the ordinary African people. He was not particularly happy with the fact that his principal identity was formed by his poetry in Ebonics, but it was his most authentic voice.

He started to write poetry but found it difficult to find a publisher, so he took out a loan to publish his first book, *Oak and Ivy*, in 1893. He was fortunate enough later to read his poetry at the World's Columbian Exposition in Chicago, Illinois, where he was praised by Frederick Douglass and other prominent African

Americans. By 1896, when his second book, *Majors and Minors*, was published it was remarked upon by the white critic William Dean Howells. Howells soon arranged for an expanded version of the book, titled *Lyrics of Lowly Life*, to be published by Dodd, Mead. After the book was published, the tour that followed made Dunbar a household name as his fame spread.

Dunbar's poetry was racially conscious. He tried to demonstrate breadth in his writing but he never strayed far from his people's struggles. In the poems "Douglass," "The Colored Soldiers," and "Black Sampson at Brandywine," he praised African Americans for their heroic deeds. His poems were icons of sincerity and cultural authenticity. In 1895 Dunbar started a correspondence with Alice Moore, another poet, and the communication between them led to marriage three years later. The marriage ended in 1902 but during the time they were married, Paul and Alice Dunbar were a celebrity couple in the African American community. Dunbar soon contracted tuberculosis and an addiction to alcohol. This combination of disease and addiction brought a catastrophic end to his brilliant career.

In the last several decades of the twentieth century, scholars and readers started again to consider Dunbar's life and work. Dunbar is a prominent figure in the African American literary world not only because he was one of the first black authors to create an audience that stretched across racial lines but also because his ability to use the language of the African American community in classic poetry made him a rare literary genius. When he died in 1906 he had also written two novels, *The Fanatics* and *The Sport of the Gods*, and completed a career-defining book, *Complete Poems and Short Stories*.

# KATHERINE
# DUNHAM
1909–

**K**atherine Dunham was born in 1909 in Chicago, Illinois, to Fanny June Taylor and Albert Dunham. She attended public schools in Chicago and showed an appreciation of dance at an early age. She left high school to attend Joliet Junior College, only to discover that her real interests were cultural. She enrolled at the University of Chicago, where she received her Ph.D. in cultural anthropology. Since she was interested in dance, she taught dance and worked as a librarian to pay her educational expenses. Soon she was able to create a dance troupe that she named the Chicago Negro School of Ballet.

One of the key events in her life was when she received a Guggenheim Award for travel to the Caribbean to explore the cultural and social dimensions of African-based dance styles and techniques. She was drawn to the artistic traditions of the people of Jamaica and Haiti; both countries accepted her and taught her many traditional and sacred dances. A Jamaican maroon settlement (descendants of runaway Africans during slavery) allowed her to witness Koromantee, the sacred war dance. Later, in Haiti, Dunham participated in the sacred rites of voodoo. She became one of the leading exponents of the Haitian culture in America. Dunham promoted Haitian arts, culture, and dance, and the Haitian government recognized her contributions by giving her many awards and honors. In fact, Dunham became an honorary citizen of Haiti.

Dunham produced several books, including *Journey to Accompong* (1946), *A Touch of Innocence* (1959), *Kasamance* (1967), and *Islands Possessed* (1969). Mastering the techniques of African

Caribbean dance, she developed her own technique, called the Dunham technique for modern African dance. Dunham was essentially an intellectual, a scholar of culture who understood that in order for the African people to advance their cultural idea, it had to be widely understood and appreciated. She saw herself as a proponent of the African culture as expressed in the Caribbean. An opportunity to work for the Illinois Project of the Federal Writers' Project from 1935 to 1940 helped her to appreciate oral traditions as well as the written word.

Using a combination of scholarship and art, Dunham created choreography and dance performances that represented her belief in the vitality of Africa in the Americas. She finally formed the Katherine Dunham Dance Company in 1940. The company became famous, touring and presenting dances she created on the basis of her studies in African Caribbean cultures. Among these early dances were *L'Ag'Ya* (1938), *Le Jazz Hot* (1939), *Tropics* (1939), *Tropical Revue* (1943), *Shango* (1945), and *Bal Nègre* (1946). A prolific artist, writer, and choreographer, she performed in shows and films from New York to California. She was featured in the Broadway musical *Cabin in the Sky* (1940) and the motion picture *Star-Spangled Rhythm* (1942).

Seeking to have more security, in 1945 she started the Katherine Dunham School of Dance and Theater in New York City. The school gave performances and offered courses in the Dunham technique as well as other subjects of culture and history. She was the first African American woman to choreograph an opera when she created the dances for *Aida*, for the New York City Metropolitan Opera during the 1963 to 1964 season.

After twenty years her company closed. Dunham left to represent the United States at the Festival of Black Arts in Senegal. Once in Senegal, and because of her use of the French language, she was able to secure a position as a cultural adviser for the Senegalese government. In this position, she helped create and train the National Ballet of Senegal.

By 1967 Katherine Dunham was affiliated with the Edwardsville campus of Southern Illinois University, where she developed and directed the Performing Arts Training Center. She retired from the university and served as an informal consultant and adviser to many African dance companies from her home in St. Louis.

Dunham received numerous honorary degrees and awards from cultural magazines, journals, professional organizations, as well as the Albert Schweitzer Music Award (1979), the Kennedy Center Award (1983), and the Distinguished Service Award of the American Anthropological Society (1986).

# DUKE
# ELLINGTON
## 1899–1974

**E**dward Kennedy Ellington was born to a middle-class black family in Washington, D.C., in 1899. He attended public schools and quickly exhibited a genius for the piano at the age of seven. By the time he was fourteen, he was playing music professionally. Ellington had his own band by the time he was twenty years old. Playing for local clubs and at community dances, Ellington soon gained a reputation as an outstanding pianist.

When he was twenty-three years old, Ellington went to New York City to explore the bustling jazz scene. In New York Ellington found a growing jazz community and numerous venues for his performances. He played a variety of spots, comedy theaters, orchestra shows, and nightclubs. He also explored work on Broadway with music for the comedy *Chocolate Kiddies of 1924*.

In 1926 Ellington was leading a band with eleven members and experimenting with different styles of jazz. No longer wedded to the soft, syrupy style of his Washington days, he now experimented with various improvisational styles. Soon he became a leader of the Harlem "stride piano" style of play that had been pioneered by James P. Johnson and Willie "The Lion" Smith. Playing the stride, the pianist would divide the keyboard into three ranges, playing the two lower ranges with the left hand. Striding, the pianist's left hand would alternate between a single bass note at the bottom and chord clusters struck up higher. Thus, the left hand established a powerful beat and created the tune's harmonic structure while the right hand played the melody and solo improvisations. Ellington was the master of the florid style of striding.

New York soon belonged to "the Duke." He was able to obtain a contract with the Cotton Club in 1927, and the combination of Ellington's band and the Cotton Club's prestige and class made both Ellington and the club nationally famous. Writing and composing music at a rapid rate, Ellington soon became the most prolific black composer of his time. By the time of his death in 1974, the Duke was the most productive composer in America's history, with more than twelve hundred compositions to his credit. He surpassed the work and fame of the bands of King Oliver and Fletcher Henderson in the late 1920s.

Ellington used his position in the jazz world to make his own statements about African American culture. He sought opportunities to highlight the African culture as he knew it, to celebrate its creativity, and to project the artistic and cultural strength of the African American community. He often gave his compositions cultural identifications, such as "Black and Tan Fantasy," "Black Beauty," "Creole Rhapsody," "Symphony in Black," and "Black, Brown, and Beige."

In 1935 Ellington wrote "Reminiscing in Tempo," a unified composition that filled four album sides, written to commemorate his mother's death. His most famous compositions of the 1930s were "Mood Indigo" (1930), "It Don't Mean a Thing If It Ain't Got That Swing" (1932), "Sophisticated Lady" (1933), and "In a Sentimental Mood" (1935).

Duke Ellington's closest collaborator was the great Billy Strayhorn, who joined the Ellington band in 1938 and remained with it for thirty years. He created the work "Take the A Train" in 1941. Strayhorn was a stabilizing influence on the Ellington sound, often creating compositions that carried the Ellington sound as well as those by Ellington himself.

During the Second World War, Carnegie Hall honored Duke Ellington for his musical genius and band leadership. Ellington, as always, tried to place this event in the context of African American history, and he created the forty-four-minute-long "Black, Brown, and Beige: A Tone Parallel to the History of the American Negro." It was not a critical success though it was an ambitious project.

Ellington won the Grammy Award in 1966 for "In the Beginning, God." He created a second sacred piece in 1968 called "Second Sacred Concert." This was in keeping with Ellington's sense of the spiritual in the African American community. He never left the struggle for civil rights, which he had joined in the 1940s. Actually, his musical *Jump for Joy*, written and performed in 1941, was really an attack on the stereotyping of African Americans. He was a committed and determined activist against racism, using his art to make his case.

In 1951, two months before he premiered *Harlem*, Ellington wrote to President Harry S. Truman asking him to allow his daughter, Margaret Truman, to serve as the honorary chair of the premier event. Ellington explained that the proceeds would go to the National Association for the Advancement of Colored People (NAACP) to help fight for Truman's objectives of stamping out segregation, discrimination, and bigotry. Of course, Truman's office refused the offer without comment.

President Richard Nixon presented Ellington with a Medal of Freedom at a gala seventieth birthday party in 1969. Ellington learned that he had lung cancer in 1973 but continued to work and write compositions even after he was hospitalized. When he died, sixty-five thousand people came to view his body, and ten thousand to fifteen thousand came to the funeral. In subsequent years Ellington's reputation has continued to grow. He is rightly acclaimed as one of the greatest of American composers.

# JAMES
# FORTEN
## 1766–1842

**J**ames Forten was born in colonial Philadelphia, of free parents, in 1766. He was intensely interested in the political issues of his day, including the War of Independence. Forten was only ten years old when the Declaration of Independence was signed in Philadelphia, but by the time he was fifteen he was a powder boy for the Continental Army and was captured by the British while serving on an American ship. The British took him to England and imprisoned him for seven months.

Once freed, he was allowed to return to the United States, where he took an apprenticeship with the sailmaker Robert Bridges. When Bridges retired, Forten purchased his company and quickly expanded it. Forten soon became an inventor of a device used to make the handling of sails easier. The business was successful, and Forten became one of the wealthiest Africans in the Americas, amassing a fortune of more than one hundred thousand dollars and employing more than forty men. He became increasingly active in the social and political life of the black community. When Richard Allen and Absalom Jones walked out of the white St. George Methodist Episcopal Church in November 1787, Forten was with them. Later, he joined with Allen in forming the African Methodist Episcopal Church in 1793.

Dubbed the "merchant prince" by some historians because of his wealth, Forten used a large portion of his personal fortune to advance the cause of African people living in Pennsylvania. In fact, he supported the abolition of slavery, donated money to the abolitionists, and worked with white abolitionists to defeat the

African colonization program of the American Colonization Society. Forten also opposed legislation in Pennsylvania aimed at restricting the immigration of blacks from the slave South. He wrote a "Series of Letters by a Man of Color" in 1813, arguing his position against the legislation.

As a cofounder of the Pennsylvania Augustine Society, dedicated to the "education of people of color," Forten etched his name in the field of education as one of the earliest campaigners for black education.

An activist all his life, Forten worked on many fronts. In 1812 he organized nearly three thousand Africans to help defend Philadelphia against the British when it was thought that the British would invade the city. He later recruited many of the seventeen hundred subscribers to William Lloyd Garrison's newspaper, the *Liberator*. Perhaps the most famous of Forten's actions was his leadership in 1817 of a conference called to protest the American Colonization Society's scheme to send Africans back to Africa. More than three thousand Africans met at the Bethel AME Church to hear speaker after speaker condemn the attempt to divide the black community by sending some back to Africa and retaining others in the South as a servile race. Forten, who had come in his carriage to the meeting from his country residence, spoke with passion about the attempt to banish Africans in America from "the land of our nativity." Forten, as the chairperson of the meeting, read the resolution that said in part: "Whereas our ancestors were the first successful cultivators of the wilds of America, we their descendants feel ourselves entitled to participate in the blessing of her luxuriant soil, which their blood and sweat manured, and that any measure or system of measures, having a tendency to banish us from her bosom, would not only be cruel, but in direct violation of those principles, which have been the boast of this republic. Resolved, that we never will separate ourselves voluntarily from the slave population."

# JOHN HOPE
# FRANKLIN
1915–

**J**ohn Hope Franklin was born in the all-black Oklahoma frontier town of Rentiesville in 1915. When he was eleven years old, his family moved to Tulsa, where his father practiced law. His father was known as one of the best lawyers in the black community because he not only resisted segregation himself, but also assisted others to fight discrimination. This had a strong influence on the young John Hope Franklin. Furthermore, the young Franklin saw how much his parents, Buck and Mollie Franklin, loved reading and writing. This was an inspiration to him. His mother was a schoolteacher who, like her husband, fought against racism every opportunity she got. In fact, she was once asked to leave a train because she refused to sit in the inferior colored section.

John Hope Franklin graduated from the public schools of Tulsa and soon left to attend Fisk University in Nashville. He was to become one of Fisk's brightest stars. He got his bachelor's degree from Fisk with honors in 1935. Six years later he walked across the platform at Harvard University to receive his doctorate degree in history.

As bright and intelligent as John Hope Franklin was when he left Harvard, much like W. E. B. Du Bois years earlier, he had to find a historically black institution that would hire him. His early professional career was spent at Fisk, North Carolina Central College, and Howard University. His career at the African American colleges was distinguished by a strong work ethic. He enjoyed teaching and believed that students at the black colleges deserved the best teachers. But Franklin was also a researcher who spent considerable time writing articles and books, even with the heavy load of teaching he had at Howard University.

In 1956 John Hope Franklin was appointed chairman of the Department of History at Brooklyn College. The department was all-white at the time, and Franklin was the first black chairman of the department. Franklin's presence in the City University of New York as the chairman of the history department at Brooklyn College did not make his life any easier as far as racism was concerned. Real estate agents refused to help him look for a house in New York. When he found a house, he could not find a bank willing to lend him the money to purchase the house. He remained at Brooklyn College for ten years and then moved in 1967 to the University of Chicago as chair of the history department

Franklin's greatness is found in his unswerving commitment to the principles of fairness, justice, and equality. He was the heir to the legacies of W. E. B. Du Bois and Carter G. Woodson in historical studies. Among his contemporaries, only Benjamin Quarles attempted to do as much in the field of African American history, and yet Quarles's achievements, as stellar as they were, do not compare to the prodigious work of John Hope Franklin. He did not speak much on the nature of injustices against Africans from some platform, but he wrote powerful books and articles correcting the errors made about Africans and their history. The most significant book written by Franklin is probably *From Slavery to Freedom: A History of American Negroes*, a book that has been revised seven times since 1947. It remains the most widely accessible book on African American history. Among the other major works by Franklin are *The Free Negro in North Carolina, 1790–1860* (1943), *The Militant South* (1956), *Racial Equality in America* (1976), *George Washington Williams* (1985), and *The Color Line: Legacy for the 21st Century* (1993).

No contemporary African American historian has received more honorary degrees than John Hope Franklin. Franklin was awarded the James B. Duke Professor of History Emeritus at Duke University in 1985. Since that time he has continued to work, adding to his long list of associations and organizations. He was the president of the American Historical Association as well as the American Studies Association. John Hope Franklin received two recognitions from President William Jefferson Clinton. He was given the Presidential Medal of Freedom in 1995, and two years later, in June 1997, when President Clinton assembled a seven-member panel to advise him about racial strife in the United States, John Hope Franklin was selected as the chair of the panel. At eighty-two years old, the stately historian of the African American people did his best to direct the nation's attention to the unfinished business of the abolition of racism.

From his early days in Oklahoma to the high honor of serving the nation in his eighties, John Hope Franklin has been a model of the best in scholarship, consciousness, and commitment to truth. Working with Thurgood Marshall in the historic brief for the school desegregation case called *Brown* v. *Board of Education,* Franklin had as a young historian demonstrated that he would be a formidable enemy of ignorance.

# HENRY HIGHLAND
# GARNET

1815–1882

Henry Highland Garnet was born on a plantation in Kent County, Maryland, in 1815, with all the expectation that he would discover his greatness even in the midst of enslavement. His grandfather, a former king in Africa, was one of the leaders of the slave community in Kent County. In 1824 Garnet's father escaped from the plantation with his family. They made their way to New York City, fearing that if they stopped in Philadelphia they would be recaptured. Garnet's father became a preacher in the African Methodist Episcopal Church. The young Garnet attended the African Free School. He soon took to the sea as a sailor and then returned to work as a farmer's apprentice before returning to school, where he studied with the abolitionists Theodore S. Wright and Peter Williams Jr., who ran the Canal Street School for African Children.

When he graduated from the Canal Street School, Garnet and several other young blacks, including abolitionist and nationalist Alexander Crummell, enrolled in a newly established academy in New Canaan, New Hampshire. About two or three weeks after the school opened, white racists destroyed it and threatened the African students with guns. Garnet and Crummell escaped from New Canaan and immediately left for the Oneida Institute in Whitesboro, New York, where both studied theology. Garnet completed his studies in 1840.

Garnet established his residence in Troy, New York, and became a preacher committed to abolitionism. His church became a station on the Underground Railroad. After two years preaching in Troy, Garnet married Julia Williams in 1842. When he was ordained a Presbyterian minister in 1843, it was as if he was given permission to achieve his national reputation. He appeared at a conference in Buffalo, New York, where he made his debut in national politics with his speech at a Buffalo convention for African Americans. The speech was called "Address to the Slaves of the United States of America," but Garnet's real audience was the assemblage of African American leaders, whom he urged to fulfill God's will by seeking the abolition of enslavement. He invoked Christianity as he called for a slave insurrection. Garnet's speech placed him in direct contact with the free African leadership in the country, and his speech brought about a radical shift in the country. Garnet's remarks brought him into direct conflict with Frederick Douglass, who favored the more gradualist approach to abolition, advocated by William Lloyd Garrison, that involved appeals to fair play. A heated debate followed, and Douglass's motion narrowly carried the day.

Garnet's address made him famous. He was considered the most revolutionary of African orators. He gained national recognition for his speech. The address was published, by which time even Douglass supported a slave uprising. In 1850 Garnet left for a tour of Europe, where he hoped to enlist support for his causes, which now included a boycott of cotton. Cotton, the chief product of the South, was essential to the slave economy. It must be said that Garnet did not succeed; he wanted so much to have his people free. He also served as a delegate to the World Peace Congress in Frankfurt, and in the next few years he favorably impressed English and Scottish congregations and antislavery societies to whom he spoke.

Presbyterians in Scotland raised funds for Garnet to minister to blacks in Jamaica, where he arrived in 1853. Sickness forced him to return to the United States in 1856, whereupon he became pastor of Shiloh Presbyterian Church in New York City. He was soon elected president of the newly created African Civilization Society. The organization sought to repatriate Africans to the continent. It was something that had need of a leader, and

Garnet was a leader. He spoke with such eloquence on the subject of abolition that he was soon in demand as a speaker.

Garnet and Douglass confronted each other over and over again on the issues of colonization and self-determination. Where Douglass seemed almost eager to bring the white abolitionists into his circle, Garnet believed that blacks had to take the leadership for their own freedom. Garnet, however, had strong allies, such as Alexander Crummell and Martin Robison Delany, in his Pan-African movement.

As the Civil War broke out, Garnet saw the opportunity for Africans to join in the fight for liberation. He was one of the people who persuaded Lincoln to allow blacks to fight. However, he found Lincoln rather lukewarm on the issue of black freedom. Nevertheless, Garnet kept up his public agitation for the Union Army to enlist black troops. Nothing could keep Garnet from his commitment to end slavery by any means. Garnet's life, church, and friends were threatened, but he preached anyway. Even the draft riots by whites in 1863 did not take him off the mission. In 1864 he moved his ministry to Washington, D.C., where, on the anniversary of the ratification of the Thirteenth Amendment, he became the first African American to speak before Congress.

Garnet was an active campaigner after the Civil War for the empowerment of the African people. He served in the Freedmen's Bureau. Throughout the 1870s he became disappointed at the federal government for refusing to distribute land to the freed people, and he eventually settled into an uneasy retirement in New York. His wife, Julia, died in 1871, and he later married Sarah Thompson.

By 1881 the federal government asked Henry Highland Garnet to serve as minister to Liberia. He had been in poor health for some time, but having long entertained the dream of traveling to Africa, he accepted the offer to serve. He died the following February, in 1882.

# MARCUS
# GARVEY
## 1887–1940

**M**arcus Mosiah Garvey was born in St. Ann's Bay, Jamaica, on August 7, 1887, and died on June 10, 1940, in London, England. Marcus Garvey's parents were Marcus and Sarah Garvey, subsistence farmers. His father also did stonework as a mason. Garvey left school at the age of fourteen and started working as a printer's apprentice. At sixteen years of age, the teenage Garvey was well versed in the anticolonial rhetoric of the day. He became a nationalist listening to the various speakers who demanded that the British cease their oppression of the black masses. He felt the tension in the atmosphere when he moved to Kingston, the capital city. But he was restless, and after several years working as a printer, learning the skills of propaganda and information dissemination, Garvey traveled to Limon, Costa Rica, where he continued his political activities while working as a timekeeper for the United Fruit Company.

Living in Costa Rica sparked in Garvey an interest in the lives of African people everywhere. This was the first time he was outside of Jamaica, and the large Jamaican population in Costa Rica was a natural environment for his political ideas. He began setting the foundations for his later years as an international leader by creating the Universal Negro Improvement Association (UNIA) and African Communities League (ACL) in Limon in 1910. Situating himself as a radical believer in the African race's rise from poverty, Garvey committed himself to travel throughout Central America to see the conditions of black people. Everywhere he traveled he saw African people at the bottom of the social, economic, and political ladder. In 1913 he traveled to England and put his printing and writing skills to use working for Dusé Mohammed Ali on the Pan-African journal *Africa Times and Orient Review*.

One year later Garvey returned to Jamaica and set up the Jamaica chapter of the Universal Negro Improvement Association. Convinced that Booker T. Washington, then the most famous African American, had the right answer to uplift the African race through industrial training, Garvey sought to create the same type of movement in Jamaica. He wanted an organization that would embody the best principles of African humanity.

Marcus Garvey traveled to New York on March 23, 1916, with the idea that he would create a national movement in the United States that could support his plan. He wanted to raise funds by lecturing in the United States and Canada. Booker T. Washington, whom he had planned to meet, had died the previous year, so Garvey lectured on the theme of self-help and self-determination. In 1917 Garvey created a stir in Harlem as a street speaker. Garvey was able, after developing a considerable following in New York, to incorporate the UNIA and ACL in New York and move into its headquarters, Liberty Hall. Black people came by the hundreds to hear the Jamaican-born lecturer inspire the crowds with his calls for African economic advancement. Garvey was the master of the platform in Harlem. No speaker could match him in art, argument, and passion. He felt as if the burden of the entire African race was on his shoulders, and when he stood to speak in Harlem he spoke with the idea of one aim, one purpose, and one destiny for black people.

Garvey's audience was the disaffected as well as the middleclass blacks who had worked their way into the good life of New York following World War I. They were convinced that racial consciousness was necessary, since the European war had demonstrated that Europeans considered race and nation to be important. Africans in the Americas did not have the same type of commitment to race and nation as the whites, and

Garvey believed that this had to be changed. Whatever the possibilities might have been after the war, racial violence in the South created a climate of racial hatred and bitterness. Blacks were tired of being defenseless and felt that the nation had turned its back on its African citizens. Garvey was the most articulate spokesperson of the African American community during this time. He was determined to show the hypocrisy of the whites in speaking about democracy yet denying blacks freedom and equality.

Marcus Garvey was the greatest symbol of the African people during the first quarter of the twentieth century. He stimulated racial pride and consciousness and created the opportunity for business and commercial ventures based on African culture. Even today, when we think of Garvey we have to think of his larger-than-life image as a savior of the race at a time when blacks were being lynched, brutalized, denied the right to vote, and discriminated against in the job market of the north. Garvey could thunder, "There shall be no solution to this race problem until you yourselves strike the blow for liberty." All across the nation there were black people who took up the challenge to strike the blow for liberty. They paid their dues, bought their UNIA uniforms, marched, demonstrated, and attended rallies. Soon, blacks everywhere were joining the movement. Chapters flourished in the United States, Canada, Liberia, England, and the Caribbean. Almost immediately, Garvey launched the Negro Factories Corporation in 1918. This organization supported the development of black-owned businesses, including a black doll factory, which employed more than a thousand workers. The UNIA also published the *Negro World* weekly, which became the most widely distributed African news publication of its time.

The most challenging venture for the UNIA/ACL was the steamship enterprise called the Black Star Line. It was created to transport people and produce between the United States and Africa or the Caribbean. There were three ships, the most famous of which was the SS *Frederick Douglass*, and all were owned and operated by black people. Garvey's inspiration and drive led Africans to develop an enthusiastic campaign for self-renewal. Optimism was alive in the African world because of his tremendous belief that Africans could demonstrate sufficiency and courage in the face of all obstacles. To this end he led his organization to create symbols of independence, icons of power, and motifs of history that reflected the history of the African people. Because of the generosity of his gifts, all African American history after Garvey is nothing more than a commentary on Garveyism. He examined every facet of the life of the African in the Americas and all questions were submitted to the authority of experience. Every issue that is raised either in support of or against African American nationalism, Pan-Africanism, integration, or separation of the races is a statement for or against Garvey's philosophy.

By the time the UNIA held its huge meeting in August 1920 at Madison Square Garden, Garvey had become a household name among African Americans in the urban areas of the north. He had surpassed the leaders of the National Association for the Advancement of Colored People (NAACP) in his popularity. By the force of his personality and character he had demonstrated that the NAACP's emphasis was on integration with whites, and Garvey argued that this was a dead end. He believed that the idea of "colored people" was an idea that did not have any substance because the African was "a Negro" and he wanted to show that the Negro race was equal to any other race and people on the earth. When twenty-five thousand people assembled in the huge Madison Square Garden under the banner of the UNIA, the event brought Garvey more attention than ever before. From that moment forward, the United States government and Garvey's enemies outside of the UNIA would do everything in their power to dishonor his operation. What was worrisome to the national government was the fact that an African, without the support of the white media, had ascended to such heights in the popular imagination of the African American people.

The convention was successful. Marcus Garvey was elected president-general of the UNIA, and the Declaration of Rights of the Negro Peoples of the World was written and disseminated. In addition, the formal leadership structure of the organization was proposed and accepted, chapters were established with commissioners for each chapter, and resolutions were approved. Among the demands made by the Garvey movement was that black schoolchildren should be taught African history.

Perhaps one of Marcus Garvey's greatest gifts was his ability to identify the values and the cultural motifs that resonated with the African people. He produced several cultural symbols that galvanized the membership. An anthem was created called the "Universal Ethiopian Anthem"; a flag of the colors red, black, and green was made and presented to the members; and small industries were created as places for workers to make a living. Furthermore, Garvey dispatched representatives to Liberia to investigate the possibilities of colonies in West Africa.

The failure of the Black Star Line in 1921 was an ominous sign that the UNIA would have financial problems. Accusations of mismanagement were beginning to circulate in the organization. The constant criticism of some middle-class African American members, as well as the United States government's interest in the organization, led to in-fighting and disaffections, yet Garvey carried on his mission of trying to unite the African race. In 1922, however, Garvey was indicted by the federal government for mail fraud related to the sale of stock for the Black Star Line. He was convicted and given a maximum prison sentence of five years by Judge Julian Mack, who claimed to be a member of the NAACP, but was not. Garvey appealed, and in 1925 he lost his appeal and was sent to the federal penitentiary in Atlanta, Georgia.

Amy Jacques Garvey, his second wife and the mother of his two sons, Marcus and Julius, led a national campaign for Garvey's release. In addition to running the organization, she edited and published two volumes of his speeches and writings titled *Philosophy and Opinions of Marcus Garvey* (1923 and 1925) as a way to raise money for legal support. In 1927 the petition drive succeeded and Garvey was released from prison but immediately deported to Jamaica and was barred from reentering the United States. Many people believed that he had been framed by the American government in the first place, and when he was released from prison and immediately shipped out of the country, it confirmed their opinion that he was considered too charismatic for the government to permit him to remain. The organization limped on without its most powerful leader. Garvey called two conventions in Jamaica and started two publications: *Black Man*, a monthly magazine, and the *New Jamaican*. However, he was not able to control the different international branches from Jamaica. From Harlem his ardent supporters continued to promote the aims of the UNIA and to publish the *Negro World* into the 1930s. Offices of the UNIA dwindled but some have continued into the twenty-first century at places as far apart as Limon, Costa Rica, and Philadelphia, Pennsylvania. Garvey soon turned to Jamaican politics, running for the colonial legislative assembly and losing in 1930. His biting political rhetoric and organizing made him a thorn in the side of the British authority. Still, he was able to win a seat on the municipal council of Kingston.

Intending to take his fight for the rights of Africans to the heart of the British Empire, Garvey moved to London in 1935. He found London difficult for Africans and finding a job that would pay adequately was a constant challenge. Nevertheless, through financial sacrifice he held annual conventions in Canada and continued his work in publishing. The skill he had acquired as a young man working as a printer's apprentice rescued him from poverty. He worked with Duse Mohammed Ali and his publications, hoping to bring about an international revolution in the African world. Garvey died on June 10, 1940, after suffering two strokes.

Marcus Garvey's influence in the African world is monumental. He touched so many aspects of the lives of Africans that his impact in art, music, social ideals, philosophy, economic empowerment, and self-determination constitutes the primary foundation of the modern African's response to European hegemony. No African hated oppression more than Garvey, and no African fought so valiantly to see the African people rise from poverty, oppression, and subjugation. He was, as one poet said, the bright star of African redemption.

# PRINCE
# HALL
1735–1807

**P**rince Hall was born in 1735, most probably in Boston, Massachusetts. He died in 1807 at the age of seventy-two. He was born into slavery as the property of William Hall, a leather processor and dresser. Prince Hall, taking the name of his slave owner, was taught how to dress and protect leather.

In 1762 Prince Hall joined the predominantly white Congregational church on School Street in Boston. He married Sarah Ritchie, an enslaved woman, on November 2, 1763. On April 9, 1770, Prince Hall received his freedom from William Hall as a reward for twenty-one years of faithful service. On August 22, 1770, after the death of Sarah Ritchie, Prince Hall married a second time. His new wife was Flora Gibbs of Gloucester, Massachusetts. Their son, Prince Africanus, was baptized on November 14, 1784, at the New North Church in Boston. Hall was married once more to a third wife, Zilpha Ward, on June 28, 1798.

Three years prior to his marriage to Zilpha Ward, he was initiated into Freemasonry by a member of a British army lodge on March 6, 1775. The lodge was a part of the 38th Foot Regiment located near Boston. Hall was one of fifteen Africans initiated by the British. A British Mason, Sgt. John Batt, who initiated the men, issued a limited "permet" on March 17, 1775, that allowed them to meet as a lodge. They were also permitted to "walk on St. John's Day," and "to bury their dead" in the Masonic tradition. On July 3, 1775, African Lodge No. 1. was formed under a permit issued by John Rowe, provincial grand master of North America. It, too, was a limited permit. The Revolutionary War divided the

African community, with some supporting the colonial government and others supporting the rebellion. By March 2, 1784, the
Africans had grown weary of having limited permits, so Prince
Hall, as master of the lodge, wrote to William Moody, most worshipful master of Brother Love Lodge No. 55 in London, England, asking for full recognition. He received no response to his
letter. Undaunted, he wrote a second letter as master of African
Lodge No. 1 on June 30, 1784.

A charter, dated September 29, 1784, was issued for Africans
to establish a lodge, but it did not arrive in Boston until April 29,
1787. The charter specifically authorized the organization in
Boston of African Lodge No. 459, a "regular Lodge of Free and
accepted Masons, under the title or denomination of the African
Lodge," with Hall as master, Boston Smith as senior warden, and
Thomas Sanderson as junior warden. Prince Hall was charged
with the responsibility to follow all the rules and orders of the
Book of Constitution meticulously and to keep a regular account
of the lodge's proceedings.

A second African lodge, Hiram Lodge No. 4, in Providence,
Rhode Island, which had received a copy of the proceedings at
Prince Hall's African Lodge No. 459, was chartered on June 24,
1797. The third lodge was established in Philadelphia in September 1797, with Absalom Jones as worshipful master and
Richard Allen as treasurer. Prince Hall was responsible for
establishing these three lodges and ensuring their adherence to
the procedures and rules of the Book of Constitution. By the year
2000 there were forty-five African grand lodges and nearly six
thousand lodges with six hundred thousand members, attesting
to the great contribution Prince Hall made to the organization of
Africans in America. After the death of Prince Hall in 1807, the
African Grand Lodge changed its name to the Prince Hall Grand
Lodge and united the Supreme Councils of the Northern and
Southern Jurisdictions, the Ancient Egyptian Arabic Order of
Nobles and Mystic Shrine, as well as all auxiliary bodies in
honor of Prince Hall.

Hall made five leather drumheads that indicate that he was a master craftsman as well as an astute organizer with a gift for symbolism. His influence on the African population in the early history of the United States was considerable, because he was also dedicated to the freedom of Africans from enslavement. His name appears alongside that of three other Masons, out of eight Africans, who signed a petition on January 13, 1777, to the Massachusetts State Legislature requesting them to abolish slavery as incompatible with the cause of the Americans fighting for liberation from Britain.

Massachusetts referred the matter to the Congress of the Confederation, which refused to act on the matter. In fact, abolition of slavery in Massachusetts did not occur until a state judicial decision was taken in 1783. Nevertheless, Hall was energetic in his campaign to have all vestiges of the slave trade out of Massachusetts. He was outraged that three African men were kidnapped by slave catchers on February 6, 1788. On February 27, 1788, Hall drafted a blistering petition to the legislature, signed by twenty-one Masons, protesting the seizure of the men, which included one Mason. The petition denounced the slave trade as injurious to human rights. By March 26, 1788, the state legislature was ready to pass an act "to prevent the slave trade, and for granting relief to the families of such unhappy persons as may be kidnapped or destroyed from this Commonwealth." Soon, letters from Governor John Hancock of Massachusetts and the French consul in Boston obtained the releases of the three black men, who had been taken to the island of Saint-Barthélemy in the French West Indies. The African Grand Lodge was responsible for organizing a celebration in honor of the returned men in Boston in July 1788. Hall's impact on the activities and festivities was profound, as he had been the moving spirit behind the release of the men.

Hall took it upon himself, without being named or asked, to defend the interests of Africans in Massachusetts. During the time of Shays's Rebellion, a western Massachusetts uprising laid to excessive land taxation and economic depression, Hall had written Massachusetts governor James Bowdoin on November

26, 1786, telling him that the African Masons were "peaceable subjects to the Civil powers where we reside and would not participate in any plot or conspiracies against the state." Hall believed that this was necessary so that the government of Massachusetts would not take any actions against the African population for the unrest. By January 4, 1787, he was led by the conditions of Africans in Massachusetts to propose to the Massachusetts legislature an idea for a separate state abroad with its own African leadership. This was probably the first written request for a colonization scheme in Africa. Prince Hall was clearly convinced that the situation for Africans in Massachusetts would not lead to happiness and tranquility. Thus, nearly a quarter of a century before Paul Cuffe's voyage to Africa in a quest for a colonial home for African Americans, Prince Hall had broached the idea with the Massachusetts legislature, who simply received it and forgot about it.

Taking his civil responsibilities seriously, Prince Hall voted and paid his taxes. He tried to get support for public education, petitioning the Massachusetts legislature on October 17, 1787, that "means be provided for the education of colored people," inasmuch as black people paid taxes just as white people did. Nothing happened to this petition and, like others, it died a silent death in the chambers of Massachusetts government. Seeing that education was necessary for advancement in knowledge and understanding, in 1796 Hall requested that the selectmen of Boston establish a separate school for black children. Boston's leaders agreed to the request but could not find a building for the school. Prince Hall asked that the school be started in his home in 1800, since the city leaders could not find a place for the school even after four years. By 1806 the school had become so successful the two teachers had to secure larger quarters at the African Society House.

Prince Hall was an unusual man who had taught himself to read, write, and do mathematics, and who was eager to educate African youth in Boston. He was the founder of the first school for African children in Boston and might reasonably be called the first African intellectual in the Boston area. He was the chief instigator of petitions to the Massachusetts legislature for black rights, writing the words in his own hand and of his own composition. When he died it is said that his possessions included sundry old books that may have assisted him in his education. He wrote two major essays that showed a great deal of erudition. One was written June 25, 1792, in Charlestown, and the other was written on June 24, 1794, at Menotomy (West Cambridge), Massachusetts. The 1792 essay emphasized good living, a belief in the one Supreme God, love, benevolence, good deeds, good behavior, and abstinence from excessive drinking. The 1794 charge was an assault on the enslavement of Africans and the discrimination that he had seen on the streets of Boston against Africans. He asked his audience to remember how God had rescued "our African brethren" from even worse treatment in the French West Indies. Deprived of education, Africans learned to advance themselves through meditation, observation, and repeating psalms, hymns, and sermons. Hall's legacy as an activist and organizer is imprinted in the fabric of African American history.

# FANNIE LOU
# HAMER
## 1917–1977

**F**annie Lou Hamer was born in 1917, the youngest of twenty children of sharecroppers Ella and Jim Townsend in Montgomery County, Mississippi. She started working in cotton, picking and chopping, at the age of six. When she was thirteen, she quit school to work full-time in the fields. She enjoyed physical work but she loved to read even more. There was nothing unholy about physical labor, she would often say, but there was something wrong with white people ruling over black people and taking all of their money. She did not have a strong education, to be sure, but she had a basic ability to read and a stronger skill of understanding. Fannie Lou Hamer was also gifted as a speaker. Very early in her life, people could tell she would be able to handle herself in any confrontation with others. She had a quick wit and a sharp tongue.

Like so many children of her age and community, she spent the bulk of her childhood in material poverty. The family house had neither heat nor plumbing. Although they had food from the farms they tended and their own gardens, the family members' diets consisted of a rather monotonous diet of pork, grits, rice, and sweet potatoes. Hamer learned very early not to complain, but to work hard to make a difference. She believed that she could change her status and that of many of her peers through her hard work. This was her spiritual quest. Her leg had been broken during infancy and was never professionally repaired and she ended up with a lifelong limp.

Many of her siblings moved to the north for work during the

years of World War II. Fannie Lou remained in the South and married Percy Hamer, a local farmworker, in 1944. They moved to a small, unpainted shack on a cotton plantation near Ruleville, Mississippi. For nearly twenty years, Hamer lived the life of a farmworker without major incident. In the summer of 1962, however, this would all change. Hamer went to a mass meeting organized by the Student Nonviolent Coordinating Committee (SNCC), which had recently begun organizing in the Mississippi Delta. African Americans in the Mississippi Delta lived in some of the poorest conditions in the United States. SNCC sought to register nearly a half million African American voters by over-turning the obstacles that had been placed in their way by the Mississippi registrars of voters. African Americans were being denied their constitutional right to vote by various devious means, such as requiring voter registration tests of African American voters, poll taxes where the potential voter had to have a copy of the previous year's poll tax receipt, dismissals from jobs, and violence against voters. After the SNCC meeting, Fannie Lou Hamer was fired up and went along with seventeen other people to attempt to register to vote in Indianola, Missis-sippi. The white registrar pulled out the constitutional test and gave it to all seventeen of the potential registrants. All failed. No blacks ever passed the test.

By the time the African Americans returned home, the word had been spread by whites that they had tried to vote. When Hamer got to her house, her white boss tried to extract from her a promise that she would not try to register to vote again. She refused to give him that promise and he immediately fired her from her farm job. He then told her and her husband that they would have to leave the plantation house. "They kicked me off the plantation," she later recounted, "they set me free. It's the best thing that could happen. Now I can work for my people."

Hamer was hired by SNCC as a field-worker among the poor people of the Mississippi Delta. Her job was to help register as many people as possible. She soon became a major voice in the South because of her powerful oratory and her inspiring singing.

She was the symbol of courage, resistance, and defiance of the white South. She did not escape prison. In June 1963 she was unjustly jailed and severely beaten in Winona, Mississippi, while returning from citizenship classes. The white sheriff even had black male prisoners beat her in an effort to humiliate both the black men in prison and the civil rights activist. SNCC was outraged, and the country became aware of the sufferings of Fannie Lou Hamer. She spoke about the conditions she experienced and demanded that the government do something about them. Soon the FBI intervened and the Justice Department was able to get a trial against the jailers for assaulting Hamer. An all-white local jury found the jailers not guilty.

By 1963 Fannie Lou Hamer was a major figure in the Council of Federated Organizations (COFO). COFO was the activist arm of the alliance between SNCC, the National Association for the Advancement of Colored People (NAACP), and the Congress of Racial Equality (CORE). These organizations came together to fight for the Freedom Vote, a statewide effort in Mississippi devoted to registering thousands of African Americans. The potential voters were given "freedom ballots" that served as voting guides when they went to cast their votes. More than eighty thousand voting guides, designed to help potential voters know where to vote, how to mark ballots, and what rights they had, were given out. The concept of the Freedom Vote led to the idea of the Freedom Summer, and Fannie Lou Hamer was right in the midst of it. She gave hundreds of hours to SNCC in 1964, working in voter education. She became the most powerful voice in the voter registration movement in Mississippi. About this time she, along with others, founded the Mississippi Freedom Democratic Party (MFDP) as an alternative to the racist Mississippi Democratic Party. There were no blacks in the Mississippi Democratic Party organization, and the MFDP challenged it to change its policies. It was only a matter of time before Hamer started her own run for Congress, as the candidate of the MFDP. This was a catalyst to registering thousands of black voters. Hamer did not win the nomination, but she created so much interest in the Mississippi electorate that she gained national attention and prominence.

The Mississippi Freedom Democratic Party sought to seat a delegation at the 1964 Democratic National Convention. This attempt, spirited and rational in its logic, failed. But the rejection of the MFDP's delegation did not prevent Hamer from condemning racism in Mississippi and hypocrisy in its democratic process. She became even more outspoken in her attacks on the white racial hierarchy that controlled the Mississippi Democratic Party.

Hamer's sacrifice resulted in great changes in Mississippi. She was able to see an African American, Robert Clark, elected to the Mississippi legislature in 1968. Furthermore, she had witnessed the passing of the 1965 Voting Rights Act three years earlier. By 1968 the Mississippi delegation was integrated. Fannie Lou Hamer did not rest on her laurels, nor did she gloat over the fact that she had forced so many changes in Mississippi. She went right back to her earlier work as a farmhand and soon established the Freedom Farm, a cooperative project with other farmers. She directed the Freedom Farm for five years, from 1969 to 1974, providing poor African Americans with food and jobs.

Fannie Lou Hamer received honorary degrees from Morehouse College and Howard University, and won numerous other awards for her work. Although she never won any major recognition from white America, Fannie Lou Hamer's commitment, political savvy, personality, and charisma were recognized by the Congressional Black Caucus in 1976. When Fannie Lou Hamer died in 1977, the African American community mourned the death of the woman who had sung the old African American spirituals like they were her own creations and whose spirit had politicized her Mississippi neighbors like nothing else in history.

# LORRAINE
# HANSBERRY
## 1930–1965

Lorraine Vivian Hansberry was born in Chicago, Illinois, in 1930, the youngest of four children. Hansberry was born into a high-achieving family. Her father, Carl Augustus Hansberry, was a real estate broker, and her mother, Nannie Perry, was a schoolteacher and political activist.

Lorraine Hansberry's family experienced some crucial changes during her childhood. In 1940 Hansberry's father sued to overturn the restricted covenant law that prevented African Americans from purchasing homes in some areas of the city. The case went to the Supreme Court as *Hansberry* v. *Lee* and was decided in favor of Carl Hansberry, but racism remained prevalent in the real estate market anyway, and Hansberry grew discouraged, feeling that African Americans would always have to fight against prejudice in the United States. He emigrated to Mexico, leaving his family in Chicago.

This greatly affected the young Lorraine, who remained in the United States and entered college at the University of Wisconsin in Madison—only to find the education stifling and limiting. She took courses in theater, dramatic productions, and stage construction. Hansberry recounted her days at the university in her book *To Be Young, Gifted and Black*, published in 1969. In this book Hansberry related how impressed she was with dramatists, and it was at the University of Wisconsin that she learned of the works of Sean O'Casey and other playwrights. These had an impact on her life that would send her to the artistic world.

Feeling that she could not fulfill her wishes in the Midwest she traveled to New York City and settled in Harlem, the jewel of the African American cultural experience. She could not find a position in the arts or theater, although she had recently taken up painting. Securing a position as a journalist, however, she was able to support herself as an associate editor of the monthly paper *Freedom*, later transformed to *Freedomways*, which was headed by Paul Robeson. Surrounded by activists, artists, and writers, Lorraine Hansberry stepped into a world created by the great singer, actor, and activist Paul Robeson and learned as much as she could about the issues confronting America. In 1953 she married activist Robert Nemiroff, who became her manager and literary executor.

Hansberry's greatness is unique. She was a young writer, gifted with talent, frustrated and conflicted by racism and discrimination, brought to consciousness in the arena of political writing at an early age, and she had the audacity and genius to write *A Raisin in the Sun*. This became her most famous play. Her father's experience with restricted covenants in the 1940s was something that she knew about, and in the 1950s such covenants were still prevalent throughout the United States, so she wrote the play to highlight the continuing racism in the housing sector. The play premiered at the Ethel Barrymore Theatre on Broadway on March 11, 1959. Lloyd Richards directed the play, which starred Sidney Poitier and Ruby Dee. The play was a success, running for 583 performances.

*A Raisin in the Sun* made history as the first Broadway play written by an African American woman and the first play on Broadway directed by an African American since the turn of the century. The acclaim that came to Hansberry was phenomenal and timely. She was the first black woman and the youngest person to receive the New York Drama Critics Circle Award. Two years after the play opened on Broadway, it was turned into a movie and received a nomination for best screenplay from the Screenwriters Guild. Several additional awards and recognitions were given to the movie. The film also received a special award at the Cannes Film Festival. By 1973 the play had become one of the most recognized works by any African American, and its addition to the canon of literary creations from the African American community was sealed by its many performances and critical acclaim. In fact, a musical based on the play, *Raisin*, won the Tony Award in 1973. Hansberry wrote a second play that made it to Broadway, *The Sign in Sidney Brustein's Window*, in 1964, but it did not receive the critical recognition of her first Broadway play. However, Hansberry had grown quite ill, and the play was kept running by private gifts until Hansberry's death. Several productions by Robert Nemiroff, including *To Be Young, Gifted and Black* (1969), and *Les Blancs* (1970), further established Hansberry's intellectual and artistic genius.

It seemed that Lorraine Hansberry burst upon the literary scene with an entire catalog of works she wanted to create. She wrote the historically oriented work *The Movement: Documentary of a Struggle for Equality* (1964), and the memoir *To Be Young, Gifted and Black: Lorraine Hansberry in Her Own Words* (1971). She also published several articles in the new *Black Scholar, Village Voice, Freedomways*, and the *National Guardian*. Without question, she saw herself as a campaigner for the rights of African people and felt, even as she was dying, a commitment to the activism that was her family's tradition. She was a remarkable human being whose flight over the literary landscape in America was quick and purposeful, like that of an eagle. Hansberry set the tone for the next generation of African American writers and gave voice to the underrepresented in her constant demand for democracy. Her death in 1965, at the age of thirty-five, was widely considered untimely.

# DOROTHY
# HEIGHT

1912–

**D**orothy Height was born in Richmond, Virginia, in 1912. Her family moved to Pennsylvania when she was young. After high school she enrolled in New York University, where she earned her bachelor's degree. In 1933 she earned a master's degree from the same university. Her major was educational psychology, and when she completed her college education, she received a job as a social worker with the United Christian Youth Movement. This was the position that led to her interest in organizing women. Spurred by her association with many important women, including Mary McLeod Bethune and Eleanor Roosevelt, Dorothy Height was motivated to be a leader of women.

Height left the United Christian Youth Movement in 1937 to accept a position with the Harlem Young Women's Christian Association (YWCA). From that position Height would move swiftly to leadership positions, because of the force of her character, her education, and her commitment to the betterment of women's lives. Nothing defined her life more than organizing women. She held a conference in 1946 and presented an argument for the YWCA to integrate its programs and activities. This decision was formally taken at the conference, and the association became one of the first national service organizations to express its commitment to bringing African Americans into every aspect of its operation.

Dorothy Height came to her activism by conviction and mentorship. In November 1937, while attending a social function at which Eleanor Roosevelt was to be a major speaker, she met Mary McLeod Bethune. In many ways Bethune saw Height as her protégée and worked to bring her into the National Council of Negro Women (NCNW), the coalition of black women's groups founded by Bethune, as a potential leader. Since Dorothy Height was the epitome of the clubwoman—that is, a woman committed to holding small meetings of like-minded women to handle social and welfare issues in the African American community—she was prepared to follow Bethune's example. She was a sorority activist, the president of Delta Sigma Theta sorority from 1947 to 1956. When she left the presidency of Delta Sigma Theta, she was elected president of the National Council of Negro Women, serving as president of the organization for more than four decades.

Height's leadership as the major African American female organizer was unquestioned for many years. The NCNW provided her a platform from which to articulate the interests of African American women and families as no other political or social leader could. Anyone who wanted to appeal to the clubwomen of the African American community had to consult Dorothy Height. She gave of her time and energy freely, believing that there was no more worthy a cause as fighting for the rights of the women and families often forced to the margins of American society.

Dorothy Height did not work for honors, but she received numerous awards and honors for the passion and intellect she placed in the work for justice and fair play for African American families. More than twenty universities have awarded her honorary degrees, and she has received more than fifty awards from local, state, and national organizations. In 1989 she received the Citizens Medal Award for Distinguished Service.

# MATTHEW
# HENSON
## 1866–1955

**M**atthew Alexander Henson was born in 1866 and raised in Maryland. He always wanted to travel. After the death of his parents, he sailed around the world for six years as a hand aboard the *Katie Hines*, a merchant ship. When he returned to the states, Henson took a job working in a hat store in Washington, D.C. By 1887, at the age of twenty-one, he was able to accompany Adm. Robert E. Peary, the renowned scientist and explorer, on a mission to survey a canal site in Nicaragua. Henson was to make seven expeditions with Peary, becoming his most loyal coexplorer. Peary once said that he found Henson indispensable because of his determination, courage, sense of mission, and willingness to risk his life to accomplish his goals. Henson's gifts were as a translator and an interpreter. He was a navigator in the Arctic and a translator among the Inuit people.

Matthew Henson reached the North Pole on April 6, 1909, in an expedition led by Peary that included four Inuit explorers. This expedition claimed to have reached the North Pole before any other. Henson reached the North Pole forty-five minutes before the sick and tired Peary, but because Peary was the leader of the expedition, historians usually credit him with the discovery. Nonetheless, scholars have concluded that the expedition may have been a few miles off of the exact North Pole.

When Henson wrote *A Black Explorer at the North Pole* in 1912, he recorded, in graphic terms, his impressions of the journey to the North Pole. It was clear that Henson was a major presence in the expedition. Although he received limited attention at the time for his achievements in 1913, President William Taft recommended him for a post at the United States Customs House in New York. Whereas Peary became famous for the North Pole expedition, Henson's exploits remained forgotten for a long time. However, in 1944, during World War II, Henson received a joint medal from Congress honoring the Peary expedition to the North Pole. Six years later President Harry Truman honored Henson for his adventure to the North Pole, and he was finally admitted into the select Explorer's Club. Henson received increasing respect in his own community, becoming a fixture in the recitations of great African Americans at black colleges. Five years later, in 1955, Matthew Henson died without fanfare. In 1986 Henson was commemorated on a United States postage stamp. Descendants of Peary and Henson from their relationships with Inuit women were united with their American relatives in the early 1980s. In 1988 Matthew Henson was reburied in Arlington National Cemetery in Virginia with full honors as an American hero.

# CHARLES
# HOUSTON
## 1895–1950

**C**harles Houston was born in 1895 in Washington, D.C. He was the only child of William and Mary Houston, who raised him to be proud of his heritage. He attended the public schools of Washington, including the prestigious M Street School. After completing high school, he entered Amherst College in Massachusetts. Having always achieved academically, Houston continued his strong record of accomplishments at Amherst, although he was the only African American in the class of 1915. He was elected to Phi Beta Kappa while at Amherst.

Houston began his professional career as a teacher at Howard University in Washington, teaching part-time during World War I. He joined African American college students in pressuring the United States government to open separate officers' training schools for African Americans. Most African Americans who served in the army ended up in menial jobs; this made Houston angry, and, while he wanted to serve his nation, he wanted to serve in a capacity that recognized the achievement of educated African Americans. The young Houston was ecstatic when the United States War Department established an officers' training camp in Des Moines, Iowa. In June 1917 Houston reported to the camp. As he had done in high school and college, he studied diligently, earning his commission as a second lieutenant. The army sent him to France, where he saw little action, but experienced a lot of racism.

When Houston returned home during the Red Summer of 1919, he was convinced that the fight against racism had to be intensified. But he believed that he needed more education in

order to be able to assist in the struggle against racism. He entered
Harvard Law School, where he excelled as a student. Making history at Harvard, he became the first black student elected to the
*Harvard Law Review.* When he graduated from Harvard in 1924,
he traveled to Europe, studying in Madrid, Spain.

When he returned to the United States, Houston took a position in his father's law firm. As a way to keep his legal skills
sharp, Houston taught evening classes at the Howard University
Law School. He came to the attention of Mordecai Johnson, the
first African American president of Howard University, who
invited Houston to head the law school. Howard University Law
School, however, had been denied accreditation by the American
Bar Association.

Houston revitalized the school by hiring more-qualified faculty,
creating seminars and workshops, and redesigning the curriculum
to concentrate on litigation against racial discrimination. Among
the law professors hired were Thurgood Marshall and Oliver W.
Hill, future civil rights giants. Houston's young cadre of professors
emulated his energy and vigorous attention to high standards. After
two years, in 1931, the school received its new accreditation.

Howard became the premier center for socially relevant law
and conscious and committed lawyers. Since Charles Houston
had worked with the legal committee of the National Association
for the Advancement of Colored People (NAACP), he was now
eager to test the theories that he and his colleagues had worked
out at the university. Walter White, the executive secretary of the
NAACP, had often called upon Houston for legal advice. Now
White wanted Charles Houston to agree to assist in the defense
of George Crawford, a black man accused of murder in Virginia.
Blacks were not allowed to serve on juries in that state during
the 1930s. Houston lost the case against juries that excluded
blacks, but kept Crawford from being executed.

In 1935 Houston accepted White's invitation to become
NAACP chief counsel. Thus, Houston had a platform that would
allow him to craft the legal foundation for the civil rights movement as well as to train the cadre of young African American

lawyers who would challenge the bastions of segregation through American law. A report was commissioned by the NAACP to discover the best route for equality before the law. It was called the Margold Report. This report suggested gradualism as the principle by which blacks would gain equality. Houston differed with this assessment, believing that education should be the primary battlefront. Houston saw three areas that had to be addressed, as they exemplified the discrimination in education: (1) unequal pay scales for black and white teachers, (2) disparity in transportation based on race, and (3) inequality in opportunity for graduate study at state-supported, segregated institutions. This third approach proved successful in creating the three Supreme Court cases that provided the ammunition to overturn *Plessy* v. *Ferguson,* the 1896 Supreme Court decision that created the "separate but equal" doctrine.

Charles Houston was the architect of the civil rights strategy against legal discrimination. Thurgood Marshall, Houston's protégé and successor, called him "the engineer." Marshall recognized that without the brilliance of Charles Houston, the civil rights movement never would have been placed on a legal foundation. He essentially invented civil rights law. For this reason, he remains one of the most influential American lawyers of the twentieth century.

Houston's health began to deteriorate in the late 1930s. By 1938 he had stepped down as chief counsel of the NAACP. He rejoined his father's law practice with an interest in economic justice. Houston represented two railroad unions and challenged discriminatory actions by government negotiators and contractors. He resigned from the Fair Employment Practices Committee (FEPC) in 1945 in protest over its lukewarm support from the government.

Charles Houston, the "lose your head, lose your case" lawyer, was also a hardworking and hard-charging personality, although he had a calm demeanor. He was hospitalized for a severe heart attack in 1948 and died in 1950 at the age of fifty-five. He was survived by his second wife, Henrietta, and their only child, Charles Hamilton Houston Jr.

# LANGSTON
# HUGHES
1902–1967

$L$angston Hughes was born in Joplin, Missouri, in 1902. The next year, his father abandoned the family for Mexico, where he thought racism would be less pervasive than in America. Subsequently, the young Hughes spent most of his time with his maternal grandmother, who lived in Lawrence, Kansas. It is believed that her first husband, one of the followers of John Brown, was killed in the attack on Harper's Ferry, Virginia, in 1859. Her second husband was the brother of the activist abolitionist John Mercer Langston. The African American community of Lawrence was committed to political freedom and activism; most of the African Americans who had moved into Kansas had done so to escape the slave conditions in the southern states. Pap Singleton had led a movement of thousands of African Americans into Kansas, and the resulting populations were strongly convinced that the only way to retain their freedom was to fight to protect their rights. Hughes's maternal grandmother kept him close to the aspirations of that community.

When he attended elementary school in Lawrence, Hughes became interested in reading stories. He enjoyed the short story form and was considered one of the best young readers in his classes. The support of his teachers was an inspiration for him to continue his literary interest. As a teenager he moved with his mother to Lincoln, Illinois, and then to Cleveland, Ohio. This proved to be a difficult period for him, since he was away from the warm, comforting environment of his grandmother; yet it allowed him to test his skills in writing among a larger group of children. He was elected the class poet and edited the high school's literary magazine during his senior year. By the time he graduated from high school, in 1920, he was already considered a future world-class poet by many of his schoolmates. Langston Hughes was going to be a famous writer. It was not clear in Langston Hughes's mind where this fame would originate; the only thing he knew was that he loved to write poetry and short stories. After graduation from high school, his father asked him to spend a year in Mexico. On the way to Mexico, as the train crossed the Mississippi River at Memphis, Tennessee, Langston Hughes wrote "The Negro Speaks of Rivers." This poem was published in the June 1921 issue of the *Crisis*, the official publication of the National Association for the Advancement of Colored People (NAACP). It was immediately hailed as a singular example of African American poetic genius. Here, a young man, barely nineteen years of age, had condensed the entire history of Africans into a few powerful lines that captured the cadence, rhythm, emotions, and metaphors of a noble people. What could be more revealing of greatness than the ability to see into the soul of a people during the troubled times of the early 1920s, when lynching of African men was something of a national pastime?

By the time Langston Hughes left Mexico for New York City, to enroll at Columbia University in the fall of 1921, he knew he wanted to be a poet. He remained at Columbia for only one year and devoted his time in the big city to trying to write poetry and short stories. He took odd jobs in order to make ends meet, including a stint on a merchant ship that took him along the west coast of Africa. He also traveled to Europe on a steamer. But the one constant was his writing about the experiences of African American people. He could capture a feeling, a phrase, an idea with such succinct lines that most African Americans would feel that he had written the words in their own voices. He was the most accomplished poet in the African world. His works were published in numerous journals and newspapers in the African American community. The *Crisis* and *Opportunity*, two popular journals, accepted his works regularly. By the time he returned to the United States in 1924, his reputation as a poet was established. The next year he won first prize in *Opportunity*'s poetry contest with his poem "The Weary Blues." In 1926 Alfred A. Knopf published *The Weary Blues,* Hughes's first volume of poetry.

Soon his influence was not just national but international, as black writers in Senegal, Haiti, and Liberia sought to emulate his works. He was dubbed by the press as the leader of the Harlem Renaissance, when, in fact, this was a title he did not encourage. Yet everyone recognized the exceptional talent of the young poet who had published a book with a major publisher by the time he was only twenty-four years old.

Hughes created a style of his own that was widely read in all cultures. One of the tremendous advantages he had over many African American poets of his generation was his travels and his readings. He used all styles and forms, but soon discovered in his own traditions, particularly the idioms of Paul Laurence Dunbar, the way to evoke the essence of his people. This was his brilliance and his art. He found the rhythms of black speech especially poetic and incorporated them into many of his poems.

With speech having a powerful influence on Hughes's work, it is easy to forget that music was also a principal base of his poetic tone. He knew that one could sing his works, as poets often sang poetry in ancient African cultures, and though he wrote the poems to be read, they were lyrical enough to be sung. The themes were from the urban culture of the African American. When he wrote the powerful essay "The Negro Artist and the Racial Mountain" in 1926, he tried to set the standard for themes that might be covered in African American writing. What other writers liked about Hughes was his ability to explain the culture in such a way that there was no reason to make any excuses for using blues, jazz, Ebonics, or other icons of the culture. He was the cultural keeper par excellence.

Finally, ready to settle down and complete his education, in 1926 Hughes enrolled in Lincoln University in Lincoln, Pennsylvania. He graduated from Lincoln in 1929.

By 1930 his novel *Not Without Laughter* was ready for publication. When the novel came out later that year it was clear that Hughes would make his mark not as a novelist but as a poet. He made enough money to visit Haiti, the USSR, and Carmel, California. Each of these places held special attractions to him. He liked the African culture he found in Haiti and was impressed with the possibilities of a strong black government in the Caribbean. He went to the Soviet Union to see what communism offered the African American. And in Carmel, California, he found solace, friends, and a place to continue to write. His first collection of short stories, *The Ways of White Folks,* written in Carmel, was published in 1934. Hughes tried many forms and genres of writing. He found success with several plays, including *Mulatto,* which opened on Broadway in 1935 and was the longest-running Broadway play by an African American until Hansberry's *A Raisin in the Sun* opened in 1959. He committed himself to writing an autobiography, *The Big Sea,* and the book was published in 1940. In 1942 he started his weekly column for the Chicago *Defender*, one of the most popular African American weeklies. His character, Jesse B. Semple, or "Simple" as he was affectionately called, commented on everything that had to do with African American life in the United States. Simple showed how ridiculous racism was and how stupid the racist had to be in order to practice it. He was the representative of the ordinary wisdom of everyday African Americans.

Langston Hughes was one of the earliest African American writers to make a living from writing. The 1947 Broadway musical *Street Scene* brought him enough money to purchase a house in Harlem. He published many collections of poetry and some anthologies of African American writing, but his second autobiography, *I Wonder as I Wander* (1956), came as an unexpected gift to the literary establishment, filling in the gaps that appeared in his first autobiography and continuing the story of his life.

Using his talent to capture the style and flavor of the African American community, Hughes wrote several plays in the 1960s, using the gospel music that was succeeding the spirituals in the churches. Thus, *Black Nativity* (1961) must be seen as one of his most enduring contributions, since it is played every holiday season at many theaters. But he also wrote a play dealing with the civil rights movement, *Jericho-Jim Crow* (1964). Langston Hughes was—by virtue of his immense talent, his deep respect for his people's culture, his considerable corpus of work, and his command of the rhythms of the ordinary African American—the greatest poet of his people during the twentieth century.

# ZORA NEALE
# HURSTON
## 1891–1960

**Z**ora Neale Hurston was born in either Eatonville, Florida, in 1901 or Notasulga, Alabama, in 1891. The first date is the one claimed by Hurston and the latter is claimed by recent scholarship. Raised in Eatonville, Florida, near Orlando, Hurston was educated by the segregated schools of her town. Eatonville was a distinctive community, one of the all-black towns created throughout Florida and other states in the South by free blacks during the period of enslavement and continuing into the early twentieth century. There was a special security that African Americans often felt in towns like Eatonville; it was without the daily racial discrimination and harassment of other towns. Zora Neale Hurston imbibed the culture of her youth, listened to the old men who sat at the corner stores, remembered the narratives of faith told by women in the kitchens, went to the churches and heard the praises to "de Lawd," and sat at the feet of her family members as they told her stories about their youth. She saw the resources, spiritual and social, of a people who did not possess much materially but who were rich in personal relationships and inner resources. The narratives of her youth were the stories that would fuel her literary career, particularly in her novels and short stories.

*Dust Tracks on a Road,* her autobiography, was written in 1942. In that work Hurston reveals that her mother died when she was thirteen years old, and that she then began to work as a young maid for a traveling theater group. She was educated on the road, whenever she could find a school that would accept her, but in the end she was finally able to earn a high school degree from Morgan Academy in Baltimore in 1918. She then entered Howard University and attended classes at the university until 1924. She published a story, "John Redding Goes to Sea," in *Stylus*, Howard's literary magazine in 1921.

Hurston was attracted to the literary world and believed that it was necessary for her to go to New York to actually become a writer. In 1925 Hurston moved to Harlem and joined the movement of writers that became known as the Harlem Renaissance. Alain Locke selected her short story "Spunk" for inclusion in his volume *The New Negro*, published in 1925. This was a good year for Hurston: she also received awards from *Opportunity* magazine, the Urban League's journal, in May 1925.

Because of her writing ability, energetic promotion of her talents, and innate genius, Hurston was granted a scholarship to study at Barnard College. When she entered Barnard, the sister college to Columbia University, she was so impressed by the work of Franz Boas, the anthropologist, that she became one of his most enthusiastic students. As the only African American studying at Barnard, Hurston had some lonely times but she eventually received her bachelor's degree in 1928. Now she was interested in the folklore of her own people, having been shown the methods of acquiring intimate knowledge of the lives of people through anthropology. She did not give up her writing of fiction, she simply combined the two disciplines, writing fiction as though she was writing folklore and writing folklore in the same style as she would write fiction. Interested in the customs of African people in other countries, she went to Haiti and Jamaica during the Great Depression to do fieldwork for a comparative study of the Caribbean and the American South. She received fellowships from the Rosenwald and Guggenheim Foundations, as well as private funding, to support her research. Her research led her to publish the books *Mules and Men* (1935), an innovative collection of African American folklore; *Tell My Horse* (1938), insights into the popular Haitian religion Vodun; and *The Florida Negro* (1938), funded by the Federal Writers' Project.

The latter work never found a publisher, but Hurston kept coming back to the information in her speeches and writings.

Zora Neale Hurston did not lack ideas for publications. She was steeped in African American culture as a literary source and found a constant well of good material in the lives of ordinary African Americans. She published four novels between 1934 and 1948, including the powerful novel *Their Eyes Were Watching God* (1938).

She was outspoken and often controversial. Her attitudes about integration, which she did not favor, angered some blacks. Conversely, her celebration of African American culture without political objectives upset some writers, who called her a modern-day minstrel.

With the rise of socially conscious writers like Richard Wright, Hurston's work was ignored, and it became difficult for her to support herself on her writings. She returned to Florida and tried desperately to have some of her manuscripts published, but to no avail. She took menial jobs, far below her qualifications but the only positions available to African Americans in the 1940s, in order to support herself. She died of a stroke on January 28, 1960, in a welfare home.

Largely due to Alice Walker and Robert Hemenway, Hurston's work was revived in the 1970s, and she became one of the most well-known figures of the Harlem Renaissance. Her novel *Their Eyes Were Watching God* became one of the most popular novels by an African American author, outstripping the famous novel *Invisible Man,* by Ralph Ellison, as a recommended book by American literature professors. Janie, the central figure in the novel, lives a life of seeking and searching until she looks into herself and finds peace. Numerous female African American writers—and some male writers—claim Hurston as a literary influence. While ignored in her later life as a writer, in death she has become, according to critics and the public, one of the greatest writers of all time.

# JESSE
# JACKSON
1941–

**J**esse Louis Jackson was born in 1941 in Greenville, South Carolina, the son of Helen Burns and Noah Robinson. Burns was an unwed teenage mother who was herself the child of an unwed teenage mother. Jackson's mother and grandmother loved him, and he grew up in relative poverty while his biological father, who refused to accept him as his child, remained one of the more well-to-do African Americans of Greenville. Jackson found acceptance from his stepfather, Charles H. Jackson, who adopted him as his own son in 1957. Jesse became a promising athlete and scholar in high school, and both Charles and Helen were very proud of their son. When he finished high school in 1959, Jackson received a football scholarship to study at the University of Illinois. He soon left the university to return to the South because the coach refused to let him play quarterback, a position he had starred in at high school. Jackson enrolled at North Carolina Agricultural and Technical University in Greensboro, North Carolina. At the university he became quarterback of the football team as well as president of the student body.

North Carolina Agricultural and Technical University was one of the campuses actively involved in the protest for civil rights. Jackson, a student leader, became involved in the protests and demonstrations that were raging around the campus. He led a protest against the local whites-only libraries, theaters, and restaurants. Struck by the moral leadership of preachers who railed against the practice of segregation, Jackson saw the ministry as a road toward leadership in America. He graduated in 1964 and immediately accepted a scholarship from the Chicago Theological Seminary. He married Jacqueline Brown, went to school, worked at his studies, and could not keep away from the drama of the demonstrations going on in the South. He volunteered to go to Selma, Alabama, in March 1965. Selma changed his entire life. Martin Luther King Jr., the president of the Southern Christian Leadership Conference (SCLU), was leading a march, and Jackson led a group of divinity students down to Selma to support the march. Jesse Jackson emerged as a strong supporter of King, a charismatic speaker in his own right, and a person of immense capability.

Jesse Jackson left school and joined the SCLC as one of its leading voices. He gave up the seminary to learn on the streets with his mentor, Martin Luther King Jr. He headed the Chicago branch of Operation Breadbasket, an organization created to develop the economic potential of the African American community. Jackson was elected national head of the organization in 1967.

After the death of King in 1968, Jackson's relationship with other members of SCLC turned sour. Some felt that he had overreached his position by trying to wrest the organization away from older leaders. Nevertheless, Jackson continued to press his own case for national leadership, developing a base in the Chicago area that gave him a strong national footing. He persuaded several corporations in Chicago to hire more African Americans, and in 1971 decided to create his own organization, called Operation PUSH. He continued to work with certain activities of the SCLC, such as Resurrection City, serving as the mayor of the project.

Operation PUSH, which stands for People United to Serve Humanity, was dedicated to raising the economic standards of the African American community. Jackson was in his own element when he created PUSH. He was its chief proponent, its inspiration, its motivator, and its chief lobbyist. Indeed, he created the now ubiquitous motto, "I Am Somebody."

Having his own organization afforded Jackson an enormous

platform. He could speak on any issue, consult with politicians, support political candidates, denounce those he thought were against the interests of African Americans, and create obstructions for segregationists and racists. He was a national leader. When he declared himself a candidate for the Democratic nomination for president in 1983, he sincerely believed that he had a chance at the nomination. He ran in 1984 and then again in 1988. His theme was compassion, and he worked to build a "rainbow coalition" of people of all races that would speak to the many ills of the society.

He faced charges of anti-Semitism because of his association with Nation of Islam leader Louis Farrakhan, and for calling New York City "Hymietown." He apologized for the remarks but for a while was unable to live them down. Although he did not win the nomination in 1984, he remained committed to fighting against racism and anti-Semitism. At the National Democratic Convention, he gave an impassioned speech that galvanized the audience with shouts of "Keep hope alive," "Keep hope alive." The audience took up the chant; Jackson had made his point.

With many whites willing to join his organization and numerous Latinos wanting to ally themselves with him, Jackson formed the National Rainbow Coalition in 1986. He lost the nomination again in 1988 to Michael Dukakis, who may have had a chance to win had he placed Jackson on his ticket as the vice presidential candidate.

Jackson was indefatigable as a civil and human rights leader for more than thirty-five years. He supported his son, Jesse Jr., as a congressman from Illinois. In the meantime, Jesse Jackson Sr. made many diplomatic missions on behalf of Americans. He has brought back many prisoners of war from Iraq and Syria. He resumed leadership of Operation PUSH in 1996. During the 2000 presidential campaign, Jackson was one of the biggest supporters of Vice President Al Gore. Jackson's work to get out the vote produced one of the largest turnouts of African Americans in any presidential election. However, soon after the election of President George W. Bush, it was revealed in the press that

Jackson had fathered a child by one of his organization's workers. Soon thereafter he was attacked by Reverend Wyatt T. Walker, a former top aide to Dr. Martin Luther King Jr., for not repenting and showing remorse for fathering a child out of wedlock. The controversy damaged Jackson's standing in the civil rights establishment but nothing could take away the years of work that he contributed on behalf of the African American community. In 2000 Jackson was on the front line in Florida, trying to get all the votes counted in the presidential election. He remains an established figure in the pantheon of African American civil rights.

# MAE
# JEMISON
1956–

**D**r. Mae C. Jemison was born in Decatur, Alabama, on October 17, 1956, the youngest of three children. When she was three years old, her family moved to Chicago, Illinois. Introduced to the world of science by her family members, Jemison took to anthropology, biology, and astronomy at an early age. She graduated from Morgan Park High School in 1973. At sixteen years of age, Jemison entered Stanford University. In 1977 Jemison received degrees in chemical engineering and African American Studies, a powerful combination of study and research, demonstrating her ability to handle both the hard sciences and the social sciences. She then enrolled at Cornell University and received her doctorate in medicine in 1981, proving that she was a gifted intellectual.

After earning her medical degree, Jemison did postgraduate training at the University of Southern California Medical Center. She worked in a refugee camp in Cambodia as a medical volunteer. Relocating to California from New York, she became interested in the Peace Corps and took the job of medical officer for Sierra Leone and Liberia. Her responsibility was to manage the health delivery system for Peace Corps and United States Embassy personnel. Her background includes work in the areas of nuclear magnetic resonance spectroscopy, reproductive biology, and printed wiring board materials. Such was her versatility that she also worked on the hepatitis B vaccine, schistosomaisis, and rabies. In addition, she mastered Russian, Swahili, and Japanese. She was a general practitioner and attending graduate engineering classes in Los Angeles when she was named to the astronaut training program. She completed her astronaut training in 1987.

Jemison flew her first flight as science mission specialist on STS-47, *Spacelab*-J, in September 1992. This was the first space flight by an African American woman. She was coinvestigator for the bone cell research experiment on that mission. In completing her first space flight, Jemison logged 190 hours, 30 minutes, and 23 seconds in space.

In 1993 Mae Jemison resigned from NASA to found the Jemison Group, Inc. She is a professor of environmental studies at Dartmouth College in New Hampshire. The singularity of Jemison's historical achievements has made her one of the greatest icons of the African American community.

# JACK
# JOHNSON
## 1878–1946

J ohn Arthur Johnson was born in Galveston, Texas, in 1878. His parents, Henry and Tina, were laborers who did menial work. His father was a school janitor and a porter at the rail station. By the time he was ten years old, John Arthur Johnson was out of school. He tried to help his parents by doing small jobs around the city of Galveston. He was a painter, a dockworker, a baker, and a horse trainer before he discovered a job that would inspire him and catapult him into greatness. In a way, he followed his father into the janitorial field, working as a janitor at a white gymnasium. This work excited his imagination and he started to train himself to fight. When the gymnasium was closed and he was cleaning it, he used the equipment to strengthen his body. Soon he started fighting in Galveston and rose quickly in the local community as the best African American fighter.

When he was nineteen years old, he turned professional. His record was spectacular: in 113 fights he lost only 8, and he continued fighting for thirty-five years. The reports on Johnson were specific: he was physically imposing, had powerful arms and legs, and could deliver a knockout with one blow. In addition to the reports of his athletic prowess, Johnson was also considered a smart fighter with the ability to defend himself from the best punchers and to counterpunch with withering speed and definite results.

In a 1903 bout with "Denver Ed" Martin, Johnson proved that he was the best African American fighter in the country and was crowned the unofficial black heavyweight champion. Nevertheless, in the eyes of the white world, Johnson's victory over Martin was a black affair. Whites did not consider him capable of fighting the best white heavyweights; still, they were afraid to give him a chance to fight them. The greatest white American boxers of the time were John L. Sullivan and Jim Jeffries, but both refused to get into the ring with Johnson. They either complained that black boxers would bring a bad reputation to the sport or that blacks could not take a punch. Nevertheless, they did not rush to prove their points by fighting Johnson.

The international boxing community was able to arrange a fight between the heavyweight champion Tommy Burns and Johnson on December 26, 1908. Johnson had waited for a long time for this fight. He was thirty years old by the time of the championship fight in Sydney, Australia. Johnson's defeat of Tommy Burns was an electric shock to the boxing world. It was broadcast throughout the world as one of the biggest sporting events of the era.

Johnson wore his championship belt proudly and flamboyantly. "White Hopes," as they were called, rushed to retake the title from him. Within two years he had defended the championship five times, each time defeating the challenger. Many whites were angry that a black man had taken the championship, so they called upon Jim Jeffries to come out of retirement to retake the title. This was to be the return of the "Great White Hope."

The two fighters met on July 4, 1910, in Reno, Nevada. Johnson clearly and thoroughly whipped Jim Jeffries. Race riots caused by angry white outbursts against blacks over the defeat of Jeffries created tension throughout the nation. Whites could no longer hide behind the veneer of white physical superiority because Jeffries, the "Great White Hope," had been defeated by Jack Johnson.

Johnson was not accorded the respect that he expected. In fact, he was condemned for beating the white hope. He did not demonstrate any of the stereotypical traits of African American subservience. Whites hated him for what they considered his arrogance. He showed no deference to his white opponents, defeating them with devastating punches. Johnson often got in the ring laughing at his opponents. He intimidated other fighters with the wink of his eyes, his glittering gold teeth, and his triumphant smile while standing over opponents on the floor.

Jack Johnson's personal life often created more controversy than his behavior in the ring. In 1913 Johnson was convicted of violating the Mann Act, which forbade transporting women across state lines for immoral purposes. It was meant to control prostitution. However, Johnson had traveled across state lines with his wife, Etta Terry Duryea, whom he married in 1911, and Lucille Cameron, whom he married in 1912 after Etta's suicide. The marriages to both women, who were white, were considered crimes since Johnson and his wives traveled across state lines for various boxing matches. Jackson and Lucille Cameron left for France to escape a prison term. He worked performing boxing and wrestling exhibitions in Paris. Two years later he traveled to Havana, Cuba, to defend his championship. He lost the title in April 1915 to Jess Willard. Deciding to clear his name, although he still disagreed with the law, he served a year in prison in 1920 when he returned to the United States. Four years later Johnson divorced Lucille Cameron and married a third white woman, Irene Pineau. He was killed in an automobile accident on June 10, 1946, in Raleigh, North Carolina.

Jack Johnson's greatness rests on his courage and self-determination in the early twentieth century to challenge any person who would restrict his rights as a human being. In many ways, Johnson demonstrated the irrational nature of white fears about race as well as white beliefs about racial superiority. Johnson's ability to take on the best white fighters and defeat them soundly had a lasting impact on the African American and white communities in the United States.

# JAMES WELDON
# JOHNSON
## 1871–1938

J ames Weldon Johnson was born in 1871 in Jacksonville, Florida, to literate, working-class parents. His birth, six years after the Civil War, to literate African parents meant that he would have a unique upbringing among Africans. His mother had been born in Nassau, Bahamas, and had lived in New York City prior to moving to Jacksonville. His father was a waiter at one of Jacksonville's resort hotel restaurants, but this did not prevent him from reading the Greek philosophers, studying Spanish, and appreciating poetry. Since both parents were well-read, they taught James and his brother, John Rosamond, the value of reading classic Western literature. In addition, they took their children on trips to the Bahamas and to New York, giving them a broader perspective on racial conditions and a greater understanding of the progress that was being made by African people. Although Johnson was educated in a school for African Americans that went only to the eighth grade, he soon enrolled at Atlanta University for preparatory and college work. This was the experience that allowed him to use the background given to him by his parents to excel. He took Latin and Greek, mastering both languages, and spent his seven years at the institution very profitably. He wrote poetry, started writing essays, and became a critic of literature while a student at Atlanta University. He would emerge as a composer, novelist, and major poet because of his brilliant mind.

Johnson graduated from Atlanta University in 1894 and accepted a position as a principal of a school in Atlanta. While black grammar schools typically went only to the eighth grade,

Johnson added the ninth and tenth grades to his school. He found that improving the education of the young black student was the best way to overcome the deficit of decades of impoverishment and deprivation. It was a hard, serious business, and he spent lots of time discovering new ways to deliver educational advantages to his students. Yet he was not satisfied and his intellectual appetite yearned for more mental challenges. In 1895 he started a newspaper, the *Daily American*, which gave him an opportunity to use the talents that he had developed while attending Atlanta University. This newspaper was politically progressive, and its name gave an indication that Johnson was eager to assert the agency of African Americans. It was not the *Daily African* or the *Negro American*, but the *Daily American*. He soon saw, however, that he needed to study the law in order to be able to defend African Americans from racial injustice. He studied law as an apprentice and finally passed the bar in 1898. Johnson was well on his way to becoming a truly exceptional activist, one who was educated in literature and law, in passion and reason. Johnson became the premier intellectual of the Harlem Renaissance, a period of artistic and literary flourishing from the 1920s to the 1940s. No one was as prolific as Johnson during this time when his poems, song lyrics, traditional sermons, and historical essays underscored his intellectual leadership.

Two decades before the beginning of the Harlem Renaissance, James Weldon Johnson and his brother, John Rosamond, collaborated on the creation of the African American national anthem, "Lift Every Voice and Sing." Written in 1900 to commemorate the life of Abraham Lincoln, the song was first performed by a high school in Jacksonville, Florida, and became a popular success across the nation. Johnson soon moved to New York City, where he studied literature at Columbia University.

James Weldon Johnson was made consulate for Venezuela in 1906, after throwing his political support to Theodore Roosevelt and becoming one of the most visible African American Republicans. For eight years he was a diplomat, serving in both Venezuela and Nicaragua.

Johnson's knowledge of diplomacy was to aid him in dealing with the political and social issues that would later confront him as the leader of the NAACP. He married Grace Nail in 1910; started work on his book *Autobiography of an Ex-Colored Man*, a novel about a light-skinned black who passed for white in America; had it published anonymously in 1912 while he was still a Central American consular; and ended his diplomatic service in 1913.

Seeking to jump-start his career in literature, his first love, Johnson took a position as contributing editor for the *New York Age*, an African American weekly. He was a skilled writer against racism, segregation, and ignorance. His education and culture were useful tools in his position with the newspaper. He soon had a poetry section in the newspaper and attempted to foster what he considered to be great literature.

It was during Johnson's impressive work with the *New York Age* that he came to the attention of the president of the National Association for the Advancement of Colored People (NAACP) and W. E. B. Du Bois, the editor of the *Crisis* magazine. They wanted Johnson to work with them on the development of the young organization. Johnson proved ready to assume a more dynamic role in the African American community, and in 1916 he became the NAACP's first field secretary, with duties that included organizing chapters in all major cities. Soon he had brought a young Atlanta native, Walter White, into the organization. White would become one of the most formidable leaders of the organization. Johnson's work and that of Walter White took place during the most intense period of lynching against African Americans. Any African American could be taken by vigilantes and lynched. The Red Summer of 1919 was so brutal for the African American man that many leaders, including Johnson and White, took it upon themselves to speak out forcefully against this barbarity.

The legacy of Ida B. Wells, the Silent Protest Parade in 1917, and the 1919 publication of *Thirty Years of Lynching* could not overcome the resistance in Congress to the Dyer Bill, which sought to make lynching a federal crime. In 1922 the African American community was disappointed when the Dyer Bill was defeated. Although it was defeated, Johnson had spent valuable energy fighting to get it approved by Congress. He was the principal lobbyist for the bill, and his enthusiasm brought him much attention. The NAACP rewarded him by offering him the post of executive secretary in 1920. Johnson took the position with the idea of making it a significant platform for defending African American rights.

James Weldon Johnson proved himself to be a man of unusual talent. He ran the organization, devoting much of his time to legal activities, but he also kept up his intellectual output as a writer. He edited three anthologies, *The Book of American Negro Poetry* (1922), *The Book of American Negro Spirituals* (1925), and *The Second Book of Negro Spirituals* (1926). His book *God's Trombones* (1927) was a powerful work that revealed the persistence of the traditional sermon in the African American psyche. When he retired from the NAACP in 1930, he published a work of social history, *Black Manhattan* (1930). Three years later Johnson wrote a memoir, *Along This Way* (1933); and a year later, a collection of essays, *Negro Americans, What Now?* (1934). His third and final poetry book was *St. Peter Relates an Incident: Selected Poems* (1935). He was killed in an automobile accident in Maine in 1938 at the age of sixty-seven.

# JOHN H.
# JOHNSON

1918–

J ohn H. Johnson was born in 1918 in Arkansas City, Arkansas. His mother left Arkansas in 1937 and moved to Chicago. She worked long hours as a domestic to make ends meet. Young John H. Johnson went to the public schools of Chicago and excelled at his studies. He was eager to achieve so that he would eventually be able to assist his mother. Johnson was elected president of the student body at DuSable High School, where he also edited the school newspaper. When he graduated from high school, he entered Northwestern University and took courses at the University of Chicago. Johnson's mother was a major influence on his sense of responsibility, work, and discipline. During the 1940s he developed an idea that would catapult him into the forefront of African American business. Johnson accepted a job working for Supreme Liberty Life Insurance Company and started collecting information about the African American community for Harry Pace and Earl B. Dickerson, senior officers of the company. He eventually became chairman of the board of Supreme Life Insurance Company. However, it was in the collection of news that Johnson made his mark. Johnson collected so many news items about the black community that he was convinced there was enough happening in the African American world to warrant a publication devoted exclusively to the community. He borrowed money, using his mother's furniture as collateral, to publish the first issue of *Negro Digest*. The initial five hundred dollars would lead to a great story of wealth accumulation in the African American community.

Initially, Johnson reprinted articles that had already been published, but he quickly turned his attention to publishing original pieces. In October 1943 First Lady Eleanor Roosevelt wrote an article for *Negro Digest*. The magazine soon had to print more than fifty thousand copies. Not only was Johnson able to repay his loans, but he also had enough money to see his mother comfortably retired by 1944.

Johnson created *Ebony* magazine in 1945 to satisfy the desire for a glossy, celebrity-type African American magazine. It was immediately successful as a concept, but a failure financially. Whereas the *Negro Digest* had been easily published and widely circulated, the launching of *Ebony* was a challenge. Johnson discovered that he did not have enough money to meet the higher costs of production and distribution, so he had to rely on creativity. He was able to secure advertising from white companies that catered to black audiences. In addition, Johnson used the network of black churches for distribution of the magazine. It soon became the centerpiece of the Johnson publishing enterprise. In 2001 the circulation of *Ebony* was more than 2 million. *Negro Digest* was discontinued in 1951; the company relaunched it in 1965 and renamed it *Black World* in 1970. Unable to generate market share in the African American community, the *Black World* was closed for good in 1976. *Jet*, a small weekly that featured entertainment, celebrity items, and sports, was produced in its place.

*Jet* was quite successful and became an international success by 2001, with a circulation topping 1 million and distribution in forty countries. It provided readers with thumbnail reports, short entries of hot information, and news bits about entertainers and athletes. It did not engage in high-level or deep discussion of political or social issues.

The Johnson formula has been criticized widely by the African American intelligentsia, who have argued that with so many blacks reading the news in *Ebony* and *Jet*, the Johnson companies could have had a different political impact on the community. However, Johnson rarely listened to the voices of the intellectuals, since the company made money with its formula. In 2001 the company employed 2,358 people, had a total circulation for all of its publications of 3.25 million, and had earnings of $330 million. The company has remained in the family, with John H. Johnson as the publisher and chief executive officer, Eunice W. Johnson as secretary-treasurer and producer-director of the *Ebony* Fashion Fair, and Linda Johnson Rice as the president and chief operating officer. The Johnson holdings include the publications *Ebony, Jet, EM: Ebony Man,* and *Ebony South Africa,* the Supreme Beauty Products, and the *Ebony* Fashion Fair.

# PERCY
# JULIAN
## 1899–1975

**P**ercy Lavon Julian was born on April 11, 1899, in Montgomery, Alabama, and died in Chicago on April 19, 1975. During his life, he became an important African American chemist because of his pioneering effort in synthetic drugs such as cortisone.

Julian was one of six children of James Sumner Julian, a railway clerk, and Elizabeth Adams Julian. The Julian family was committed to the idea of education as the path to freedom and opportunity. James and Elizabeth encouraged their children to excel in school. Given the fact that the education of African American children at the time was limited, the achievements of the six children were spectacular. Each of the children eventually earned either an M.A., Ph.D., or M.D. degree.

Percy Julian set a high standard for a child educated at State Normal School for Negroes when he graduated in 1916 as the leading student in his class. He immediately entered Indiana's DePauw University in Greencastle. Although Julian had been urged to excel by his parents and had the example of his siblings who loved education, he still found DePauw challenging. It required him to take high school courses to augment his college classes. Fortunately for Julian, he had learned to work hard as a child and did not have any trouble studying and working to support himself in college. His family, although encouraging, could not afford to finance his education, so Julian took that upon himself. Confronted by the DePauw curriculum, he established his intentions very early to become one of the best students at the college. He succeeded in becoming a member of the Phi Beta Kappa academic honor fraternity. Moreover, he graduated as class valedictorian from DePauw in 1920.

Percy Julian had earned his first degree and intended to pursue a doctorate in chemistry. However, he saw up close the racism of American education when he watched white students with lesser academic records receiving graduate fellowships, while he was ignored. During the early twentieth century American racism was quite overt, and many people believed that the country was not "ready" to accept a black person with a Ph.D. in chemistry. Denied entrance into a doctoral program because of his race, he took a position teaching chemistry at Fisk University in Nashville, Tennessee. Finally, after several years of teaching chemistry, he succeeded in obtaining an Austin Fellowship to study chemistry under the guidance of E. P. Kohler. He leaped at the opportunity and earned an M.A. degree in organic chemistry from Harvard in 1923. Leaving Harvard, he took a job at the West Virginia State College for Negroes. In 1927 he went to Howard University as professor and head of the Department of Chemistry, the premier position for an African American chemist at that time.

But Percy Julian was not finished with his education. Since the time he graduated from DePauw in 1916 he had wanted to obtain a doctorate. In 1929 the Rockefeller Foundation gave him a fellowship to study at the University of Vienna in Austria under Ernst Späth, who had won recognition for synthesizing nicotine and ephedrine. Julian assisted Späth in synthesizing hormones, vitamins, and naturally occurring drugs. When he left Vienna in 1931 he had earned a Ph.D. degree.

He resumed his work at Howard University until he was asked by DePauw to return as a faculty member at his undergraduate college. Thus, nearly twenty years after he left DePauw, Percy Julian returned to study the development of drugs to prevent glaucoma. William Blanchard, who had been a mentor to Julian, was eager to find ways to treat patients with glaucoma but could not find enough naturally occurring physostigmine. It was Julian's work to determine how the drug worked in the body that produced a breakthrough in the treatment of glaucoma: in 1935 he discovered a method to create synthetic physostigmine. This established his reputation as a brilliant scientist.

Afterward, Blanchard suggested that Julian be made head of DePauw's Department of Chemistry. The white faculty members at DePauw would not concur, and Julian soon left for a post as chief chemist with the Glidden Company, a manufacturer of paint, varnish, and other chemical products. In 1936 Percy Julian became the first African American to hold the highest chemist's post in an American industry. There were to be other breakthroughs in Julian's work. He used soybeans (the substance he had used in synthesizing physostigmine) to develop a synthesis of Reichstein's Substance S, which enabled the mass-production of the arthritis drug cortisone.

While at Glidden he pioneered a new process for using soy protein in paints and papers that generated large profits for the company. The protein was used as fire-retarding foam that helped save many lives on ships and planes in World War II (1939–1945). Furthermore, Julian's chemical team performed syntheses of progesterone and testosterone, the female and male sex hormones.

Eager to create his own company and to establish an African American company that was a leader in chemistry, Julian left Glidden in 1963 and created Julian Laboratories. He made the company international by opening offices in Mexico City as well as in Chicago. Julian Laboratories became known for the production of synthetic cortisone, first from soybeans and then from yams. His labs were the best in the world for the production of drugs synthesized from yams. He sold the company in 1964 to the U.S. pharmaceutical company Smith, Kline, and French.

# ERNEST
# JUST
1883–1941

One of the best scientists of the twentieth century was Ernest Everett Just, who was born on August 14, 1883, in Charleston, South Carolina. He died on October 27, 1941, in Washington, D.C. Just was greatly influenced by his mother, who moved the family from Charleston to James Island when her husband died. Ernest Just was four years old when his mother was widowed. She devoted her life to the care and education of her children, working in the dirty and dangerous phosphate fields to make enough money to feed and clothe Just and his siblings. A committed believer in education, Mary Just taught her children to read and write, and eventually started her own school. A woman with a visionary style, she convinced the neighbors to attend the church she founded in the community and to create farming cooperatives. She performed these activities with the energy of a prophet. Little Ernest Just did not believe anything was impossible. His mother had taught him that African Americans could achieve whatever they wanted to achieve.

Soon young Just had completed all the courses of study that were available in the James Island Gullah community in South Carolina. Mary Just knew that her son was bright and enthusiastic about learning, so she wanted to find the best school for him, given the circumstances of their lives. They were African Americans who lived in the deepest part of the American South, a very reactionary place. So Mary Just did some research and decided to send her son to Kimball Union School in New Hampshire. It was a preparatory school known for its openness to African American students. When Just got to Kimball Union in 1900, he discovered that he was the only African American student. Just had come from a rural southern background where his mother engaged in hard work to raise her children, and he was so inspired by his mother's example that he wanted to succeed despite the racial harassment he sometimes experienced at Kimball Union.

He took a course of study where he was immersed in the European classical tradition in language, oratory, rhetoric, and logic. By the time he was a senior at the school, Just had emerged as the leading student in the school. He was the editor of the school's yearbook as well as the commencement speaker for his senior class. Ernest Just had taken the hardships of his youth and used them as a foundation for excellence. In 1903 he entered Dartmouth College. As at Kimball Union, Just was the only African American in his class. He found the racism at Dartmouth far more daunting than at Kimball. Most students isolated him socially and refused to include him in any extracurricular activities. This situation served to make him more determined to excel in academics. He was lonely, but he felt that his time at Dartmouth would be better spent in the libraries than in pursuing social interests to no avail.

When Ernest Just graduated magna cum laude in biology, after taking extra courses in sociology and history in 1907, he had made history for African Americans and had reasserted that the African was the equal to anyone in science and academics. He was elected to Phi Beta Kappa.

Just left Dartmouth and took a position as a teacher of rhetoric and English at Howard University. Two years later he switched to teaching biology and zoology. Just brought to his job at Howard the same enthusiasm for intellectual pursuits that he had exhibited at Kimball Union and Dartmouth. The students loved him, and he was considered one of Howard's best teachers. He helped the students at Howard organize the Omega Psi Phi fraternity in 1911. Teaching was rewarding, but it did not satisfy Just's insatiable appetite for knowledge in the scientific field. He had to balance his love for teaching with his desire to pursue science as a researcher, so he spent his summers at the Marine Biology Laboratory in Woods Hole, Massachusetts. His research interests were fertilization of marine animal eggs and embryology. His friend and colleague Frank R. Lillie, a white scientist, urged him to pursue a doctorate. After four years of long-distance study, Just received a Ph.D. from the University of Chicago. He continued to work at Woods Hole and eventually published a distinguished textbook, *Biology of the Cell Surface*, and fifty scientific papers. His affiliation with Woods Hole would last for twenty summers. Just tried to do both teaching and research, and by virtue of his commitment to scholarship and science became one of the best teachers of his generation and perhaps the greatest cell scientist of his day.

Just traveled to Europe, lecturing and studying intermittently for ten years. In 1940, during World War II, he was in Nazi-occupied France, where he was briefly detained. Just died the next year, after trying to convince the Howard University leaders that his travels, paid for by philanthropy and his own family, were necessary for his scholarship. Ernest Just left an indelible impact upon the practice of science in the African American community, and his dedicated work in the interest of advancing knowledge must be seen as a model for other scientists and scholars.

# MAULANA
# KARENGA
1941–

**M**aulana Ndabezitha Karenga was born in Parsonsburg, Maryland, on July 14, 1941, and was given the name Ronald McKinley Everett by his parents. Karenga attended the public schools of nearby Salisbury, Maryland, but completed high school in York, Pennsylvania. In 1958, after graduating near the top of his high school class, he moved to Los Angeles. Soon thereafter he enrolled at Los Angeles City College, where he became the first black student body president. As a student leader, he was immediately thrust into the forefront of the emerging civil rights movement. Assuming leadership in the African American community, Karenga devoted attention to the peace movement and the struggles against capital punishment. While in college he embraced black nationalism and Pan-Africanism, expressing a belief in the self-determination of people of African descent. He immersed himself in the works of major black thinkers, such as W. E. B. Du Bois, Marcus Garvey, Kwame Nkrumah, Aimé Césaire, Sékou Touré, Julius Nyerere, and Edward Blyden.

In 1961 Karenga enrolled at the University of California, Los Angeles (UCLA). At UCLA, Karenga concentrated on the study of continental African and African American culture and social thought. Reflection on the state and condition of Africans motivated him to formulate the outlines of a philosophy based in African culture, which he came to call *Kawaida*.

He was greatly influenced by his meeting with Malcolm X in the early 1960s, and embraced some of the tenets of Malcolm's philosophy. Many people accept the Organization US, founded by Karenga in 1965, as the legitimate heir and keeper of Malcolm's legacy. Maulana Karenga earned his bachelor's degree in political science from UCLA in 1963, and his master's degree in political science with a specialization in African studies in 1964. He began work on his doctorate in political science but withdrew from his studies to join the black freedom movement after the Watts Revolt of 1965.

During this period, in what became known as the Black Power movement, Karenga began to emerge as a national leader. In 1965 he founded the Organization US (meaning "us, African people"), a social and cultural change organization, and began to advocate cultural revolution as an indispensable aspect of the liberation struggle. Having developed his Kawaida philosophy and the related *Nguzo Saba* (The Seven Principles), he created Kwanzaa, the Pan-African holiday, in 1966 to promote these principles and the communitarian African philosophy out of which they evolved. These principles are *umoja* (unity), *kujich-agulia* (self-determination), *ujima* (collective work and responsibility), *ujamaa* (cooperative economics), *kuumba* (creativity), and *imani* (faith). Through the Organization US and his Kawaida philosophy, Karenga helped shape some of the major movements since the 1960s.

Karenga's books on Kawaida philosophy offer an analytical discussion of his philosophy as well as a view of the course of its development, as seen in *Essays on Struggle: Position and Analysis* (1978), *Kawaida Theory: An Introductory Outline* (1980), and *Kawaida: A Communitarian African Philosophy*. In these works, the reader sees Karenga's initial emphasis on nationalism, Pan-Africanism, and African socialism turn into a broader conception of Kawaida as "an ongoing synthesis of the best of African thought and practice in constant exchange with the world."

After the decline of the Black Power movement in the 1970s, Karenga returned to university life, finishing his doctorate in political science at United States International University in 1976 and teaching at various universities as a visiting professor.

Contributing to the scholarly discourse on the field and mission of black studies, Karenga worked with his colleagues to build the National Council for Black Studies and wrote *Introduction to Black Studies* (1982), generally considered the standard introductory text in the discipline.

Turning to the study of ethics and classical African culture, Karenga focused on ancient Egyptian ethical texts. His magnum opus is an 803-page dissertation entitled *Maat, the Moral Ideal in Ancient Egypt: A Study in Classical African Ethics* (1994), which he wrote for his second doctorate in social ethics at the University of Southern California. Two of his other works in this area are *Selections from the Husia: Sacred Wisdom of Ancient Egypt* (1984) and *The Book of Coming Forth by Day: The Ethics of the Declarations of Innocence* (1990).

One of the most significant figures in African American history, Maulana Ndabezitha Karenga's greatness is based upon the fact that he is the single most important intellectual influence on African American culture since the 1960s. The impact of his ideas and work can be seen in the development of various social and intellectual movements. These movements include Black Studies, Black Power, the black arts movement, the Simba Wachanga (Young Lions) youth movement, Afrocentricity, ancient Egyptian studies within black studies, rites of passage, independent black schools, and the 1995 Million Man March, for which he wrote the official mission statement. Karenga is best known for creating the African American and Pan-African holiday Kwanzaa and authoring the definitive book on the subject, *Kwanzaa: A Celebration of Family, Community, and Culture* (1988). Over the past thirty years he has earned hundreds of honors and awards, including an honorary doctorate from the University of Durban-Westville, South Africa.

During the 1980s Karenga was influenced by Senegalese scholar Cheikh Anta Diop's work on ancient Egypt. Karenga's own scholarship in ancient Egyptian culture is a part of a larger project of Africana studies, where he seeks to recover and reconstruct classical African cultures in order to enrich contemporary discourse.

Continuing this work, he authored *Odu Ifa: The Ethical Teachings* (1999), a collection and translation of the ancient sacred text of the Yoruba, a group of West African peoples, with accompanying commentary. As with the *Husia,* his interest here is in using an ancient classical African text to address the compelling issues of contemporary times from an African-centered perspective.

He currently serves as professor and chair of the Department of Black Studies at California State University, Long Beach; executive director of the African American Cultural Center in Los Angeles, California; and chair of the Organization US and the National Association of Kawaida Organizations.

# MARTIN LUTHER KING JR.

1929–1968

**M**artin Luther King Jr. was born Michael King on January 15, 1929, in Atlanta, Georgia. He was the eldest son of Martin Luther King, a Baptist minister, and Alberta Williams King. The senior King served as pastor of Ebenezer Baptist, a large Atlanta church that was founded by Alberta Williams King's father. King Jr. was ordained as a Baptist minister at age eighteen.

King attended local segregated public schools, where he excelled. By the time he was fifteen years old he was admitted into Morehouse College; he graduated in 1948 with a bachelor's degree. King's first degree was in sociology, belying the fact that he would soon study theology. He left Atlanta in 1951 to attend Crozer Theological Seminary in Chester, Pennsylvania. From Crozer, he was attracted to the theological school at Boston University, where he studied with the leading theologians of the day and eventually earned a doctoral degree in systematic theology in 1955.

King was an excellent student, gravitating easily to the work of the liberal and progressive theologians and studying the life and thoughts of Mohandas Gandhi. He had been intellectually mentored by Benjamin E. Mays, the president of Morehouse College, to seek the most intelligent explanations for the human condition. King believed that Morehouse had prepared him for Crozer and Boston.

Coretta Scott, a music student and native of Alabama, was studying music in Boston when King met her. They were married in 1953 and had four children. His first position after leaving Boston University in 1954 was the pastorate of the Dexter Avenue Baptist Church in Montgomery, Alabama.

King entered Montgomery at a time when the grievances of the black community were mounting by the day. The community had long complained that the segregationists had pushed them to the limits. The Women's Council, under the leadership of JoAnn Robinson, had approached the white city fathers and petitioned them for relief from the strict racist policies of the city. Black men and women were routinely mistreated and abused. White bus drivers were known to physically beat black passengers who did not give their seats to whites. There were many reasons for the black community to be angry.

On December 1, 1955, Rosa Parks, the secretary of the local branch of the National Association for the Advancement of Colored People (NAACP), was ordered by a bus driver to give up her seat to a white passenger. She refused and was arrested by the police and taken to jail. From that day forward, the Montgomery black community was in revolt against racism. The local leader of the NAACP, Edgar D. Nixon, seized the opportunity to launch a campaign that would bring down segregated buses. The arrest of the highly respected Rosa Parks, who was a seamstress in a downtown department store, was the catalyst for the end of segregation.

Nixon, in his wisdom, sought someone to be the spokesperson for the community who could pull everyone together in a citywide protest. Martin Luther King Jr. had recently arrived in Montgomery and had immediately established a reputation as a powerful orator and a brilliant thinker. King was elected the president of the Montgomery Improvement Association (MIA), the organization that called for a bus boycott.

The protest was sustained by the energy that King and other leaders, including Reverend Ralph Abernathy, generated within the movement. The Montgomery bus boycott lasted for more than a year, during which time the white segregationists intensified their attacks on the homes and churches of the black leadership. King's home was firebombed, and others had their homes threatened. In February 1956 Fred Gray, a young Montgomery

attorney, filed a lawsuit in federal court on behalf of the Montgomery Improvement Association, seeking an injunction against
Montgomery's segregated buses. The federal court ruled in favor
of the MIA, ordering the city's buses to be desegregated, but the
white authorities of the city government appealed the ruling to
the United States Supreme Court. The Supreme Court upheld the
lower court decision in November 1956, and King was immediately thrust into the national limelight. He had taken on the
movement as a challenge to the structures and institutions of the
racist South and had become, by virtue of his intelligence, energy,
and dignity, the embodiment of the fearlessness that was to
accompany all future demonstrations against segregation. He
wrote a book about the bus boycott and called it *Stride Toward
Freedom* (1958).

One year later, in 1957, King was one of the founders of the
Southern Christian Leadership Conference (SCLC), an organization of black churches and ministers that were allied against the
racist practices of the South. The members of the SCLC saw segregation and racism as being in opposition to the laws of God.
They framed their objectives in moral and ethical terms. King
was made the president of the organization and became its
leading theorist. He used all of his training in theology school to
devise a philosophy of nonviolence that would provide the ratio-
nale for demonstrations, marches, and rallies.

Martin Luther King Jr. did not forget the numerous partici-
pants in the demonstrations and marches against injustice. He
was eager to point out that the moral authority of the movement
came from the work of Protestants and Catholics, Jews and gen-
tiles. There was an egalitarianism in his thought and action that
made it possible for all people of goodwill to join in the movement against evil.

In 1959 he visited India and studied more determinedly
*Satyagraha,* Gandhi's principle of nonviolent persuasion. This
would become King's principal strategy for demonstrations and
protests, but he would discover its limitations where the numbers were not large enough to have an impact on the racist struc-

ture. This was precisely the case in northern suburban areas, where the populations of African Americans were limited. In 1960 King moved his center of operation to Atlanta and became a cominister with his father at the Ebenezer Baptist Church in Atlanta. The work as president of SCLC was taking more and more of his time, and he wanted his wife and children to be closer to his family and the base of his work. He led several campaigns in the early 1960s against segregation. In 1961 SCLC went to Albany, Georgia, a bastion of segregation, and led protests against all forms of segregation in restaurants, buses, hotels, housing, and schools. In its visibility it was a national campaign eliciting assistance from across the nation. However, the strategy of nonviolent protest seemed to fail in Albany as money ran out for bail. The police chief of Albany had decided to arrest hundreds of people if necessary and to make them pay bail.

In the spring of 1963, the SCLC, eager for a victory, joined forces with Reverend Fred Shuttlesworth, one of the ministers who had worked with King in 1957 in organizing the SCLC, to nonviolently defeat the segregation of Birmingham, Alabama. The Birmingham police commissioner, Eugene "Bull" Connor, had a reputation for violence. By May 1963 King and the SCLC decided it was time to test Bull Connor, to see what he would do if hundreds of schoolchildren joined the marches. This was an escalation, but it was also predicated upon the belief that the youth had to be involved in the struggle to overturn segregation. It was not simply an idea to use the children as cannon fodder. Nevertheless, the officers of the SCLC could not believe the ferocity of the Birmingham police under the direction of Bull Connor. Police officers with attack dogs and electric prodders and firefighters with high-pressure water hoses mowed down the demonstrators, pinning some of them against the walls of downtown buildings. The photographs of the Birmingham demonstration became one of the most powerful weapons in the hands of the SCLC. King made good use of the Birmingham demonstration. He was arrested and thrown into jail as the leader of the group. In prison he penned what is the most carefully thought out essay on his philosophy. The "Letter from a Birmingham Jail" articulated all of King's principal arguments. He contended that it was the duty of human beings to break unjust laws and that no laws made by men should be greater than the laws made by God.

King had called upon the white ministers of Birmingham to take the leadership in fighting against the racist practices of their churches' members. Soon, the white leaders of the city were pressured to negotiate the end of segregation.

The victory in Birmingham intensified the call for a national march that would support civil rights legislation in Congress. On August 28, 1963, King delivered the keynote address to a mass audience of more than 250,000 civil rights followers, including labor and business leaders. The "I Have a Dream" speech became the anthem of the civil rights era. His oratorical style was suited for the moment and his beautiful metaphors, delivered in the slow, deliberate cadence of a black Baptist preacher, shook the foundations of American society. In fact, the speech may be one of the most famous ever given in American history.

The Civil Rights Act of 1964, which prohibited segregation in public accommodations and discrimination in education and employment, was a direct result of the pressure put upon Congress by the moral high ground that had been taken by King and his coworkers. It was to be expected that he would be nominated for the Nobel Peace Prize. He was awarded this honor because of the high standards he had set in leading the moral protest and outrage against segregation.

The Battle of Selma would be another defining moment for King. In 1965 the SCLC joined a voting-rights protest march from Selma, Alabama, to the state capital of Montgomery, more than fifty miles (eighty km). When the marchers started their demonstration, the police pounced upon them with batons and tear gas. It was one of the bloodiest marches King had participated in since the Birmingham protest, becoming known as Bloody Sunday. People came to Alabama from around the country to resume the march, once they saw on television that the demonstrators had been beaten. The federal court gave the marchers a victory by placing an injunction on the police. They were told they had to allow the demonstrators to march. In two weeks the marchers started again and with three thousand people entering Montgomery, three hundred who had marched the entire distance, the crowd in Montgomery gave a loud cheer. King spoke to twenty thousand people at the Alabama capitol about the struggle for civil rights. He was eloquent and inspirational, but he did not forget the toll that had been taken on the demonstrators.

Soon thereafter the Voting Rights Act of 1965 was signed into law by President Lyndon Johnson. The act suspended (and amendments to the act later banned) the use of literacy tests and other qualification tests that had often been used to prevent African Americans from registering to vote.

King soon turned his attention to the Vietnam War. His opposition to the Vietnam War (1959–1975) caused many people, including President Johnson, to accuse him of ingratitude. But King was clear that injustice anywhere should be fought and he was not about to turn his back on the injustice of Vietnam.

Challenged by the growing cadre of young civil rights spokespersons, King spoke to the disaffection that existed within the black community. Stokeley Carmichael (later Kwame Ture) articulated a view that blacks needed to fight for black power. Malcolm X had been killed in 1965, and many young people saw his philosophy of black nationalism as the key to a self-determining and self-defining African American community. King remained committed to nonviolence and turned his attention to economic issues, including the persistent poverty of the black community. Throughout 1966 and 1967 he planned the Poor People's Campaign to pressure national lawmakers to address economic justice.

When King went to Memphis, Tennessee, in the spring of 1968, he wanted to demonstrate his support for the striking black garbage workers. On April 4, 1968, Martin Luther King was shot and killed by James Earl Ray. Ray later pleaded guilty to the murder and was sentenced to ninety-nine years in prison. More than one hundred cities erupted in a frenzy of anger as

African Americans burned cities and destroyed businesses in the aftermath of the of King's assassination. Several years later the Martin Luther King Jr. Center for Social Justice, a research and training institute, was established to commemorate the life of the nonviolent philosopher. In addition, January 15 was made a national holiday to celebrate the life of one of the greatest moral leaders of the nation.

# EDMONIA
# LEWIS

1843–?

It is believed that Edmonia Lewis was born in either New Jersey, Ohio, or New York in either 1843, 1844, or 1845. There is no certain place or date of her birth reported in the literature. However, what is certain is that Edmonia Lewis, the offspring of an African American man and a Native American Ojibwa woman, was the first female sculptor of African American and Native American heritage to be recognized in modern art.

Edmonia Lewis used the historical experiences of African Americans as the principal pathways to her artistic achievement. She created the famous piece *Forever Free* (1867, Howard University Gallery of Art, Washington, D.C.), which was apparently based on the emancipation of millions of Africans after the Civil War. The piece, carved in marble, shows a man and a woman who have just heard that they were free. The woman is kneeling, her hands clasped, and the man is resting his foot on the ball that held them in bondage. He is shown raising his arm to reveal the broken shackle and chain around his wrist.

The record of Edmonia Lewis's time at Oberlin is clear. She entered Oberlin in 1859 and made excellent grades in drawing. She was the best artist in her class and excelled at drawing human figures. She had gone by her Ojibwa community name, Wildfire, until she enrolled at Oberlin, where her name was changed to Mary Edmonia Lewis. All of her artwork, paintings, drawings, and sculptures were signed with the single name *Edmonia*. She soon got into difficulty at Oberlin, when a teacher missed some paintbrushes and it was believed that Edmonia had stolen them. She was accused of theft. Furthermore, two girls got quite ill after drinking some mulled wine given to them by Lewis. She was accused of attempted murder in those cases. On both counts Edmonia was found not guilty, yet she was not permitted to graduate.

Believing that Boston was a more enlightened community, Edmonia moved there in 1863. She used her contact with the famous abolitionist William Lloyd Garrison to gain an introduction to the sculptor Edward Brackett, who became her first mentor. In the rich tradition of Boston's antislavery community, Lewis found the time to develop medallions with portraits of the abolitionists and Civil War heroes. She modeled these in clay and cast them in plaster. One of the more famous pieces was the *Bust of Colonel Robert Gould Shaw* (1865, Museum of Afro-American History, Boston, Massachusetts). In this piece she depicted the young, white Bostonian as he led an all-black battalion, the 54th Massachusetts Volunteer Regiment. The work immediately caught on, and sales of replicas of the work made enough money for Edmonia to travel to Italy, where she established an artist's studio in Rome in 1865.

Lewis found that her work in Rome improved her skills. She was able to focus on the content of her pieces as she had never been able to do in the United States. The crowning point of her artistic career was when she completed the work *The Death of Cleopatra* (1876, National Museum of American Art, Washington, D.C.), and it became a sensation at the Philadelphia Centennial Exposition of 1876.

What is so creative about Lewis's depiction of Cleopatra is that she does not abstract the death of Cleopatra, but shows Cleopatra seated upon her throne. She holds the poisonous snake in one hand and shows a limp second hand. This is a fairly realistic portrayal of Cleopatra, not the general sentimentality that had been the normal case with artists.

The highly acclaimed Lewis was reported as still living in Rome in 1911. The date and location of her death are not known.

# ALAIN
# LOCKE
## 1885–1954

Alain Leroy Locke was born in 1885 in a middle-class Philadelphia family. His paternal and maternal families had descended from a long tradition of free Africans. He was a model student in high school, demonstrating a love of music and literature at an early age. He mastered both the piano and the violin while maintaining high grades. Locke entered Harvard University in 1904 and was elected, for his scholarship, to the honor society Phi Beta Kappa. In 1907 he received his bachelor's degree in philosophy magna cum laude.

A few months later he received the Rhodes Scholarship, becoming the first African American to study at Oxford University as a Rhodes scholar. It would be nearly fifty years before another African American would be named a Rhodes scholar. He studied philosophy at Oxford and then at the University of Berlin.

He was not a narrow intellectual; Locke was opened to all fields of study, becoming known as one of the first multidisciplinary African American scholars. His love of research and scholarship was to drive his leadership during the Harlem Renaissance. The scope of his intellectual interests and the depth of his understanding of the major currents of the day made him one of the most celebrated African American scholars of his era. He loved his culture and believed that the great men and women of the African American community would create a "new Negro" who would be cosmopolitan, broad, progressive, and culturally dynamic.

When Locke returned to the United States in 1911, he spent a few months looking for the right position but finally joined the faculty of Howard University as a professor of philosophy and English in 1912. With the exception of a sabbatical in 1916 and 1917 to complete his Ph.D. in philosophy at Harvard, Locke remained at Howard until his death. Locke was considered a brilliant philosopher, but his reputation is usually based on his work in the field of literature and anthologies.

In 1923 the National Urban League, recognizing the incredible talent of Alain Locke and knowing that the NAACP could count on James Weldon Johnson and W. E. B. Du Bois, asked Alain Leroy Locke to contribute a series of essays on various topics to its journal, *Opportunity*. The essays made him more famous as a scholar, and two years later, in 1925, the National Urban League asked him to edit the March issue of a national magazine, the *Survey Graphic*, whose editors wanted to publish an issue devoted to race. When Locke accepted the idea, he immediately began to look for African Americans who were at the top of their fields in literature, social thought, and poetry. The issue he created proved to be a major success. It was subtitled *Harlem: Mecca of the New Negro,* and included nonfiction, fiction, and poetry by writers such as Anne Spencer, W. E. B. Du Bois, James Weldon Johnson, Langston Hughes, Countee Cullen, and Jean Toomer. Locke soon turned it into a book, *The New Negro,* published eight months later. *The New Negro*, the authoritative statement of the Harlem Renaissance, included pieces by Claude McKay, E. Franklin Frazier, Zora Neale Hurston, Angelina Grimke, Jessie Fauset, William Stanley Braithwaite, Kelly Miller, and J. A. Rogers. Artwork by the well-known artist Aaron Douglas spoke to the developing artistic sensibility of the African American community. The book answered the critics of African American genius by demonstrating that the African American could produce exceptional work in any area of art, philosophy, or literature.

Locke had a strong belief in the cultural connection between Africa and African Americans. He believed that it was the art of Africa and African America that would show the connection between the two sides of the Atlantic. This allowed him to define African American culture on the basis of the visual arts. As a collector and critic of African and African American art, Locke established himself as the principal artistic judge of African and African American art. Locke founded the Associates in Negro Folk Education to assist in publishing African American scholarly books in the 1930s, because he felt the American public deserved to know the depth of African American thought. Using the Associates of Negro Folk Education, Locke published *Negro Art: Past and Present* and *The Negro and His Music*, both in 1936, and the comprehensive, illustrated volume *The Negro in Art: A Pictorial Record of the Negro Artists and the Negro Theme in Art* in 1940. The latter work is one of his most recognized works.

Alain Locke published his first article on philosophy in 1935, at the end of the Harlem Renaissance. By this time he was already fifty years old and had spent years reading the European philosophers and concentrating his thought on the nature of African American life and culture. He did not have any training in African philosophy and could not write authoritatively on the subject itself, but he was skillful and astute enough to know that African art held the key to many African concepts. Consequently, he turned his attention to the development of ideas that related to aesthetics in the African world.

Continuing to publish excellent anthologies, in 1942 Locke coedited a work called *When Peoples Meet: A Study in Race and Culture Contacts*. This book went a long way toward reinforcing the reputation that Locke had nurtured as an intellectual with a broad understanding of human culture. *The Negro in American Culture,* a work that Locke believed would capture his entire philosophical enterprise, remained unfinished at his death in June 1954. Afterward, Margaret Just Butcher published a work that was a smaller version of the book envisioned by Locke. It was universally considered to be Butcher's—not Locke's—work.

Nevertheless, the philosophical and cultural history of African Americans could not be written without Alain Locke. He is the greatest African American philosopher of his age and the person who almost single-handedly brought respectability to the scholarly profession in the black community. Locke takes his place alongside the most significant African American scholars of the twentieth century. However, his importance as a personality extends beyond his academic interests since he became, by virtue of his leadership, the symbol of the Harlem Renaissance.

# JOE
# LOUIS
## 1914–1981

**J**oseph Louis Barrow was born in 1914, the son of sharecroppers, on a small farm near Lafayette, Alabama. He was the seventh of eight children. Soon after his birth his father, Munroe Barrow, was sent to a psychiatric hospital. Although Joe Louis was told that his father had died, he learned later that his father had lived for two decades after he was committed.

His mother, Lillie Barrow, trying to make ends meet for all of her children, remarried another farmer. In 1924 the entire family left Alabama and moved to Detroit, Michigan. After the family reached Detroit, Louis's stepfather found work rather easily. However, Louis found school tough because he was older and bigger than the children in his classes. His education in the South had been poor and he found a challenge in the assignments given to him by his teacher. Joe Louis soon developed a stammer in his speech, which some believe may have been the result of the embarrassment he felt in school. He started skipping classes to study carpentry and to watch boxers at a local gymnasium. By the age of seventeen, he was out of school and training himself to box.

Joe Louis started his amateur career in an impressive fashion. He lost his first boxing match, but soon had a string of forty victories during the next three years—and only four defeats. He won the national amateur title in 1934 and turned professional soon afterward. His first managers were two African American businessmen, John Roxborough and Julian Black. They suggested that he drop the Barrow from his name to make it easier to remember. They also hired Jack Blackburn, a former light-weight fighter and well-regarded trainer.

Roxborough and Black sought to keep their boxers away from the controversies that had engulfed the championship held by Jack Johnson from 1908 to 1915. Louis's managers wanted him to demonstrate courtesy in the ring and shyness around the press. They tried to keep him from anything that would distract from his greatness. Louis was told to stay away from drinking, smoking, and being seen alone with white women.

In the 1940s Joe Louis was the most celebrated African American athlete. He surpassed Jack Johnson in the African American community as an icon, because he had values that were more in keeping with the vast majority of African Americans. His boxing career was spectacular. He won twenty fights with no losses during the first year he fought professionally. Hearing Louis's fights on the radio became a ritual in the African American community as people listened to every account of his blows against whites.

One of the most memorable fights in Louis's career occurred on June 19, 1936. On that day Louis met German boxer Max Schmeling, a former world champion, in New York's Yankee Stadium. This was during the time that the German leader, Adolf Hitler, was threatening various countries in Europe and expressing the superiority of the German people. The press reports called Schmeling a representative of a fascist government and Louis a symbol of democracy. In the twelfth round, Schmeling knocked out the heavily favored Louis, sending him to the canvas in his first professional loss. The Germans seized upon Schmeling's victory as proof of the superiority of the Aryan race.

Louis returned to the ring and had seven straight victories, securing the right to fight heavyweight champion James Braddock on June 22, 1937, in Chicago's Comiskey Park. Braddock was a skilled boxer, and he knocked Louis to the ground early in the fight, but Louis gained strength as the fight continued and in the eighth round knocked Braddock to the canvas. Still only twenty-three years old, Louis had become the heavyweight champion of the world. The war in Europe was nearly breaking out when a second Louis-Schmeling fight was organized. In the very first round Louis went to work on Schmeling and soon scored a stunning knockout. Louis took his place as one of the most popular athletes in America and, indeed, much of the world.

However, because of poor investments and free spending, Louis was heavily in debt. He defended his title almost monthly during most of 1941 and 1942. This was an impressive demonstration of Louis's physical stamina.

In 1942, with World War II (1939–1945) under way, Louis entered the United States Army and boxed in nearly one hundred exhibition matches for the troops. Joe Louis became a voice against segregation in the army during the war. He used his position in the nation to call attention to the mistreatment of the African American soldier, and in so doing became a black spokesman.

When the war was over, Louis fought Jersey Joe Walcott in 1947. Walcott knocked him down twice, but in the end Louis won a controversial split decision victory. Later Louis knocked Walcott out in a rematch.

In 1949, at the age of thirty-four, Louis retired but had to return to the ring to fight because of his financial situation. He fought several times, losing twice, once to heavyweight champion Ezzard Charles and, in a knockout on October 26, 1951, to Rocky Marciano. Louis then retired for good with a final record of sixty-eight wins, fifty-four by knockout, and three losses. He married Martha Jefferson in 1959, following three earlier divorces. In his final years, Joe Louis worked in Las Vegas as a greeter at casinos. He died in 1981.

# THURGOOD
# MARSHALL
## 1908–1993

**A**ll great lawyers do not make great judges, but judges are, more often than not, lawyers first; nonetheless, no lawyer in African American history has stood as tall as Thurgood Marshall. He was born in 1908 in Baltimore, Maryland, and spent most of his life living in Washington and New York. When Marshall was born, Baltimore was clearly a racially divided city, and the lessons of segregation were everywhere. Blacks were discriminated against in housing, in employment, and in education. Inequality was inherent in the system of racial separation that favored white privilege.

When he was a young man, Marshall's father said to him, "If anyone calls you nigger, you not only have my permission to fight him, you got my orders." Marshall's parents were not rich. They were hardworking people who believed in making the best out of the circumstances of their lives. William Marshall worked as a waiter at an all-white private club. Norma Marshall was a grade school teacher in the Baltimore public schools. Marshall credits his parents with giving him a strong sense of confidence, African American pride, and personal dignity. This did not mean that Marshall would not get into trouble with his teachers. He often said that he was not the most obedient student. In fact, he called himself "a hell-raiser." When he was punished by one teacher who forced him to read passages from the Constitution of the United States, he said it probably laid the foundation for his interest in the law.

He would eventually become the first African American justice on the Supreme Court of the United States. However, appointment to the Supreme Court was not automatic in Marshall's career. He set a stunning course of legal achievements that gained him recognition nationally as one of the most brilliant legal minds of his time. In fact, he was considered great before he was appointed to the Supreme Court. The African American community did not feel any different about Thurgood Marshall's chance for being in the panoply of greatness because he was appointed to the national bench. Before he assumed his seat on the High Court, his legal agility had already helped millions of African Americans exercise their rights to education. Furthermore, he had already served nearly thirty years as a public-servant lawyer for the National Association for the Advancement of Colored People (NAACP), on the federal bench, and as a solicitor. He was pre-eminently a man of the people, and he was loved universally because of the issues for which he fought. In 1993 his body lay in state, only the second justice so honored; the first had been Chief Justice Earl Warren, who wrote the majority opinion in Marshall's most celebrated case, *Brown* v. *Topeka Board of Education.*

Marshall graduated from Baltimore's Douglass High School and entered Lincoln University, less than a hundred miles away in Oxford, Pennsylvania. At Lincoln, Marshall was an outstanding student who graduated with honors in 1930. Having a love for the law, he wanted to pursue legal education at the University of Maryland in his home state, but he was denied admission because of his race. He would later sue the university to overturn its segregated admission policy. In *Murray* v. *Maryland*, Marshall was able to defeat the policy that enabled Maryland, one of the earliest southern states, to outlaw race as a criterion for admission. He went to law school at Howard University in Washington. Among the influences on his career was the outstanding civil rights lawyer Charles H. Houston, who was the vice dean of the law school and the first chief counsel for the NAACP. Houston was also the first African American to win a legal case before the United States Supreme Court. Marshall joined Houston's NAACP law office after he graduated magna cum laude from Howard in 1933. Five years later Marshall was named chief counsel of the NAACP, replacing Houston. Marshall succeeded one of the most dynamic lawyers of the day. Houston was an activist lawyer and believed that the only way the NAACP would make advances against segregation as a policy would be to challenge the racists in the courts. The NAACP was dedicated to challenging inequality in housing, education, and employment, and had won many local cases since its inception in 1909. However, Marshall took the legal argument to the core of the racial privilege philosophy. This meant that he challenged not just inequality between segregated facilities, but segregation itself.

Marshall's new strategy would have an immense impact on the nature of the civil rights struggle. In effect, he changed the entire movement from a concentration on local challenges to a more substantive challenge of the structure that supported the local laws. What this meant was that Marshall had to direct his attacks on the law that was created by *Plessy* v. *Ferguson* (1896), a case that established the legality of segregated railroads by declaring them constitutional as long as there were equal facilities for blacks and whites. But Marshall showed an intense dislike for all segregation laws and started pressing the court to decide if there could ever be "separate but equal" anything. Cases such as *Sweatt* v. *Painter* in 1950 suggested that the Supreme Court was not satisfied with the "separate but equal" rule. Marshall saw the weakness and went for the jugular vein of the system. He was convinced that the principle of segregation was the final column in political and social inequality. It had to be toppled.

The legal case argued by Marshall that brought down the segregation column was *Brown* v. *Topeka Board of Education*. This was a historic case, because it used all of the most recent social and behavioral sciences to argue that it was impossible to have separate but equal schools. Marshall also sought to prove that African American children were harmed by the malicious practice of racial segregation, which gave them inferior schools. The Supreme Court was unanimous in its decision to outlaw state-imposed segregation and set guidelines for eliminating it with all deliberate speed. The

constitutional victory had far-reaching significance for the structure of the American society. It meant that the state laws that supported separate but equal facilities, institutions, and opportunities
could be struck down. This was a powerful decision.

Thurgood Marshall was a productive lawyer, bringing thirty-
two cases before the Supreme Court. His record of wins before the
Supreme Court was impressive; he lost only three cases. As a
judge for the U.S. Court of Appeals, to which he was appointed
by President John F. Kennedy in 1961, he wrote 112 opinions, not
one of which was overturned by appeal. Marshall was appointed
the chief counsel of the nation, that is, solicitor general of the
United States, by President Lyndon Johnson in 1965. Two years
later Marshall was nominated for the Supreme Court. Taking the
jobs as solicitor general and as Supreme Court justice was difficult for Marshall, because he felt bad about abandoning his colleagues in the civil rights struggle. Remaining active, however,
Marshall did not lose his energy for writing essays, in addition to
legal opinions, once he got to the Supreme Court. On the court,
Marshall wrote the majority opinions for *Bounds* v. *Smith* (1977),
which defended prisoners' rights to assistance and libraries; and
*Stanley* v. *Georgia* (1969), which protected the rights of individuals to possess pornography. In writing about *Stanley*, Marshall
said, "If the First Amendment means anything, it means that the
state has no business telling a man, sitting alone in his own house,
what books he may read or what films he may watch." Thurgood
Marshall was often placed in the role of the "great dissenter,"
standing alone or with a minority of judges for the rights of the
poor and oppressed. He saw the Court grow more conservative
during the 1980s, yet he argued against the death penalty. In a
sixty-three-page dissent in *San Antonio School District* v.
*Rodriguez*, a 1973 case in which the majority decided that
unequal funding of urban and suburban school districts, based
upon their disparate tax bases, was constitutional, Marshall
asserted "the right of every American to an equal start in life."

On the bench Thurgood Marshall was a judge who often
questioned lawyers with sharp barbs of legal opinions, but in his

private life he was known as a great storyteller, regaling his family and friends with jokes and gossip. He was beloved by those who appreciated his passion for justice and his love for life. Even his conservative colleagues on the Supreme Court respected his wisdom, energy, and judgment. President Johnson could not have found a more appropriate person to serve as the first African American on the High Court. Marshall was gifted with words, reason, and a sense of fair play, and, more than all of this, he had a great understanding of his place in American history. He was feared by those who were the enemies of justice. His ability to overcome discrimination and segregation through the law meant that he developed a strong capacity and personal will to see the world made better for human beings. He was able to sustain the hope of African Americans by his determined action against all forms of human oppression. He truly did all that he could do with the gifts at his disposal.

# BENJAMIN E.
# MAYS

## 1894–1984

**B**enjamin Mays may be called the intellectual father of Martin Luther King Jr. Of course, he had a reputation for intellectual vigor and philosophical speculation long before King became a student at Morehouse College. Benjamin Mays was the son of Hezekiah and Louvenia Carter Mays, both of whom had been enslaved Africans. He was born on August 1, 1894, in Ninety-Six, South Carolina. Mays attended Virginia Union University in Richmond, Virginia, for a brief time and then transferred to Bates College in Maine, where he earned a bachelor's degree in 1920.

Mays was ordained a Baptist minister in 1921. His intellectual interest in religion and his commitment to the ministry led him to seek an advanced degree at the University of Chicago's Divinity School, where he received a master's degree in 1925. Ten years later he would earn a doctorate. While completing his doctorate, he took a position as dean of the School of Religion at Howard University. He is credited with revitalizing and reviving a program that was essentially dead. Mays was an active dean, increasing enrollment, modernizing the library, and developing outreach programs to the community. When the quality of the faculty improved, with most either having or seeking terminal degrees, the school was given one of the highest rankings by the American Association of Theological Schools.

His success at Howard led the trustees of Morehouse College in Atlanta to appoint Mays president of the college in 1950. He served in that position for seventeen years. When he retired from Morehouse College in 1967, Mays recalled that his tenure at the college was enriched by his relationship with students, especially with Martin Luther King Jr., who credited Mays with being his intellectual mentor. King attended the college from 1944 to 1948. King later said that Mays was his spiritual mentor and intellectual father. One of the important pieces of advice that Mays gave King was about ethics and civil rights. Mays believed that racism was evil and had to be fought with ethical means in order for the people of God to retain the moral upper hand. King took this advice to heart. In his later years Mays criticized the radical organizations that preached self-defense, believing that nonviolence was the only way for African Amerians to gain rights and remain morally correct.

Mays was also a scholar of the African American Church, and published works that spoke to his understanding of religion. He coauthored (with Joseph W. Nicholson) a survey of the African American Church in a dozen cities, *The Negro's Church* (1933). In 1938 he published *The Negro's God as Reflected in His Literature*, in an effort to determine how the ordinary African American writer depicted the image of God in novels, essays, and poetry. In addition to his scholarly activities, Mays was also an activist in church politics, working with the National Baptist Convention and various ecumenical groups, including the National Council of Churches and the World Council of Churches. As one of the most profound voices for justice and interracial cooperation in the organizations, Mays sought to facilitate interracial harmony and understanding. His aim was to demonstrate that the Christian religion could accommodate the commitment to equality and justice. He served on the Atlanta Board of Education after his retirement, becoming its president in 1970. In 1982 the National Association for the Advancement of Colored People awarded Mays its highest honor, the Spingarn Medal. When Mays died in Atlanta on March 28, 1984, he had become a legend within his lifetime.

# ELIJAH
# McCOY
## 1843–1929

**E**lijah J. McCoy was born on May 2, 1843, in Colchester, Ontario, Canada, as one of twelve children born to Africans who had escaped enslavement in Kentucky. Living in extreme poverty, McCoy's parents emphasized education to their children as the surest means of betterment. When he was fifteen, McCoy's parents sent him to study mechanical engineering in Edinburgh, Scotland, training that was impossible for blacks to get in the United States. After finishing his schooling in Scotland, McCoy returned to North America in 1866 with the hope of obtaining an engineering job.

Although a trained engineer with impressive credentials, McCoy was unable to find work in his field because of his race. He was forced to accept a job as a locomotive fireman with the Michigan Central Railroad, a position that required no engineering knowledge. The job demanded only that he shovel coal into the engine and apply oil in the moving parts of the machine. McCoy found the work unchallenging and sought other, more productive forms of occupation.

It had long been considered a problem that railroad engines were unable to lubricate themselves. When in need of lubrication, the machines had to be shut off entirely, causing a loss in time and money. As this was a regular necessity, the industry found profit nearly impossible to realize. In his free time, McCoy began to consider solutions to this problem, and after two years, he developed the "lubricating cup" for steam engines that allowed the continuous flow of oil on the gears without having to shut down the machine. Lubrication became an automatic process.

McCoy received a patent for his lubricating device in 1872. The lubricating cup was essential to industries throughout the world, and those in possession of the valuable cup were said to have "the real McCoy." The lubricating cup was his most successful and well-known invention, although McCoy also obtained patents for an automatic sprinkler, an ironing table, and other products, eventually acquiring fifty-eight patents in his lifetime. By the time he died in Eloise, Michigan, on October 10, 1929, he had acquired a reputation among blacks and whites as one of America's most inventive minds.

# CLAUDE
# McKAY

1890–1948

**C**laude McKay was born in Jamaica in 1890 and lived until 1948. He was a poet, novelist, and essayist who heralded several of the most significant literary transitions in African American culture. McKay's protest poetry of the late 1910s and the early 1920s represented the best example of the spirit that was to become the Harlem Renaissance. Readers were treated to intense and powerful treatments of the conditions of African people in the United States and Jamaica. McKay became, by virtue of his genius, one of the key leaders in modern Jamaican and African American literature. His novels were deeply complex and highly textured regarding the situations, political and cultural, that confronted Pan-Africanists trying to forge a new identity in the arts. McKay was the major literary influence in the African American community during his early years. His early poetry in the language of Jamaica and his fiction set in Jamaica were intricately connected to all innovative developments of Jamaican writing in the 20th century.

McKay's parents, Thomas Francis McKay and Hannah Ann McKay, farmed in the area of Sunny Ville, Jamaica, the town in which McKay was born. They succeeded in growing enough crops for their own subsistence as well as produce to sell. Claude McKay's brother, Uriah Theodore, a schoolteacher, and Walter Jekyll, an expatriate Englishman, were very encouraging when they read his early poetry. In fact, they convinced McKay that he had an important future in the literary world. This fueled McKay's literary ambitions. Because he was so eager to learn and also mastered the English language as it was taught to him in Jamaica, McKay received more education than was customary for black farm children in Jamaica at that time. However, there were not many opportunities for a black youth in Jamaica who had literary ambitions. He finally took a job as a police constable in Kingston in 1911.

McKay published two collections of poetry, *Songs of Jamaica* and *Constable Ballads*, in 1912. These poems emerged largely out of McKay's experience as a constable, which he found alienating, along with urban life in general. He felt uncomfortably located between the Jamaican elite and the great mass of the urban poor. Many of the concerns of McKay's later work, such as the opposition of the city and the country, the problems of exile, and the relation of the black intellectual to the common folk, first appear in these poems.

McKay moved to the United States in 1912 to attend Tuskegee Institute in Alabama. After brief stints at Tuskegee and Kansas State University, McKay was dissatisfied with the education he was receiving and left for Harlem. In Harlem he wrote poetry while holding several menial jobs, including working on a railroad dining car. This period of McKay's work is best remembered for his militant protest sonnets, notably "If We Must Die," considered by his contemporaries, such as James Weldon Johnson and Walter White, to be the beginning of the Harlem Renaissance. He also wrote many poems of exile, such as "Flame-Heart" and "The Tropics in New York," in which he nostalgically invokes a tropical landscape and the desire to return to a remembered community. Even many of the protest sonnets can be considered exile poems, because a break between the poem's speaker and his original community is often at the root of the speaker's anger. Much of McKay's early poetry was collected in the book *Harlem Shadows* (1922).

In 1919, at the close of the First World War, McKay moved to Europe, where he joined the new communist movement. His American experience had left him feeling that capitalism was corrupt, antihuman, and racist. He saw communism as an alternative to the evils of racism and colonialism. One of the advantages for the young McKay in London was the opportunity to work on Sylvia Pankhurst's pro-communist newspaper, *Worker's Dreadnought*. After two years in England, McKay returned to the United States, landing at New York in 1921, just as Marcus Garvey's movement was stirring the political and social ambitions of African Americans. McKay had experience as a writer, having worked at *Worker's Dreadnought*, and therefore he was able to secure a position as coeditor with Mike Gold of the progressive journal the *Liberator*. This was not to be a good position for McKay, since Gold did not want him to exercise the normal authority of a coeditor and felt threatened by McKay's aesthetic and editorial opinions. So after a few months at the journal and with personal disagreements on the rise between the two coeditors as well as other members of the journal's board, the strong-willed McKay left the journal in 1922.

Claude McKay's credentials as a communist propagandist were outstanding from the standpoint of the international communist hierarchy, so he was invited as a delegate to the Fourth Congress of the Communist International (Comintern) in 1922. At this international meeting, McKay used his moment on the stage of communism to declare that the "Negro question" was central to the world revolutionary movement. This was a stirring moment because it signaled to the world communist movement that Africans would not be denied a presence on the agenda. Since McKay had confronted the same issue at the *Liberator*, he was still concerned that the communists wanted to leave the race issue off the agenda. Nevertheless, he decided to return to Europe in 1923, and for the next ten years he traveled between Europe and Africa, living in several different places, working small jobs, and publishing several books in the United States.

McKay wrote two novels during the twenties, *Home to Harlem* in 1928 and *Banjo* in 1929; both works were political in nature because McKay wanted to show how race and class existed as contradictions in capitalist societies. But he was extremely interested in the role literature could play in explaining how rural and urban African-descended people could negotiate life in the metropolitan centers of the world. In fact,

McKay was one of the first literary figures in the African world to use his pen to attack the evils of capitalism and colonialism. His passion was real and his agitation against racism and class distinctions was a part of his art.

*Home to Harlem* became the most popular novel up to that time in the history of publishing by a person of African descent. McKay was seen as a major voice of African American culture. The novel centers on two men, an intellectual Haitian expatriate named Ray, and an African American longshoreman, who was also a World War I veteran, named Jake. Ray is a worrier and feels that the African American community does not relate to him and he cannot relate to it because of his European education. He is alienated, isolated, and angry. Jake, on the other hand, is calm, spontaneous, and capable of negotiating the social and political situations he finds himself in without worry. In the novel Ray and Jake become close friends working in a dining car. In the novel *Banjo,* Ray appears again with another character, the African American musician Lincoln Agrippa Daily, who is also quite normal. In effect, Banjo, the musician, has a better grip on reality than Ray, who cannot quite find himself. The novel is set in Marseilles and features black longshoremen, sailors, and itinerant workers from Africa. What McKay argues in his novels is that the black intellectual had to return home to the ordinary life of the people in order to be real and connected to community. His final novel, *Banana Bottom* (1933), takes this theme even further. The main character of *Banana Bottom* is Bita Plant, a European-educated Jamaican woman. Plant returns to her native village in Jamaica and eventually rejects European culture and the Jamaican elite.

By the time McKay returned to the United States in 1934, he was a celebrity. While he had started to move away from communism during the early 1930s, he had already established his credentials as a firm antiracist. However, now he turned his energy toward anticommunism, becoming active in the movement against communism. In his last books, *A Long Way from Home* (1937) and *Harlem: Negro Metropolis* (1940), McKay attacked the Communist Party of the United States of America

(CPUSA). In the autobiographical work *A Long Way from Home*, McKay sought to position his own search for intellectual and political freedom as a growth away from communism. In *Harlem: Negro Metropolis*, he attacked African American intellectuals of Harlem for being intimidated or deceived by the CPUSA in the late 1930s and early 1940s. McKay secured a job as a member of the Works Project Administration's Federal Writers' Project in New York during the late 1930s and attempted to organize an anticommunist writer's group in Harlem. He had come full circle in his political positions and at the end of his life he was more and more alienated from the mainstream of African American intellectual thought. His earlier works had been hard-hitting critiques of the society, but his last years were spent trying to influence others to fight against the "Godless communism." He became a Roman Catholic in 1944 and wrote new poetry that he was unable to publish. However, he had already established himself as one of the major writers of African American history.

# OSCAR
# MICHEAUX
1884–1951

**O**scar Micheaux was born on January 2, 1884, outside of the town of Murphysboro, Illinois. He was one of thirteen children. Always struggling to understand his plight as a young African American, Micheaux believed that it was necessary to leave rural Illinois and journey to the large city of Chicago to make his way in life. He was only seventeen years old when he went to Chicago and got a job as a shoe shiner. Soon thereafter he secured a job as a Pullman porter, considered at the time to be one of the best positions a young, undereducated African American could possess. Micheaux was careful to save his money, and within a few years he had saved enough funds to invest in the South Dakota frontier. His idea was to develop a homestead in the new territory and secure a place for himself. He was among the few African Americans to go to South Dakota in 1904 as a settler. The experience would prove valuable to him artistically.

Ten years later he had written a novel, *The Conquest: The Story of a Negro Pioneer*, that was enlarged and reissued in 1917 as *The Homesteader*. Both books were published by Western Book and Supply Company, a company established in Sioux City, South Dakota, by Micheaux. He proved to be an aggressive businessman, eager to make his mark in the commercial world. This meant that Micheaux did not limit himself to the writing or publishing of books. When the opportunity presented itself for him to enter filmmaking, as it did when a negotiation to turn his book into a film failed: He filmed *The Homesteader*, and it became his first movie in 1919.

Soon the Micheaux Book and Film Company, as his company was renamed, would become the most productive African American filming operation of the era. Micheaux was a one-man production crew, writing, directing, producing, and distributing nearly forty films over the next thirty years. His financial backers included blacks and whites who believed that Micheaux was a genius. Among his most important films from a historical point of view were *Body and Soul* and *The Exile*. In the 1924 film *Body and Soul*, Micheaux featured the great actor and singer Paul Robeson. It is believed that this was Robeson's first appearance in an American film. Seven years later, Micheaux's *The Exile* became the first full-length sound movie by an African American.

Micheaux's reputation as one of the greatest African American promoters of culture was established because he believed so profoundly that the culture of African Americans could create its own commercial audience. His faith was rewarded when he expanded his efforts to create movies that black audiences identified with and appreciated. He did not have much money, but he used his funds wisely in distribution and advertising. He was engaged in the film business from the writing of the scripts to the opening of the shows. The branch offices in New York and Chicago gave him a wider audience than he could have ever developed from Sioux City, South Dakota. As an entrepreneur, Micheaux understood many aspects of marketing. He would ask his actors to stage scenes from upcoming films as ways to raise money from the theater owners. However, most of his films depended upon his own money, ingenuity, and energy.

Few entrepreneurs or cultural promoters have faced as many obstacles as Micheaux. Yet he knew and accepted the challenge that racism as well as ignorance would be his chief opponents in the quest for an African American film tradition. In one sense the racism appeared in the difficulty he had in getting his films in major theaters. On the other hand, he often confronted African Americans who did not understand the process of making a film. Micheaux, even with the people he gathered around himself, was essentially operating alone and without a map of the celluloid territory. Thus, after achieving a measure of success with his films, he did not create an archive of his works. In addition to *Body and Soul* and *The Exile*, one can find copies of only *Within Our Gates* (1919) and *God's Stepchildren* (1937). However, when a group of African Americans opened a community movie theater called the Oscar Micheaux Theater in Buffalo, New York, in the late 1970s the founders could not find a unified body of the film works of Micheaux. The theater founders, nevertheless, celebrated the works of the greatest African American filmmaker of his time. In fact, it might be said that because of his tremendous output of books, Micheaux was the most prolific author-filmmaker ever in African American history.

Micheaux did not escape controversy in the African American community. His portrayal of negative aspects of the African American experience, including some of the stereotypes whites had often used, did not give him universal appeal. There were those in the civil rights community who believed that Micheaux was using the African American culture as a way to advance his own commercial interests. There were those who accused him of portraying a sexist, fun-loving, and happy-go-lucky African American.

Micheaux's career spanned the Harlem Renaissance and lasted until the 1940s. During this period Micheaux wrote several more books, including a new version of his frontier memoir called *The Wind from Nowhere*. He also made a three-hour epic film called *The Betrayal*, which was a commercial failure but an artistic triumph. The film was released in 1948 on the verge of the modern civil rights movement. Micheaux died in Charlotte, North Carolina, on March 25, 1951.

# DORIE
# MILLER
1919–1943

**S**ometimes heroes are made by virtue of the situation in which they find themselves. Dorie Miller, who was born on October 12, 1919, on a small farm near Waco, Texas, would find himself in Pearl Harbor on the day of the Japanese attack. He would distinguish himself and become an authentic African American hero in the process of shooting down five Japanese airplanes.

Dorie Miller's parents, Connery and Henrietta Miller, worked as sharecroppers on an eleven-hectare (twenty-eight-acre) farm near Waco. The young Miller was a farmhand at a very early age, working alongside his parents in the fields. He grew to be nearly six feet tall, muscular, and powerfully built. By the time he was in his late teens, he yearned to leave Waco and experience the wider world. He had made trips into the city from the farm to sell produce and to shop, but he had never been out of Texas. His fortune changed when he spoke to a U.S. Navy recruitment officer in Waco, and soon thereafter he joined the Navy. He was eighteen years old. His intention was to get as far away from Waco and the narrow-mindedness of the people of the area as he could. It looked to him as though the navy was the way to travel. In the early 1940s the only area of the navy opened to African Americans was the food service branch, usually referred to as "mess." The navy, like other branches of the United States Armed Forces, was segregated, and black enlisted men had limited choices. The mess area was the only area for black enlistment until June 1, 1942. The navy defied the law when the Selective Service Act of

1940 provided for the induction and training of recruits without discrimination based on race or color. It relied on white volunteers until February 1943 to avoid using African Americans. Although Dorie Miller was excited about the possibilities of travel inherent in the navy, he was disturbed that the whites gave him no opportunity to rise beyond the rank of messman.

Dorie Miller underwent all the training that was necessary to be a navy sailor during the early part of the Second World War. However, he was not permitted to take part in the combat training, and after the usual orientation period, some sea duty, he was stationed on the *Arizona.* This ship was anchored in Pearl Harbor, and was heavily bombed, on December 7, 1941. Its forward part was simply a wretched mass of blood and pain. The twisted metal, mass of flames, and dead bodies made grown men sick. People ran to escape the fire, jumping into the water, trying to survive the Japanese attack.

Dorie Miller was a messman, which meant in the American navy that he was never instructed to use a gun. But when the Japanese bombs knocked him down and he saw the destruction all around him as he regained his senses, he quickly sought out the ship's captain. Other members of the crew were leaping overboard to try to escape the devastation. When Miller found the captain, he saw that he had been mortally wounded. The messman lifted the half-dead captain and lay him down in a safer spot on the ship. Not thinking of anything other than his duty to the ship, Miller feverishly worked one of the guns until it fired, and the Japanese plane Miller targeted burst into flames and crashed into the sea. With bombs falling all around him, the courageous Miller shot down three more Japanese planes before he abandoned the ship as it was slowly sinking into the sea.

Three months later the navy recognized Dorie Miller for his bravery at Pearl Harbor. He was awarded the Navy Cross and advanced to mess attendant first class. The African American community had heard about Miller's exploits even before he arrived in Texas. When he got to Dallas and Waco, he received a hero's welcome. Ironically, he was invited to speak to a graduating class of noncommissioned officers at the Navy's Great Lakes Training School, even though neither Miller nor any other African American could have received training at the school. Instead of sending him to navy training school, the United States sent him to Bremerton, Washington, where he was to qualify as a cook.

Miller was ordered to join the small carrier *Liscome Bay* in November 1943. It sailed from Astoria, Oregon, to San Francisco, and then headed into the dangerous waters of the Central Pacific, making its way to Makin Island. It was supposed to join an attack force in the Central Pacific and help to defend that region of the world. However, on November 24, 1943, a Japanese submarine attacked the carrier sending it down with most of its crew and officers, including Miller.

Miller's death was like a light having gone suddenly dark. In the African American community, Dorie Miller was larger than life. He was a symbol of a people's courage, ingenuity, and intelligence under pressure. His heroism was spoken about in the highest councils of the American navy, and although Miller's heroics may not have changed the discrimination in the navy, his bravery did a lot to reassert the role of African Americans as human beings. It would, however, be June 1949 before the U.S. Naval Academy would graduate its first black, Ens. Wesley A. Brown. Miller has been commemorated by a Navy recruitment poster and by the Dorie Miller Trophy, awarded on October 3, 1950, by the secretary of the navy. Numerous buildings and other urban projects were named in his honor. Dorie Miller's life inspired thousands of African Americans to demonstrate their individual courage in the faces of adversity. He represents one of the best examples of unselfish service in the nation.

# GARRETT
# MORGAN
1875–1963

**T**he infant who was born on March 4, 1875, in the small town of Paris, Kentucky, would become one of the world's most innovative and successful inventors and one of the most diligent African American community leaders of his day. Garrett Augustus Morgan would go on to invent the gas mask and the automatic traffic signal.

Morgan's family moved to Cincinnati when he was fourteen years old. He became a handyman, doing odd jobs in order to make money. A few years later, in 1895, he moved to Cleveland, where he found work as a repairman for sewing machines. This work encouraged him to explore his gift for mechanics. Cleveland proved to be a good place for his skills. He started several successful enterprises: a sewing machine repair service in 1907, a tailor shop in 1909, and, following the trend of the day, a hair-straightening company in 1913. Morgan was so active as a mechanic, inventor, and organizer that he was considered a Renaissance man. He invented the "breathing device," which was a prototype of what would become the gas mask. In 1914 the National Safety Device Company awarded Garrett Morgan's Safety Hood its first grand prize.

As fate would have it, Morgan was able to demonstrate the device on July 25, 1916, when he wore it as he, along with others, rescued twenty-four trapped workers from a smoke-filled tunnel beneath Lake Erie. Morgan was awarded a gold medal for his heroism by the grateful city of Cleveland. But it was a heroic effort that would have been impossible without the gas mask. He was later given a contract from the U.S. Navy to make masks. His mask was used in World War I and by fire departments throughout the country. Yet because of racism, some people cancelled their orders for his gas masks when they discovered that he was an African American inventor.

One of the most important inventions made by Morgan was the 1922 three-way automatic traffic signal. This instrument allowed the driver to have an amber warning light prior to the red stop light. The rights to Morgan's traffic safety improvement device was bought by the General Electric Company in 1923 for $40,000 and is the direct precursor of the contemporary three-way traffic light.

Morgan was not some head-in-the-clouds inventor; he was also quite involved in the activities of the African American community in Cleveland. This is what underscored his greatness. He was a civil rights worker, organizing to fight racial discrimination in the north. Civil rights and journalism rounded out his life. He published the African American newspaper *Cleveland Call* from 1920 to 1923. He was also a standing member of the Cleveland branch of the National Association for the Advancement of Colored People. He died on July 27, 1963.

# TONI
# MORRISON
1931–

**T**oni Morrison (née Chloe Anthony Wofford) was born in Lorain, Ohio, in 1931. She attended the public schools of Lorain, Ohio, and after graduation enrolled at Howard University where she received a B.A. degree in 1953. She was accepted into graduate school at the Cornell University Department of English, where she wrote a thesis on William Faulkner and Virginia Woolf. Morrison's first academic position was at Texas Southern University in Houston, Texas. After working at TSU for two years, she left Houston to take a teaching position at Howard University in Washington, her alma mater. She was married to a Jamaican-born architect, Harold Morrison, and had two sons. After she and her husband divorced in 1964, Morrison became an editor for Random House's textbook division in Syracuse, New York. Four years later she moved to the trade division of the company and relocated to Manhattan. She became the first black female to hold the position of senior editor at Random House.

Morrison is credited with inspiring a new generation of African American female writers. Writers such as Alice Walker, Toni Cade Bambara, and Gayl Jones came to find their own success at Random House because of Morrison. In 1970 Morrison's first novel, *The Bluest Eye*, was published, and it immediately established her as a serious writer. What distinguished her writing was the florid, lyrical, full-bodied style of her prose that carried emotional and intellectual substance. Her literary style and powerful telling of the African American story has made her the most celebrated African American novelist in history. She was the first African American to receive the Nobel prize in literature.

As a master storyteller, Morrison has been able to weave the many textures of the African American culture she imbibed while a young girl in Ohio, listening to the words of her father and mother. Her mother's ability to sing the spiritual and her father's love of a good story were elements in her childhood that encouraged her to imagine what life could be. It would not be difficult for Morrison to leap from the childhood memories of her parents telling stories and singing songs to her characters telling similar stories and singing similar songs. She is a medium for the expression of the historical and contemporary elements in African American culture.

When she wrote the novel *Sula* (1973), a story situated in an Ohio town, she had no idea that it would be nominated for the 1975 National Book Award in fiction. It was simply a novel about good and evil as demonstrated in the friendship of two women in a small black community. If it could be said that *The Bluest Eye* and *Sula* were her introductions to the world as a novelist, the book *Song of Solomon*, published in 1977, brought her international acclaim. *Song of Solomon* was a Book-of-the-Month Club selection, the first such choice by an African American since Richard Wright's *Native Son* (1940). Morrison also won the National Book Critics Circle Award and was elected to the American Academy of Arts and Letters and the National Council of the Arts.

In 1981 *Tar Baby* was published and received with great literary fanfare. This novel, set in the Caribbean, continued her lyrical tradition. Her fifth novel, *Beloved* (1987), became, next to Ralph Ellison's *Invisible Man*, the most acclaimed African American novel of the twentieth century. *Beloved* is based on the true story of Margaret Garner, an enslaved African who ran away from a Kentucky plantation with her four children and, when captured, sought to kill her children rather than see them returned to enslavement. In *Beloved*, Morrison gives us an account of the obstacles faced by the ordinary African person enslaved against her will. We are introduced to the vagaries of brutality and the evil of human oppression in ways that have rarely been plumbed by other writers. The book was immediately a national best-seller and further placed Morrison in the rarefied atmosphere of literary greatness.

Morrison wrote two other novels in a trilogy on love, *Jazz* in 1992 and *Paradise* in 1998. These novels, alongside *Beloved*, constitute a meditation on the meaning of love and its relationship to other emotions. *Jazz* is situated in the period of the Harlem Renaissance and *Paradise* is set in the early twentieth century in the town of Ruby, Oklahoma, an all-black town. Receiving the Nobel prize for literature in 1993 conferred on her new stature in the Western world. She had been appointed the Robert F. Goheen Professor in the Council of the Humanities at Princeton University in 1989, where her reputation as a cultural critic equaled her respect as a novelist.

Among her most important group of essays was *Playing in the Dark: Whiteness and the Literary Imagination*, published in 1992. In addition, she has written or edited several other books on literary subjects. Morrison also wrote a 1986 play, *Dreaming Emmett*, first produced in New York.

Morrison has become an icon of literary brilliance transcending national boundaries, and in the process has demonstrated the far-reaching significance of the African American experience. What the cultural message becomes in Morrison's narrative power and intelligence clearly propel her literary excellence. Her greatness rests upon her astonishing ability to use language to convey the sentiments of the African American people.

# ELIJAH
# MUHAMMAD
## 1897–1975

**G**eorgia has contributed greatly to the pool of African American leadership. It can be speculated that the severe oppression and strict segregation in Georgia made the African more willing to risk his life and career for freedom and dignity. Elijah Poole was born in Sandersville, Georgia, on October 10, 1897, to Wally and Mary Poole, share-croppers on a white farm. Elijah was the seventh of thirteen children. His older sisters taught him how to read when he was forced to leave school in order to assist his family financially. Poole worked as a bricklayer and laborer in Sandersville and Macon, Georgia, to make money. Soon he was baptized as a Baptist and became a young preacher for rural churches in Georgia.

By 1923 Elijah Poole had experienced enough racism in Georgia that he and his family felt it was wise for him to leave the South. The harassment of African American farmers by white farmers, the burning of black homes and crops, the lynching of black men, and numerous other violations of the human rights of African Americans made it inevitable that the young, vigorous, intelligent, and determined Elijah Poole would run afoul of the white Georgia tradition. Thus, he left Georgia for the north and found a job in a Detroit automobile plant. While in Detroit, he met and studied with Master W. Fard Muhammad and the Temple of Islam, being convinced that Christianity had deceived the African American person. He could no longer accept the teachings of the Christians, since he saw deep contradictions in the language of the Bible and the way white Christians treated black people.

In 1934, when Master Wallace Fard Muhammad disappeared, Elijah, who had changed his name to Elijah Muhammad, became the leader of the organization. There has never been any concrete evidence on what happened to Fard, although there is speculation that he was born in Mecca, Arabia, and was therefore deported. Others have assumed he was assassinated. Master Fard had built the organization on the belief that the original man, the black man, would be the source of redemption for the world. But the disappearance of Master W. Fard Muhammad created such a vacuum in the leadership in Detroit that Elijah had a difficult time controlling the organization. Splitting into factions and infighting characterized the Detroit temple. Soon Elijah Muhammad moved the organization to Chicago and renamed it the Nation of Islam. Chicago was a favorable environment for Muhammad's doctrine of self-determination, self-help, and separation from whites.

For twenty years the Honorable Elijah Muhammad preached the moral and spiritual revival of African American people within the context of Islam. He believed that African Americans had to separate themselves from whites in order to prosper. An economic plan was to be developed to accompany the cultural component. In his *Essay to the Black Man*, Elijah Muhammad stressed the need to eat healthily, not smoke, support black businesses, educate black children, and practice impeccable hygiene.

To demonstrate to his followers that African Americans could achieve anything, Muhammad established a newspaper, set up restaurants, and purchased thousands of acres of agricultural lands. The newspaper the *Final Call to Islam* was replete with moral messages and news of the African world. Its name was subsequently changed to *Muhammad Speaks*. After Elijah Muhammad's death the paper took the name the *Final Call*.

The Nation of Islam under Elijah Muhammad used a rigorous recruitment effort to bring into its fold many rank-and-file, ordinary, and professional people. Thousands of imprisoned African Americans accepted the Nation of Islam's doctrine. Upon the death of Elijah Muhammad, his son, Wallace D. Muhammad,

assumed leadership of the organization. Subsequently, Louis Farrakhan, one of Elijah's most trusted lieutenants, established a
rival group seeking to maintain Elijah Muhammad's focus on
self-determination.

# JESSE
# OWENS
## 1913–1980

**J**ames Cleveland Owens was born in Oakville, Alabama, in 1913, the tenth of eleven children of Henry and Emma Fitzgerald Owens, who earned their livelihood as sharecroppers. As a child Jesse Owens was chronically ill, probably because of poor diet, substandard housing, and inadequate clothing. During several winters he contracted pneumonia, which he was forced to endure since his family lacked money for a doctor or medicine. In the early 1920s, the Owens family left the South as part of the Great Migration, and settled in Cleveland, Ohio, where Owens's father and three brothers found work in the steel mills. For the first time, Owens attended school regularly.

In a racially integrated junior high school, a white physical education teacher named Charles Riley noticed Owens's athletic ability and began coaching him in track and field. After Owens entered a vocational high school, Riley continued to coach him. Owens's success was immediate: school records in the 220-yard and 100-yard sprints and the long jump fell to his smooth stride.

In 1932 he made an unsuccessful attempt for the United States Olympic team, but by 1933 his dominance of the sport was undeniable. At a high school meet in May 1933, he set a world record in the long jump with a leap of twenty-four feet, three and three-quarter inches—an improvement of more than three inches on the old mark. A month later he helped his high school to a national track title with another world record in the long jump and a 9.4-second 100-yard dash, which tied the world record. Cleveland welcomed him home with a celebratory parade.

Owens was the first member of his family to graduate from high school. Although by most accounts his educational preparation was minimal, Jesse Owens was nevertheless heavily recruited by colleges because of his athletic prowess. Despite the fact that he was urged by the black press to choose a less discriminatory school, Owens chose to stay near home, entering the Ohio State University in Columbus. Once he arrived in Columbus, he was barred from living on the whites-only campus. Furthermore, Owens and other black athletes were forced to ride to track meets in cars separate from their white teammates.

By the spring of 1934, Owens was on academic probation, which prompted his coach to set up public speaking engagements for him—perhaps to bolster his confidence, perhaps in the belief that an African American could not be helped academically. Whatever the motivation, the chance to develop and display his charisma and charm was fortuitous; it was a strength he would rely on the rest of his professional life. In May 1935 Owens broke five world records at a single meet, earning him the title among sportswriters as "the world's fastest human."

His most dramatic moments would come the next year at the Olympic Games. The 1936 Olympic Games in Berlin were embroiled in controversy long before the athletes arrived. The Amateur Athletic Union (AAU) threatened a U.S. boycott to protest the treatment of German Jews under Adolf Hitler, and black journalists were inflamed by Nazi claims of Aryan racial superiority. The U.S. Olympic Committee, however, overruled the AAU and sent athletes to the games anyway. To many American blacks, Owens symbolized a rebuttal to Nazi racism, and he became a symbol that gained all the more importance after German boxer Max Schmeling delivered a surprising defeat to black American Joe Louis in early 1936. The 1936 Olympics were designed to showcase the glory of the Third Reich. Adolf Hitler crowed publicly about the purity of the German race and the prowess of the fatherland's athletes. The fascist press wrote disparagingly of the black athletes on the United States team. Once the competition began at the Reich Sportsfeld, however, the superiority of the

American athletes became evident. Among the greatest was
runner Jesse Owens, who broke nine records and tied two others,
making him the most important runner in Olympic history.

Owens had outstanding Olympic performances. He won gold
medals for the 100-meter and 200-meter sprints, the 400-meter
relay, and the long jump, in which he set a record that lasted
twenty-five years.

The Berlin Olympics not only placed Owens in a special category
in the United States, it made him a person of international renown.
In the 100-meter dash Owens captured his first gold medal, winning
each of his four heats with ease and tying the Olympic record with a
time of 10.3 seconds in the final. Next, Owens competed in the long
jump against German champion Luz Long. In the preliminary round,
Owens fouled on his first two attempts, with only one jump left to
make the final. Long advised Owens to jump from well behind the
takeoff board on his final attempt, and the German marked the spot
with his own towel. Owens qualified on his last jump and claimed
the victory in the final round, jumping twenty-six feet, five inches
(eight meters, six centimeters)—a new Olympic record.

Owens then won the 200 meters by a full three meters (ten
feet), setting an Olympic record of 20.7 seconds and capturing
his third gold medal. After a moment of stunned silence, the one
hundred thousand-strong audience rhythmically chanted his
name. Owens warmly acknowledged the cheers of the German
crowd. Hitler, however, hastened from the stadium. The führer
angrily refused to congratulate the African American who had
shattered the false notion of Germanic superiority. When Hitler
refused to invite Owens and other black victors to shake his
hand (an invitation that had been extended to several German
athletes), the press seized on the snub and the International
Olympic Committee rebuked the German leader. Owens led the
U.S. team in the 400-meter relay. The team won the gold medal
and set a new world record of 39.8 seconds. The relay victory
was marred by controversy, however. Owens was one of two late
additions to the U.S. squad, replacing two Jewish sprinters,
Marty Glickman and Sam Stoller, who were likely forced off of

the team because of prejudice. But Owens should have been a member of the team from the beginning.

Owens was welcomed home to a series of triumphal parades, but before long he was again confronted with American racism—forced to enter through back doors and ride at the back of buses. In addition to these indignities, this "American" hero found that no jobs were available to him. Commenting on racism in Germany and the United States, Owens later told an interviewer, "I wasn't invited up to shake hands with Hitler, but I wasn't invited to the White House to shake hands with the president, either." He was initially given several offers for public appearances, but most opportunities dissolved or turned out to be bogus. Failing to graduate from Ohio State, Owens was reduced to relying on low-income jobs and the few personal appearances he could muster for money—including carnival and circus races against horses.

Jesse Owens was not a quitter. He sought all means to make a living for himself, despite the bitter disappointments he had faced upon his return to the United States. He started a laundry business, but it soon failed. He decided to return to Ohio State to complete his degree. But after two years his grades were not much higher than they had been prior to his leaving the first time. He withdrew from college the second time. However, by the 1940s Owens was able to rely on public speaking for his income; he eventually opened his own public relations firm. In his later years Owens abstained from the civil rights movement. His conservative response to the black-power salute of Tommie Smith and John Carlos at the 1968 Olympic Games in Mexico City won him derision as an "Uncle Tom" by young black activists, but others continued to admire him for his entrepreneurial achievements.

In the end, Owens's impressive achievements—winning gold medals in the 100-meter and 200-meter dashes, the long jump, and the 400-meter relay, all in the same Olympics—went unequaled for forty-eight years, until American Carl Lewis duplicated the achievement at the 1984 Olympics in Los Angeles, California. Owens's world record in the long jump stood for a quarter century. Owens died in 1980.

# ROSA
# PARKS
1913–

On December 1, 1955, in Montgomery, Alabama, Rosa Parks was arrested for disregarding an order to surrender her bus seat to a white passenger. Her protest galvanized a growing movement to desegregate public transportation and marked a historic turning point in the African American battle for civil rights. Parks was much more than a woman who was tired. She had a history of working for civil rights in the Birmingham area. Prior to her arrest she had participated in organizations devoted to the creation of equality.

Rosa Louise McCauley was born in Tuskegee, Alabama, in 1913. She was the granddaughter of former enslaved Africans and the daughter of James McCauley, a carpenter, and Leona McCauley, a rural schoolteacher. She attended the public schools of Montgomery, Alabama, and then went to Alabama State College. In 1932 she married Raymond Parks, a barber, and they both became active in Montgomery's chapter of the National Association for the Advancement of Colored People (NAACP).

The Parks family was very involved in the agitation for justice and equality for African Americans. Raymond Parks gave money and time toward the freeing of the defendants in the famous *Scottsboro* case, in which nine young black men were accused of raping two white women. In the early 1940s, Rosa Parks worked as the NAACP chapter's youth adviser, as well as, intermittently, its secretary. She joined the civil rights group in 1943 and helped to mobilize the blacks in the state of Alabama to register to vote. Working with the state president, Edgar Daniel Nixon, and other

members of the NAACP, Parks helped raise the level of consciousness among African Americans in Montgomery.

Rosa Parks worked as a seamstress for the Montgomery Fair
department store, as well as for Virginia and Clifford Durr, a progressive white couple who lived in Montgomery. It has often
been theorized that Parks's participation in a workshop on integration at the famous Highlander Folk School in Monteagle, Tennessee, might have motivated her to be more aggressive against
racism. There is no proof that this was so. Parks had a history of
activism and it is more likely that the years of petitions and
appeals to authorities had worn on her.

Segregation was a problem in all areas of public life, especially on the public buses used primarily by African Americans.
Since the buses were nearly always full with black riders, there
usually was not enough space in the segregated seating area for
black riders, thus many had to stand. Deep resentment accompa-
nied every bus trip from the black community to downtown. Furthermore, there was the indignity of having African Americans
pay their fares at the front of the bus and then to reboard through
the back door to enter the black seating area. Reports of white
driver harassment were rampant in the black community, with
stories of white drivers driving off after the passengers had paid
their fares in the front, without allowing them time to get back
in the bus through the back door and take their seats. The white
bus drivers were also like police. They could intimidate, abuse,
and arrest black passengers. Drivers had the habit of pushing
back the boundary line between the white and "colored" sections
in order to give the whites even more space during rush hour.

On December 1, 1955, Rosa Parks paid her fare in the front of
the bus, entered through the back of the bus and came to the front
of the colored section of the bus where seats were still available.
The white bus driver looked at Parks and three other black passengers and asked them to move farther to the back of the bus,
since there were whites who needed seats. Parks refused to give
up her seat; the others complied with the driver's command. The
Montgomery police were called to the bus by the driver. They

responded and arrested Parks. She was released later that night after Nixon, the NAACP president, obtained a $100 bond.

This was not the first time that Rosa Parks had encountered trouble with the bus company. She had been ordered off of a bus nearly twelve years earlier. Furthermore, three other black women had been arrested earlier that year for similar acts of defiance of segregated seating.

This was just the test case that the Montgomery chapter of the NAACP had been looking for to challenge the legality of segregated bus seating. It would prove to be historic. The morning after her arrest, Parks agreed to let the NAACP take on her case. The Women's Political Council (WPC), led by the courageous JoAnn Robinson, initiated the idea of a one-day bus boycott. Two days after Parks's arrest, the WPC had distributed more than fifty thousand fliers announcing a bus boycott, which was to take place the day of Parks's trial. Parks was convicted by the local court on December 5. The buses were almost empty that day. Refusing to pay the fourteen dollar fine, Parks had her lawyer, Fred D. Gray, appeal to the circuit court.

In the meantime, several thousand protesters crowded into the Holt Street Baptist Church to organize the Montgomery Improvement Association (MIA). They elected a young president, Martin Luther King Jr., as the spokesperson for the organization. He had just taken the job as pastor of the Dexter Avenue Baptist Church. The bus boycott was planned for one day but eventually ended up running 381 days, during which time forty-two thousand protesters walked, carpooled, or took taxis rather than ride the segregated city buses of Montgomery. The lawyers of the movement filed a case in the United States district court. The district court ruled for the plaintiffs, declaring segregated seating on buses unconstitutional. The decision was later upheld by the Supreme Court of the United States.

After the bus boycott, Rosa Parks was called the Mother of the Civil Rights Movement, but even though she was respected as a symbol of defiance, she was unable to find economic stability in Montgomery. Eventually she and her husband moved to Detroit in

1957. She struggled financially for eight years in Detroit until Congressman John F. Conyers Jr. hired her as an administrative assistant. She held that post until 1987. Her spirit unbroken by disappointments and setbacks, Rosa Parks remained a committed activist into the 1980s. She was active in the antiapartheid movement and founded the Rosa and Raymond Parks Institute for Self-Development, a career counseling center for black youth, in 1987.

A much honored and respected African American, Parks has received numerous awards and tributes, including the NAACP's highest honor, the Spingarn Medal, in 1970 and the prestigious Martin Luther King Jr. Award in 1980. Cleveland Avenue in the city of Montgomery was renamed Rosa Parks Boulevard in 1965. In 1996 President Bill Clinton awarded her the Presidential Medal of Freedom, the highest honor that the U.S. government can give to a civilian.

# ADAM CLAYTON
# POWELL
## 1908–1972

**A**dam Clayton Powell Jr. was born in New Haven, Connecticut, in 1908, and grew up in Harlem, New York, where his father was the minister of Abyssinian Baptist Church, one of the largest congregations in the nation. Powell attended the public schools of New York City and enrolled in City College. After a poor academic performance at City College of New York, Powell attended Colgate University in Hamilton, New York.

After graduation from Colgate, Powell assisted in his father's church and briefly attended Union Theological Seminary. He received a master's degree in religion from Columbia University and continued to work with Abyssinian Baptist until his father retired in 1937. Adam Jr. took over as pastor of Abyssinian. He made the church the center of political and social life in Harlem, associating with the rich and famous of the African American community.

Powell's national stature was raised when the *New York Post* quoted him on the Harlem Riot of 1935. His blunt attack on racism, discrimination, and police brutality brought him immediate national attention. Subsequently, Powell had a regular "Soap Box" column in the New York *Amsterdam News* and later the *People's Voice*, a paper Powell cofounded and published from 1942 to 1946.

Perhaps more than any preacher of his day, he employed his ministry to motivate the people toward political action. He led famous marches and demonstrations in the 1940s to protest employment discrimination against African Americans at Harlem

Hospital. Using his church as a base, he took his fight against racism to the city hall. The famous "Don't Buy Where You Can't Work" campaign against New York's stores proved to be a great weapon in breaking down discriminatory hiring barriers. Powell continued to preach the political kingdom from his pulpit in Harlem and forced the utility companies to hire black employees.

Eventually, Powell thought that the only way to guarantee the African American would have a political voice would be to run for election. In 1941 Powell won a city council seat as an independent. This gave him a dual pulpit from which to continue his challenge to discrimination. He aggravated New York City mayor, Fiorella LaGuardia, by pointing out the racism that existed in New York's public schools.

When a new congressional district was established in Harlem in 1943, Powell, having established himself as the voice of Harlem, was the perfect candidate for the position. He sought the support of the Democrats, on whose ticket he ran, the Republicans, and the Communists. He won the election and went to Washington to join William L. Dawson, a Democrat from Illinois, the only other African American sitting in Congress at the time. Neither Dawson nor his twentieth-century predecessors, Arthur W. Mitchell (D) and Oscar De Priest (R), from Chicago, had the impact that the Harlem congressman had on the nation.

The United States Congress proved to be a great arena for Powell to address the issue of racial justice. He denounced the First Lady Bess Truman for her affiliation with the Daughters of the American Revolution because it was a racist organization. His reputation among his white colleagues was not good, but he did not care so long as his power base in Harlem believed that he was speaking their opinions and their beliefs. Powell pressed the campaign against discrimination, calling it out in businesses, schools, journalism, and Congress itself. Many of the congresspersons still used the word "nigger" on the floor of the House of Representatives, and it was because of Powell that the word was finally banned in Congress. He offered the Powell Amendment, which would have denied funding to institutions that practiced racial discrimination, but it was never approved. Powell supported Republican Dwight D. Eisenhower in 1956, whom he saw as a little more progressive on civil rights than his Democrat opponent. Four years later, in 1960, Powell campaigned for Democrat John F. Kennedy. Kennedy's narrow victory coincided with Powell's rise to the position of chairman of the House Committee on Education and Labor—the first time an African American chaired such a powerful committee. Powell's committee was instrumental in passing much of the progressive legislation enacted in the 1960s, including increases to the minimum wage, protection of civil rights, and the creation of Medicare, Medicaid, and Head Start. The Powell Amendment, which had been one of Adam Clayton Powell's most eagerly sought pieces of legislation, was finally included in the landmark Civil Rights Act of 1964.

Powell faced enormous personal and political difficulties as he was experiencing his greatest popularity. His enemies attacked his lifestyle, and he was investigated by his colleagues and accused of scandalous actions and behaviors by various elements in the society. His own actions did not necessarily endear him to those out to destroy him. He was flamboyant, outspoken, and self-confident. But the most serious allegation emerged when several of Powell's aides were convicted of income tax evasion and rumors circulated that they had also given him kickbacks from their salaries. Powell was indicted for tax evasion in 1958, but his trial resulted in a hung jury and the Department of Justice declined to retry him. However, two years later Powell was again embroiled when he accused a constituent of being a "bag woman," someone who transported payoffs to police from illegal gambling rackets. The woman sued for libel and won a large judgment against Powell, who refused to honor the court's decision and its warrants. The case dragged on for years before Powell agreed to settle.

His problems multiplied when in 1966 a House of Representatives committee found he had improperly placed his wife on his committee's payroll and vacationed at committee expense in

Europe and the Bahamas. Powell maintained he was doing neither more nor less than his colleagues and was being held to a racist double standard. In a vote following the November 1966 elections, the House declined to seat Powell. He challenged the vote, and in 1969 the U.S. Supreme Court held that although Congress could expel a member, it could not deny a seat to someone duly elected by the people. Powell was finally seated after an absence of two years, but without his seniority and with his pay docked to pay for alleged financial abuses. When he died in 1972, he was still respected by the African American community as one of the greatest political leaders of his generation, although he had created numerous powerful enemies during the more than forty years of his intense attacks on white racial domination.

# COLIN
# POWELL
## 1937–

**W**hen then-President-Elect George W. Bush announced on December 16, 2000, that he was recommending that Gen. Colin Powell (Ret.) become the sixty-fifth secretary of state for the United States, he ensured that Powell would be added to the list of greatest African Americans. Powell's career had become quite public since the days when he was national security advisor to President Ronald Reagan. He had moved rather quickly from that post to become the head of the Joint Chiefs of Staff under President George Bush. Colin Powell had shown his ability to master the arts of war and diplomacy during a career of service under four presidents: Richard Nixon, Ronald Reagan, George Bush, and Bill Clinton, prior to serving under George W. Bush. He had been chair of the U.S. Joint Chiefs of Staff from 1989 to 1993. It was during this time that his leadership role in the Persian Gulf War gained him immense popularity, prompting speculation that he might run for president.

A first-generation American, Colin Luther Powell was born to Jamaican immigrant parents in Harlem, New York, in 1937. The family relocated to the Bronx early in Powell's childhood. After graduating from Morris High School in 1954, Powell attended City College of New York, where, in 1958, he received a bachelor's degree in geology. At City College he joined the Reserve Officers' Training Corps (ROTC). His academic career was unremarkable, but his tenure with the ROTC proved fruitful. He gained the highest rank achievable, cadet colonel, and upon his graduation in 1958 he was appointed second lieutenant in the United States Army. Powell received his military training at Fort Benning, Georgia.

His first posting was to West Germany, where he remained for two years, followed by a two-year period in Massachusetts. He met and married Alma Vivian Johnson, a young speech pathologist, in 1962. Alma Vivian was the daughter of a high school principal in Birmingham, Alabama. The couple had three children: Michael, Linda, and Anne Marie. Powell, now a captain, was stationed in Vietnam just months after his marriage. He received the Purple Heart after being injured by a punji-stick booby-trap set by the Vietcong. In 1963 Powell returned to the United States and moved back to Fort Benning, where he studied and worked as an instructor at the infantry school.

Dedicating himself to the military, Powell sought to move up the ladder of the military as fast as he could. He worked at being a good soldier. Subsequently, he was promoted to the rank of major in 1966. This was only the beginning of a stellar career highlighted by an impressive performance at the United States Army Command and General Staff College, where he distinguished himself by graduating second in his class. He returned to Vietnam in 1968 to work under Gen. Charles Gettys. He was wounded in a helicopter accident, but despite his injuries, he saved other servicemen from the burning site of the crash, an action that earned him his second Purple Heart and a Soldiers Medal.

On his return from Vietnam in 1969, Powell was promoted to lieutenant colonel. Two years later, in 1971, he earned an M.B.A. degree from George Washington University. One year later, he received his first political appointment as a White House fellow assigned to work in the Office of Management and Budget (OMB) under the administration of President Richard Nixon. His tenure at the OMB afforded him the opportunity to work with OMB director Caspar Weinberger and deputy director Frank Carlucci. Both men held Powell in high esteem and in later years figured prominently in his political advancement.

Powell's reputation as a troubleshooter and fix-all meant that the army could assign him to any post and he would improve it.

He was sent to a troubled infantry battalion in South Korea, where drug abuse and racial tensions threatened to paralyze the unit. The following year he was stationed in the United States, working in the Pentagon. In rapid succession he enrolled in a nine-month program at the National War College, was made a full colonel, and was assigned in 1976 to lead the 2nd Brigade of the 101st Airborne Division at Fort Campbell, Kentucky. Powell returned to the Pentagon in 1977, although not for long: By 1979 he had been promoted to brigadier general and went on to work briefly as an aide to Charles Duncan, secretary of the Department of Energy. All his experience in government was preparing him for the next assignment.

In fact, Powell's professional ascent was astounding in the sense that he seemed to just walk into a new position and know precisely what to do. His ambition was not evident—a charismatic, understated, but reassuring presence. Nonetheless, he was always on the move upward. In 1981 he took on a military assignment commanding the 4th Infantry Division at Fort Carson, Colorado. Secretary of Defense Caspar Weinberger, Powell's former superior at the OMB, then appointed him senior military assistant. His job was to act as a bridge between the Pentagon and the White House—a role in which he excelled. By mid-1986 Powell had been promoted to lieutenant general, commanding the 5th Corps in Frankfurt, Germany. The Iran-contra debacle and ensuing restructuring in Washington resulted in Frank Carlucci's appointment as national security adviser. Carlucci requested that Powell be recalled to Washington as his deputy, and, although initially hesitant, Powell agreed. Carlucci was appointed secretary of defense in 1987, and Powell received a corresponding promotion to national security adviser. In this position, Powell advocated a strong military budget but opposed the heavy spending on the space-based Strategic Defense Initiative (nicknamed "Star Wars"). He served as national security adviser until President Ronald Reagan's term ended in January 1989. In April Powell became a four-star general.

In the late 1980s Powell continued to distinguish himself in diplomatic and military coups, orchestrating groundbreaking meetings between Reagan and then-leader of the USSR Mikhail Gorbachev. In recognition of his sterling efforts, President George Bush appointed Powell chairman of the Joint Chiefs of Staff in 1989. His installation was a double triumph: He was both the youngest person and the first African American appointed to the highest rank in the military. Powell was responsible for devising the assault on Panama and Gen. Manuel Noriega, and was one of the planners for twenty-five thousand U.S. troops sent to Panama in December 1989.

When the Persian Gulf War broke out in August 1990, Powell coordinated a successful ground strategy with Gen. Norman Schwarzkopf, gaining popular approval from the American public for his effective military strategy. His capable and comforting demeanor was an added bonus at a time when television was often the public's principal source of information on the state of the war. Bush reappointed Powell chairman of the Joint Chiefs of Staff in 1991. During this time, Powell faced regional crises in Somalia and the former Yugoslavia, but had little success in guiding the administration to a clear policy in either area.

When the Democratic candidate Bill Clinton was elected president in 1992, he clashed with Powell on several issues. Clinton began exploring measures to end the ban on homosexuals in the military. Powell opposed the president's plans; it was largely through his efforts that the "don't ask, don't tell" policy was established, whereby homosexuals were allowed in the armed forces as long as they did not reveal their sexual orientation. On the issue of the military budget, Clinton and Powell also disagreed over Clinton's proposal to drastically cut the military budget.

In September of 1993 Powell retired from the military. This move fueled intense national speculation that he intended to run for president against Clinton in 1996. Powell did not refute the rumors that he could have won the presidency had he run instead of concentrating on promoting his bestselling autobiography, *My American Journey* (1995). When George W. Bush was elected president in 2000, he immediately reached out to Colin

Powell, one of the most respected government servants in history, for assistance, naming Powell secretary of state.

# A. PHILIP
# RANDOLPH
1889–1979

**A**sa Philip Randolph, founder and president of the Brotherhood of Sleeping Car Porters (BSCP), editor of the *Messenger*, and architect of the March on Washington Movement that led to the establishment of the Fair Employment Practices Committee (FEPC) and the 1963 March on Washington, was born in Crescent City, Florida, on April 15, 1889.

Although many civil rights leaders of the twentieth century focused on voting, education, and other governmental functions, A. Philip Randolph spent his long career as a labor leader working to bring more and better jobs to African Americans. After a long, successful battle to win representation for the nation's Pullman car train porters, Randolph was instrumental in the formation of the FEPC, which protected African Americans against job discrimination in the defense industries. In addition, Randolph cofounded and edited the *Messenger*, a socialist black magazine.

Asa Philip Randolph grew up in Jacksonville, Florida. He left Jacksonville to study at the Cookman Institute, where he completed his college work in 1907. It was impossible for Randolph, a literate and educated African American, to find a job in Florida equal to his talents. Thus, after a series of menial positions, this class valedictorian left the South and moved to New York City in 1911. Randolph entered Harlem prior to the Harlem Renaissance and found a job as an elevator operator. He took classes at the City College of New York and New York University, performed in amateur theatricals, and finally landed a job with a Harlem employment agency.

255

Harlem provided Randolph with lots of intellectual stimula-tion, and when he met Chandler Owen in 1914, he had found a partner with similar socialist ideals. Three years later they cre-ated the *Messenger*, a magazine whose editorials opposed the entry of the United States into World War I, and they argued for an end to racial injustice. Randolph and Owen stated that "no intelligent Negro is willing to lay down his life for the United States as it now exists."

The *Messenger* was influential because it took a more radical position than either the *Crisis*, published by the NAACP, or *Opportunity*, published by the Urban League. The *Messenger* advocated prolabor union positions and was read by many black workers, especially the all-black Pullman porters. These porters served white rail passengers in expensive sleeping cars. The Pullman Company was founded in 1865, soon after the Civil War ended, and by 1920 had become the largest single employer of African Americans. Although many of the Pullman porters were college graduates, they were discriminated against and treated unfairly at work.

It would not be long before Asa Philip Randolph would find his opportunity for a historic challenge to the Pullman Company. Thus, in 1925, Randolph began organizing ten thousand porters into the BSCP. It took him ten years to create the union in the midst of intimidation, firings, harassment, and persecution of workers. He negotiated an amendment to the Railway Labor Act and in 1935 declared victory when the company recognized the union.

Randolph achieved international stature as a labor leader because of his work in organizing the union. He fought racial injustice as the president of the National Negro Congress (NNC) during the 1930s. However, he resigned because the organization was increasingly controlled by Communists, and Randolph be-lieved that the aim of the NNC should be broader than the Com-munist agenda. He joined the efforts of the National Association for the Advancement of Colored People (NAACP) and the Urban League, becoming an ally of Walter White of the NAACP and T. Arnold Hill of the National Urban League to urge President

Franklin Roosevelt to desegregate the military. After an unsatisfactory resolution to a meeting with Roosevelt, Randolph began planning a march on Washington, D.C., by the BSCP and other groups to demand "the right to work and fight for our country." The date for the demonstration was set for July 1, 1941, at the Lincoln Memorial. President Franklin wanted to avoid a mass demonstration and asked Randolph to call off the protest, which he refused to do unless the president banned discrimination in the defense industries. Finally, after another meeting with Randolph and White, the president at last issued Executive Order 8002, which not only outlawed such discrimination but also established the Fair Employment Practices Committee to investigate breaches of the order.

Randolph continued to push for his other goal: desegregation of the U.S. armed forces. President Harry S. Truman developed a peacetime draft when he assumed office, but Randolph told him "this time Negroes will not take a Jim Crow draft lying down." In July 1948 Truman signed Executive Order 9981, finally ending the segregation of African American soldiers. During the 1950s, Randolph met with President Dwight D. Eisenhower to push for faster school integration in the wake of the *Brown* v. *Board of Education* Supreme Court decision. He planned the 1958 Youth March for Integrated Schools. Randolph's union joined the American Federation of Labor and Congress of Industrial Organizations (AFL-CIO) and he served as vice president of this newly consolidated AFL-CIO from 1955 to 1968.

The March on Washington Movement, a Randolph idea, bore new fruit in 1963 when labor and civil rights organizations came together to mobilize the largest civil rights demonstration in history. At the March on Washington, Randolph, at seventy-four years old, was the elder statesman. He called upon the crowd of 250,000 to take part in a "revolution for jobs and freedom." The next year, President Lyndon B. Johnson signed the Civil Rights Act of 1964 and awarded Randolph the Presidential Medal of Freedom. In his final years, Randolph established the A. Philip Randolph Institute, a job skills and training bureau in Harlem.

Randolph died on May 16, 1979, in New York City. Perhaps few African Americans or Americans of any other cultural background did as much to relieve the condition of the poor and dispossessed as Asa Philip Randolph.

# HIRAM
# REVELS

1822–1901

**H**iram Rhoades Revels, the son of former slaves, was born free in Fayetteville, North Carolina, on September 1, 1822. The restrictions on Africans, slave or free, were severe in states such as North Carolina and it was against the law for a white person to teach Africans how to read or write. As soon as he was able to leave the state, Revels traveled to Ohio, a state known at the time for its more liberal attitudes. He studied at several seminaries in Ohio and Indiana before becoming a minister in the African Methodist Episcopal (AME) Church. When the Civil War broke out, he was preaching for a small church in Maryland. He hurriedly went through the state encouraging blacks to join the efforts of the Union. During the Civil War, Revels not only recruited but helped organize African American regiments in Maryland and Mississippi. He taught school in St. Louis during 1863 and 1864 while he waited for the war to end. After the Civil War, he moved to Mississippi and became active in Republican politics, believing that it was the best road to complete freedom for African Americans.

Revels had learned how to organize the black masses by following the Union Army and encouraging blacks to establish institutions in the wake of the war. He was extremely successful as a persuader, getting African Americans to set up churches and schools. When he settled in Natchez, Mississippi, he found an opportunity to use his oratory and energy for politics. He rose from alderman to state senator before he was selected by the Republican Party to complete the unexpired term of the Confed-

259

erate president, Jefferson Davis, in the U.S. Senate. With this incredible irony, Revels became the first African American to become a United States Senator. After leaving the Senate, Revels served as the president of Alcorn University in Lorman, Mississippi. In 1876 he became the editor of the *Southwestern Christian Advocate*, a religious paper. He died on January 16, 1901, in Aberdeen, Mississippi.

# PAUL
# ROBESON
## 1898–1976

**P**aul Bustill Robeson was born in Princeton, New Jersey, on April 9, 1898. Although Princeton was a northern town it was strictly segregated, and Robeson's father had left North Carolina for New Jersey more than thirty years before Robeson was born. Nevertheless, the social patterns of the South found their way to the Robeson's home in the north. But the elder Robeson attended Lincoln University and became pastor of the Witherspoon Street Presbyterian Church in Princeton. Maria Louisa Robeson, Paul's mother, gave birth to five children, of whom Paul was the youngest. When Paul Robeson was six years old, his mother died in a house fire.

Five years later the elder Robeson moved the family to Somerville, New Jersey, where he became pastor of the Saint Thomas AME Zion Church. Young Paul entered the predominantly white schools of Somerville. He immediately distinguished himself as an excellent student and promising athlete. He entered Rutgers University, the New Jersey State University, in 1915, and continued his athletic and academic excellence. He was a member of the scholastic fraternity Phi Beta Kappa, and earned letters in baseball, basketball, football, and track. When he completed his senior thesis, "The Fourteenth Amendment, The Sleeping Giant of the American Constitution," it was already clear that he had a political-activist bent. He graduated in 1919 from Rutgers and the next year entered Columbia University Law School. Now that he was living in New York, his expenses were much greater than they had been in New

Brunswick, so he played professional football to earn money for law school. Robeson completed his law degree in 1923 and landed a job in a white law firm in 1924, but quit within six months because the white secretary refused to take dictation from him because of his race.

Paul Robeson was a man of many talents, and he had not placed all of his apples in the law barrel. In fact, in 1922 he had performed in the play *Taboo* and proved that he was an outstanding actor as well as a wonderful singer. Now in 1925, fresh out of a law job, he played in Eugene O'Neill's *All God's Chillun* and the play *The Emperor Jones*.

The year 1925 was Paul Robeson's year in many ways. He performed in a concert in which, for the first time, the entire program consisted of all African or African American music. This was considered a landmark. He sang spirituals, folk songs, ballads, and songs in various African languages, thus becoming the first artist to use culture in the war against racism. He soon tired of the racism in the United States and left the country for Europe in 1927. For the next twelve years he spent most of his time in Europe singing and acting, but always connecting the African American struggle with that of the working classes and poor people of Europe.

He mastered every language in which he came in contact so that he was familiar with twenty-five different European and African languages. Robeson learned the languages in order to communicate with the common people. As a musician he felt that the best way to learn the languages of the world was through the music of the ordinary people. Thus, he taught himself the many work songs of the poor people of Europe, Asia, and Africa.

Robeson was an Afrocentrist before the word was invented. He saw himself as an African in thought, practice, and behavior. It was his will to elevate the culture of African Americans to the highest levels of aesthetic appreciation. He attempted to do this single-handedly and by virtue of his great ability to teach through art. It was an impossible task, but no African American artist had ever declared with such clarity of thought and purpose that he was an African as did Robeson.

No African American artist had ever been punished, criticized, and abused by the government as Robeson was. In 1937 Robeson cofounded the Council of African Affairs with the purpose of fighting for the African masses. He worked alongside W. E. B. Du Bois and others committed to the equality of all people. His activities caused the United States government and the black establishment to criticize him for what they termed "anti-American activities." Robeson saw the Soviet Union as a champion of the working classes and this put him squarely at odds with the American government. He was a socialist, devoted to struggle, during most of the 1950s and 1960s. He was denied a passport by the United States government because he refused to say whether or not he was a member of the Communist Party.

Paul Robeson died in Philadelphia on January 23, 1976. He had lived a life too large for an ordinary embrace by the historians of his age, but he would be recorded by others as a truly magnificent figure.

# JACKIE
# ROBINSON
1919–1972

**J**ackie Robinson's greatness lay not so much in his baseball skill, though that was considerable and necessary, but in his remarkable grace under duress; that is, his ability to project the dignity of his oppressed people through the worst misfortunes and suffering.

Jack Roosevelt Robinson was born in 1919 in Cairo, Georgia, to sharecroppers Jerry and Mallie Robinson. Robinson's mother moved the family to California when he was very young. He was raised in Pasadena, California, primarily by his mother, who worked as a domestic servant. Taught by his mother to confront racism through talent, Robinson turned to athletics as a way to compete with the white children who would shout racist epithets at him and his siblings. He excelled at all sports and was eager to demonstrate his talents rather than get into physical fights and confrontations.

When he entered Pasadena's John Muir High School, Robinson starred on several of the school's athletic teams. By 1938 he was enrolled at Pasadena Junior College, where he also established himself as a great athlete. In 1940 Robinson transferred to the University of California, Los Angeles (UCLA), where he was the first person in the school's history to earn varsity letters in four sports. He became an All-America running back in football; he also competed in track and field, breaking his older brother's national record in the broad jump, and led the Pacific Coast Conference in scoring while on the basketball team. Although he was a competent baseball player, this was not Robinson's favorite sport.

When Robinson left UCLA prior to graduation in 1941, his family was not pleased because they wanted him to earn a college degree. Nevertheless, he took a job as the assistant athletic director of the National Youth Administration Camp in Atascadero, California, hoping to assist his family economically. He also played semiprofessional football for the Honolulu Bears. Soon, however, he was drafted into the United States Army. From the time he entered the army in 1942, Robinson began to sharpen his attack on racial injustice. He saw the way intelligent and college-educated African Americans were passed over for officer training. It was after the boxer Joe Louis spoke to United States officials in Washington, D.C., that Robinson was allowed to become an army officer at Fort Riley, Kansas. He was a campaigner for equal treatment in the army and could not stand the fact that blacks were asked to defend a country in which they were excluded from justice. He was transferred to Fort Hood, Texas, after he joined in a protest of the mistreatment of other African American soldiers. His army career was filled with trouble over racism. He was actually court-martialed for refusing to sit in the back of an Army bus. The army soon reinstated him, but he was honorably discharged in 1944.

While in the army, Robinson had continued to play some sports as a pastime. Soon after he was discharged, he joined a professional baseball team, the Kansas City Monarchs of the Negro American League, in 1945. They agreed to a salary of four hundred dollars a month during the season. Robinson was not accustomed to the travel schedule, the lack of accommodations, and the stress of fighting racial discrimination involved in playing for the Negro League. But he was not unaware of racism, since he had confronted it in the army as well as in California. What disturbed him most was the way the professional ballplayers were treated by whites throughout America. Nevertheless, he excelled again, batting .345 and demonstrating his fielding ability in the process.

Commissioner Kennesaw Mountain Landis, a major supporter of white-only professional baseball, died in 1944. Branch

Rickey, the general manager of the Brooklyn Dodgers, saw an opportunity to break the color barrier. It was time for a change in baseball, and the Brooklyn Dodgers dared to challenge tradition. The African American soldiers who had fought and were fighting in the world war had shown their willingness, as Africans had done in every war, to give their lives for their country. How could major baseball continue to keep black Americans from participating in the sport?

Major-league baseball was seen as the purview of whites. There were some diehards who did everything in their power to prevent the presence of African Americans in the sport. In a vote called by the new commissioner, Albert "Happy" Chandler, all the major league executives rejected the idea of blacks playing in the majors—except for Branch Rickey. The vote created a moment of crisis and set up an important challenge to the authority of the commissioner. On October 23, 1945, Rickey defied the executives' vote and signed the college-educated army officer Jackie Robinson to a minor-league contract with the Montreal Royals, a Dodgers farm team. The ice had been broken and the only thing that remained was for Robinson to play in a Dodgers uniform. In the meantime, he played in Venezuela during the winter and joined the Royals in Florida for the 1946 spring training season.

Despite unbearable conditions and rude behavior by whites, Robinson was so focused on his game that he managed to lead the Class AAA International League in batting (.349) and runs scored (113), and was largely responsible for bringing his team to the league championship. The Dodgers called him up to the majors in 1947, and he was asked to join the team at its spring training session in Cuba.

Some of Robinson's own teammates on the Brooklyn Dodgers circulated a petition to exclude him from spring training in Cuba in 1947. Dodger manager Leo Durocher challenged them to leave if they wanted to, but no one left and Robinson played. Thus, in April 1947 Robinson became the first African American in the major leagues since Moses Fleetwood Walker, who played in 1885.

However, Jackie Robinson was not just a historical figure; he actually earned his position through exceptional talent. He was rookie of the year with a .297 batting average and a league-leading twenty-nine stolen bases. Furthermore, during his ten-year tenure with the team, Robinson batted .311, led the team to six pennants and one World Series Championship, and won the 1949 National League most valuable player award. He understood that he was making it possible for African American athletes to join all professional team sports. Rarely had the sport of baseball seen a person of the integrity, courage, and character of Jackie Robinson. On and off the playing field he was an example of nobility and propriety. He knew that he was a role model for an entire nation of people and he did not want to let anyone down. He did not choose an evil word or a retaliatory spirit against those who hurled racial insults at him. It has been said that Rachel, his wife, was one of the most important influences on his personality. She was responsible for teaching him how to handle his anger when he would return from games where he had been taunted because of his race. In 1962 Robinson was inducted into the National Baseball Hall of Fame.

When he retired from baseball, Robinson became an outspoken critic of racism in the United States. He did not participate in old-timers games because it usually meant he would be the only black in the game. He became increasingly committed to social justice, talking about the lack of African Americans in the professional sports field, and seeking to improve the way Africans were treated by the society. Barely ten days before his death in 1972 he celebrated the twenty-fifth anniversary of his professional baseball debut by throwing out the first pitch in the World Series. He had a remarkable career and became one of the most beloved Americans of all time because of his singularity of purpose, poise, and expertness in achieving his aims.

# JOHN
# RUSSWURM
1799–1851

**B**orn John Brown to a Jamaican slave mother and a white American merchant father on October 1, 1799, at Port Antonio, Jamaica, he became John Russwurm when his stepmother demanded that his father acknowledge by name his paternity. Sent from Jamaica to Quebec for schooling, Russwurm was eventually taken by his father to Portland, Maine, in 1812. He attended Hebron Academy in Hebron, Maine, and graduated in 1826 from Bowdoin College, one of the first black graduates of an American college. In his graduation speech he advocated the resettlement of American blacks to Haiti, demonstrating his involvement with the current political events, since Haiti had announced two years earlier that any African person who could find his or her way to Haiti would be given land and citizenship.

In 1827 Russwurm moved to New York City, and, with the little money that he was able to save from odd jobs, he helped found *Freedom's Journal* with Samuel E. Cornish, an African American activist. It was the first black-owned and black-printed newspaper in the United States. The paper employed itinerant black abolitionists and urged an end to southern slavery and northern inequality. In February of 1829, Russwurm stopped publishing the paper and accepted a position as the superintendent of education in Liberia. In a way he was fulfilling the dream that he had articulated years earlier, migrating to a country controlled by blacks. He departed for Liberia having given up hope that African Americans would have any future equality or prosperity in the United States.

Russwurm was quite busy in Liberia. Because of his education and the fact that he had founded a newspaper, he was granted many responsibilities, including editing the *Liberia Herald* and serving as a Liberian representative, recruiting American blacks to return to Africa. Russwurm became the governor of the Maryland area of Liberia in 1836, and worked to enhance the country's economic and diplomatic position. He died in Harper, Liberia, on June 9, 1851.

# ARTURO
# SCHOMBURG
## 1874–1938

**A**rturo Alfonso Schomburg was born in 1874 in San Juan, Puerto Rico. His father was German and his mother was African. During his childhood he lived in Puerto Rico and in the Virgin Islands. He attended the Saint Thomas College in the Virgin Islands prior to immigrating to the United States in 1891. He found a job in a New York City law office. It was here that he began to have a strong interest in books about African people. He collected literary works as well as paintings by and about African people.

He took a job at the mailroom of Bankers Trust Company in 1906. He kept that position for twenty-three years. With a fairly comfortable and easy job, he was free to explore his real historical and literary interests. From 1918 to 1926, he served as the grand secretary of the Prince Hall Freemasons. Schomburg was not satisfied with the state of information and knowledge about the African world, so in 1911 he and John E. Bruce, a journalist, founded the Negro Society for Historical Research. Their aim was to publish articles on African history. Because of his active and visible campaign for African history, Schomburg was promoted as a leading spokesperson for the African people. He was elected president of the American Negro Academy in 1922. As the Harlem Renaissance was in full swing, he wrote the famous essay "The Negro Digs Up His Past" in 1925. This essay appeared in *The New Negro,* edited by the Philadelphian Alain Locke, who was considered to be the philosopher of the Harlem Renaissance. By 1926 Schomburg had amassed an enviable collection of manuscripts, books, and articles about and by African people. Other intellectuals and artists gravitated to him for information and used his library for their own research.

Recognizing the importance of his collection, writers from all over the world came to Harlem to view the artifacts and works that had been collected by Schomburg. He was relentless in his collection and in his lectures. It was his ambition to disprove the theories of African inferiority and he therefore took on all debaters and gainsayers, showing them the evidence that he had collected over the years.

Little wonder that in 1926, the Carnegie Corporation bought and donated Schomburg's collection to the Negro Division of the New York Public Library located at the 135th Street Branch in Harlem. It took six years before the city library hired Schomburg as curator in 1932. He was fifty-eight years old and he held the position until his death, six years later, in 1938. In the meantime, he had touched hundreds of people with his work, helping to define the contours of African history, setting the themes that would be discussed for decades, and influencing scores of young intellectuals. Two years after his death, the Harlem library was named the Schomburg Collection of Negro Literature and History. It was renamed the Schomburg Center for Research in Black Culture during the 1970s. The Schomburg remains, alongside the Amistad Research Center and the Spingarn Collection, one of the three most important collections of African and African American memorabilia and texts in the world.

·

# BENJAMIN "POP"
# SINGLETON

1809–1892

**B**enjamin Singleton was born in Nashville, Tennessee, in 1809 and died in St. Louis, Missouri, in 1892. Singleton's will for freedom was expressed while he was still in his teenage years. He escaped from enslavement in Tennessee and fled to Canada. However, he believed that it was better to settle in the United States in order to be able to help others escape. Thus, he settled in Detroit, Michigan. There he welcomed and accepted fugitive Africans escaping from slavery until the close of the Civil War. When the war was over, Singleton decided to return to Tennessee and lead his friends and relatives to a better land. In this regard, Singleton was one of the first truly nationalistic African Americans. He believed that it was possible for blacks to live in a free society, apart from whites, and prosper. This would consume his life; he would toil day and night toward an independent black society.

One of Singleton's strongest beliefs was that the African had to buy land. He was rebuffed in Tennessee by the white landowners and politicians who felt after the Civil War that they did not want to assist the African people in any way. If they made it to economic security, it would not be with the support or aid of the whites. Singleton was so committed to economic independence that he consulted with W. A. Sizemore and Columbus Johnson, and asked their help in promoting a migration to Kansas. They had been enslaved Africans themselves, and their conviction was as strong as Singleton's. Thus began the great drive to convince Africans to move westward. The first wave of

Africans to reach Kansas went with Singleton in 1873. Life was difficult, but it was free. The pamphlets Singleton circulated to African Americans emphasized the advantages of living in a free state and owning property. After all, the states of the former confederacy often had whites who were antagonistic toward blacks, and even the African Americans who had been elected to positions of power in politics found their lives threatened and their livelihoods jeopardized. The only solution was to migrate to a free state. Where whites controlled the political establishment, they enacted laws and participated in practices to restrict African American movement. There were Black Codes passed to control the migration and movement of African Americans. Mobs hunted down African Americans who sought to challenge the racist laws. Under such conditions and with such intense antagonism on the part of whites among whom Africans lived in the South, the only answer, as far as Singleton was concerned, was for African Americans to establish their own cities and colonies away from white people.

Singleton's most successful campaign started around 1877 and ended in 1879. By the time it had ended, several hundred Tennessee families migrated to Kansas. In 1879, two years after Reconstruction ended, twenty-two thousand African Americans migrated from Tennessee and Arkansas to Kansas. They were called the "Exodusters." So many Africans were moving from the South that by 1880 the U.S. Senate opened an investigation into this unprecedented movement. Singleton was called to testify before Congress and it was at this point that the real significance of his persuasive campaign became known. He took responsibility for the migration and referred to his role as that of "the Moses of the Colored Exodus."

An active political thinker and a man most willing to risk his life and security to gain legitimate freedom for African Americans, Singleton sought to form alliances where he thought they might be helpful in gaining access to territories in the West. He wanted to join forces with the Greenbacker political party in order to create a cooperative economy in 1880. Ultimately, however, he was disappointed with the Greenbackers and thought it necessary to organize the Chief League, later called the Trans-Atlantic Society. The purpose of this organization was to promote the emigration of Africans to Cyprus, and finally to Africa.

# MARY CHURCH
# TERRELL
## 1863–1954

Mary Eliza Church Ter-
rell's life started during
the year of the Emancipation
Proclamation and ended during
the year of the Supreme Court
decision in *Brown* v. *Board of Education.* Few people have come to
symbolize their generation as Mary Church Terrell, as she was
often called, came to represent hers.

She was born in 1863 in Memphis, Tennessee, to Louisa and
Robert Church. They eventually became fairly prosperous busi-
nesspeople, helping to form a nascent black middle class in Memphis after the Civil War. Mary Church was sent to school at
Oberlin College in Ohio, a school known at the time for its liberal and progressive leanings. After she earned her bachelor's
degree in 1884, she was slated to return to the South and serve
as the hostess and caretaker of her father's businesses. At the
time, Robert Church was reputed to be one of the wealthiest
African Americans living in the South, and he sought nothing
more for his daughter than a leadership role in the emerging
middle class. However, Mary Church wanted to become a teacher
and assist the masses of African American people through her
role as an educator

Thus, she left Oberlin and went to work as a teacher at
Wilberforce College, a school that had been established to train
young black students, in 1885. After working at the college for
two years, Mary Church moved to Washington, D.C., where she
became a teacher at the M Street High School. Still not satisfied
with her training and education, Mary Church took a master's

degree at Oberlin. Convinced that she needed to visit Europe to complete her understanding of American history, she went on a two-year tour beginning in 1888. The European trip proved useful to Church as she developed her language skills, learned to appreciate the diversity of cultures, and experienced life essentially free of the segregated customs and laws of America. Since Europe had not experienced the degree of racist hatred toward Africans that had befallen America, Mary Church felt free to explore the range of her abilities. Furthermore, she would use her European contacts to make a case for African Americans later in her career.

She returned to the United States in 1890 and married Robert H. Terrell, whom she had met when she started teaching in Washington in 1885. The next two years found her passionately involved with her husband and family. She did not teach any longer, but felt a need to stay involved in the activities of the black community in other ways. When Tom Moss was lynched in 1892, Mary Church Terrell knew that she could not remain on the sidelines. She had to be engaged in the struggle for true freedom. Moss had been a lifelong friend from Memphis, and his brutal murder was enough for her to get Frederick Douglass, at the time the most important African American living, to demand a meeting with President Benjamin Harrison. The president met with them and listened to their case for a law against lynching, but made no public statement against lynching. It was this event that caused Mary Church Terrell to move beyond the ordinary to spend the next sixty years fighting racism and organizing African American women.

In 1892 Terrell took on the revitalization of the Colored Women's League, and in 1896 led it into a merger with the National Association of Colored Women (NACW). She was elected president of this national black organization, becoming at the time the first African American to command an organization with national reach. During Terrell's presidency, the NACW organized women around issues of health, jobs, housing, and children.

Mary Church Terrell proved a major asset to the African American community. She was a member of the American Woman Suffrage Association, and from that platform she spoke for the right of women to vote. Since she was gifted as a speaker and knowledgeable as an intellectual, she was often called upon to represent African American women. She stepped up to the calling and delivered her arguments and statements on every occasion with diligence, enlightenment, and skill. At the International Council of Women conference that met in Berlin in 1904, she delivered her address in German, which stunned many in the audience. She subsequently astonished her largely white audience again by translating her own speech into French and English from the German text. There would be no end to her work or the demands on her time. She was an active associate of Frederick Douglass until his death, a supporter of Booker T. Washington's educational programs, and a colleague of W. E. B. Du Bois on the founding board of the National Association for the Advancement of Colored People in 1909.

Mary Church Terrell was an active supporter of progressive politics. She did not shy away from controversy, even though her husband was a federal judge. She spoke for social justice and equality of opportunity every chance she got and did not fear the risk of position or prestige when criticizing politicians.

When three companies of African American soldiers were dismissed in 1906 from the U.S. Army after a racial incident in Brownsville, Texas, without due process, Terrell exploded in a public attack on President Theodore Roosevelt's decision. She demanded a meeting with the secretary of war, William Howard Taft. Soon afterward the African American soldiers were given a hearing, but they were still dismissed from the army. The white soldiers involved in attacks on the black soldiers were not dismissed. It was a clear sign to Terrell that the battle for equality would have to be fought for a long time.

Mary Church Terrell was an active campaigner for all oppressed persons. She found the case of women most appealing, and between 1914 and 1945, she articulated the needs of African American women in every sector of the society. Her primary goal was to see to it that black women were adequately represented in the wartime economy. Like all antiracist fighters, Mary Church

Terrell knew that she could not rest on victories won. Since African American men had died on the battlefields of Europe and Asia, the nation needed to be reminded again and again of the sacrifice of the sons of black mothers. She vowed to never allow the national leaders to forget the sacrifice that had been made by African American people.

A final victory was won by Terrell when she had entered a segregated Washington, D.C., restaurant in 1950 with an interracial group and was denied service because she was black. The blacks in the group, including Terrell, filed lawsuits and, after a struggle of three years, the court ruled in the favor of the African Americans in *District of Columbia* v. *John Thompson*. Thus, at the age of ninety, Mary Church Terrell, the woman of steel, was bringing down the walls of segregation, undaunted by time, opposition, or age. Her death the next year ended the life of a national treasure.

# WILLIAM MONROE
# TROTTER

## 1872–1934

**W**illiam Monroe Trotter was born on April 7, 1872, near Chillicothe, Ohio, to James Monroe Trotter and Virginia Isaacs Trotter. His early life was spent in Hyde Park, a suburb of Boston. Trotter's family was deeply involved in the discussions and discourses surrounding racism, abolitionism, segregation, and white racial supremacy. He was influenced by his father, who raised him on stories of exploits by black soldiers during the Civil War, like those in the Massachusetts 54th Regiment. His father also recounted the debates and lectures of the Faneuil Hall cadre of abolitionists such as William Lloyd Garrison, Wendell Phillips, Charles Sumner, Theodore Weld, and Frederick Douglass.

Trotter's father worked at the Boston post office and sent his only son among three children to the public schools. Work in real estate and politics gave James Trotter a special insight into the political processes and the need for vigorous defense of justice, particularly when it involved matters of race. Young Monroe was the top student in his high school class, excelling in scholarship and popularity. He was elected president of his senior class. Instead of pursuing a career in the ministry, which would have pleased his mother but not his father, Monroe took a job as a shipping clerk. In 1891 he entered Harvard College, where he succeeded in achieving academically despite the Eurocentric nature of his training. When his father died during his freshman year, he had to rely on scholarships to complete his education.

When he graduated from Harvard, he took a job as a negotiator of real estate mortgages. He entered the business on his own in 1899. He was quite successful, using his training at Harvard and his father's business and political contacts to advance his career. Once his business progressed, Trotter married Geraldine Pindell, who was a descendant of an old Boston family.

Highly sensitive to matter of race and color, Trotter grew increasingly dissatisfied about the conditions of African Americans. He could not contain himself when he felt that Booker T. Washington had betrayed the African American people by settling for vocational rather than a genuine liberal arts education. Although he had planned to continue his upwardly mobile life in the quiet corners of Boston society, he was shaken by the turn of events on the racial front. As it is with men and women of principle, so it was with Monroe Trotter: he had to change directions in his life.

Trotter threw himself into propaganda, agitation, and organizing with a passion by starting a newspaper called the *Guardian*, with the purpose of maintaining an active front against the encroachment of racism. While Boston was considered one of the most liberal cities in the country, it was fast becoming a bastion of racism like other cities. At the beginning of the twentieth century, in 1902, Trotter complained that he had been forced to move twice because of racism.

Opposition in Boston did not prevent him from launching the *Guardian* with great enthusiasm, so much so that he was able to gain a circulation of twenty-five hundred within eight months. Initially the paper was coedited by George Washington Forbes, a Mississippian who had attended Amherst College. After two years Forbes withdrew from the paper because, as an employee of the city's libraries, he was vulnerable to disciplinary action if someone did not like the views expressed in the paper. In many ways, Forbes's withdrawal gave Trotter full range to unleash his violent attacks against Booker T. Washington, whom he held in contempt. He did not attack Washington when the great "Negro spokesman" was at his lowest point in popularity, but when he was at his highest. Trotter's attacks were considered foolhardy, dangerous, ill-timed, and unhealthy for African Americans by other leaders.

The *Guardian*'s articles and editorials created a national stir. Actually, the Niagara Movement, begun in 1905 and leading to the 1909 founding of the National Association for the Advancement of Colored People (NAACP), was inspired by Trotter's assaults on Washington. Du Bois understood that the Tuskegee experience, where blacks were trained to use their hands instead of their heads, would set back the process of racial integration by years if it were to become the goal of black education. Trotter drove home that point in the *Guardian*, going so far as to consider the Washington Tuskegee Machine to be the enemy of progressive race relations. The death of Washington in 1915 did not end the indictments against him by Trotter, who argued that the Tuskegee Machine did not recognize the growing deterioration of racial conditions, but rather had allowed the intolerable situation facing black people to continue. Trotter's intent was to destroy all vestiges of Washingtonian thought about race relations.

In some ways, Trotter's calls for protest, independence, and revolt did not take into consideration the difference between Boston and Montgomery at the top of the twentieth century. Yet the *Guardian* had also pointed out that Washington could speak against the universal right of African Americans to vote while having that right himself. Furthermore, Trotter could not see how the most public figure of the African American people could be a trusted advisor on southern and racial politics to President Theodore Roosevelt. Trotter feared what Washington would or could say to Roosevelt regarding the deplorable conditions of the race in the South. He did not want Washington to make Roosevelt comfortable with the racial status quo.

Prior to the death of Washington, the battle had resorted to personal insults. The Boston riot of July 1903 was symptomatic of the bad feelings between the Washington camp and Trotter. In fact, Trotter went to a speech by Washington in Boston at a church on Columbus Avenue to ask Washington some questions. Some people got out of hand and disrupted the event, Trotter was identified as one of the ringleaders, and Washington's lawyers took the case to court, eventually gaining a decision against Trotter. He was put in jail for one month as a result. His wife, Geraldine Pindell Trotter, worked on the paper while he served his time in jail. Forbes had a separate legal suit against him brought by Washington's lawyers. It was this event that forced him to leave the paper and return to his job at the library full-time.

After this incident Trotter and Du Bois became friends. They found opportunities to work together in opposition to the Tuskegee Machine. Trotter had become, by virtue of his arrest, the most public opposition to Washington. He and Du Bois would combine forces to create an organization, the Niagara Movement, that would isolate the Tuskegee Machine. But they soon found the Tuskegee Machine too powerful, and the fact that neither Du Bois nor Trotter could devote full-time energy to their organization meant that they could not wrest public and image control away from the Tuskegee Machine. Furthermore, most people who worked with Trotter, including Du Bois, found him difficult to work with. No one denied that he was a major influence in journalism and in propaganda, but in organizing he was a failure.

Trotter was at the founding conference of the NAACP in 1909, but he never considered himself a member. The early leaders of the organization, Oswald Garrison Villard and Du Bois, never reconciled with him. Trotter felt that the white money running the NAACP meant that black people would never have control of the organization. He created the National Equal Rights League, as "an organization of colored people, for colored people, led by the colored people." Trotter made this statement in 1920 to show that his organization was meant to be different from the NAACP.

Trotter was unafraid to challenge the political leadership of the nation when, in 1906, President Theodore Roosevelt summarily discharged, without honor or hearing, three companies of the black 25th Infantry following the Brownsville Riot of August 1906. Trotter then threw his support in 1908 for the Republican nomination for president to Sen. Joseph B. Foraker. In Trotter's opinion, Foraker was the only candidate who had opposed the dismissal without a hearing of the black soldiers and was consequently the only candidate that deserved black support. The everyday Republicans succeeded in getting William Howard Taft elected, yet Trotter railed that Taft had done more to increase "race prejudice and race antagonism than any man in the history of the country."

Trotter was known to confront any person he believed was antagonistic toward African American political rights. He took a delegation to the White House in November 1914 to meet President Woodrow Wilson, whom Trotter had supported, but who turned out to be an embarrassment to black supporters. Wilson resegregated the armed forces, failed to appoint African Americans to civil service positions that had been traditionally held by blacks, and turned his back on his black campaign workers. So when Trotter got to the White House, he and Wilson engaged in a powerfully emotional argument for forty-five minutes that ended abruptly when Wilson ordered the group from his office.

A lifelong campaigner against anything that smacked of racism, Trotter was arrested in 1915 for protesting the racist film *The Birth of a Nation* because of its derogatory portrayal of blacks. Later, in 1919, he journeyed to the peace conference at Versailles, France, to inject a racial equality clause into the treaty. Of course, the European powers and the American delegation ignored his appeal.

After Trotter's wife died in the influenza epidemic of 1918, he tried to manage the *Guardian* himself, but his national reputation declined in later years. He is thought to have committed suicide in 1934, on his sixty-second birthday.

# SOJOURNER
# TRUTH
## 1797–1883

**S**lavery would never be able to hold her. That was the way Sojourner Truth felt about herself and the institution of slavery. She did not like the idea that someone was considered her owner, and she refused to believe that whites were superior to her.

Truth was one of the best-known black women of her time, rivaled only by the African American abolitionist Harriet Tubman, yet her life remains surrounded by mystery. Truth, who was illiterate, left no written record apart from her autobiographical *Narrative of Sojourner Truth*, dictated to the white abolitionist Olive Gilbert in the late 1840s. Much of what we know about her was reported or perhaps invented by others. More so than Frederick Douglass, her autobiographical contemporary, Truth's life has been transformed into myth. Feminists emphasize her challenge to restrictive Victorian codes of femininity; Marxist historians proclaim her solidarity with the working class. Her spirit has been invoked on U.S. college campuses in struggles to create African American and women's studies programs. Yet most interpretations of Truth fail to understand the centrality of her evangelical religious faith.

In their writings, both Harriet Beecher Stowe and Frederick Douglass recount a central illustration of Truth's faith that occurred at a protest gathering at Faneuil Hall in Boston, Massachusetts, after the passage of the Fugitive Slave Act of 1850. Truth sat in the front row, listening to Douglass speak. Events had led him to abandon the nonviolent approach of moral per-

284

suasion, and he exhorted southern slaves to take arms and free themselves. Truth accepted his frustration but not his loss of faith in God's justice. In a voice that carried throughout the hall, she asked a single question: "Frederick, is God dead?"

By Truth's own account, this empowering faith came to her in a moment of divine inspiration after long and traumatic experiences under slavery, which included beatings by her master, John Dumont, and, according to Truth's biographer Nell Irvin Painter, sexual abuse by Dumont's wife. Religion lay at the heart of Truth's transformation from victimized slave to powerful and charismatic leader. Her decision to take the name Sojourner Truth was, in fact, the culmination of a long process of self-remaking.

It is believed that Isabella Baumfree was born around 1797 in Ulster County, New York. James and Elizabeth Baumfree had twelve children; Isabella was the youngest. From the time she was born, Isabella appeared to be special to her family as well as to her slave owners. Dutch was the spoken language among the enslaved Africans, as it was the language of the slave owners. Isabella did not remain with one slave owner. She was sold to a series of slave owners, including Dumont. She worked for Dumont for seventeen years, between 1810 and 1827. In 1811, when she was fourteen, she married another one of Dumont's enslaved Africans, Thomas. Between 1815 and 1826, they had four children, Diana, Peter, Elizabeth, and Sophia, and perhaps a fifth, who died. She was an excellent mother, developing a strong affection for her children, contrary to the intended conventions of the day, in which Africans were to have no close ties to kin.

Therefore, Isabella was devoted to the health and well-being of her children. When Peter, her son, was sold and taken to Alabama, Isabella mounted a campaign to have him returned to New York. She sued his captors to return him, and with the assistance of the Quakers, was successful. The twelve-month ordeal in 1826 and 1827 tried her patience and her sense of motherhood. She soon joined the Methodist Church, one of the only churches that would admit Africans during this time. According to her *Narrative*, she had a powerful conversion that was mystical and mysterious. She said that God revealed himself to her, coming in a suddenness like lightning and demonstrating to her that there was no place where God was not. She was dumbfounded by this mystic experience. It literally changed her entire life, and she became one of the first African mystics in America. All along Isabella was probably leaning toward the spiritual path, relying simply on the African way of life. But the conversion sent her into white communities where mystics and religious idealists dwelled. She became a reformer, seeking to make the present world better through spiritual rebirth.

It may be that she felt God had answered her prayers when New York abolished slavery in 1827. With her freedom, Isabella went to New York City with her son, Peter, to find work. The three daughters were left to care for their father.

New York City was a veritable treasure trove of opportunity. In the city, Isabella found domestic work to do for a living, while gaining a deeper knowledge of the Christian religion. She joined both the African Methodist Episcopal Zion Church and a white Methodist church. Not content with sitting in the pews and listening to others, Isabella started preaching herself. She was a strong speaker at the revival camp meetings and soon gained a reputation for holding an audience through her oratorical abilities. Her intense mystical leanings inspired her to join the self-proclaimed white prophet Matthias (Robert Matthews). She stayed with his messianic commune from 1832 to 1835. Some scholars say that she then joined or studied with the Millerites, followers of the self-proclaimed prophet William Miller, who believed that the world would end in 1843.

When the world did not end in 1843, Isabella had a profound realization—she had to break with the traditions of those who could not see the vision that she felt God had for her. She took a new name, calling herself Sojourner Truth, because she was meant to be a sojourner who would tell the truth. She preached at Millerite gatherings throughout New England. Soon, she attached herself to the Northampton Association, a utopian community in the small community of Florence, Massachusetts. It was in this little community of utopian reformers that she met Frederick Douglass and William Lloyd Garrison. Soon she started speaking out on the subjects of religious freedom and social freedom. The Northampton Association disbanded in 1846, but Truth remained in Florence for several more years. She then joined the Spiritualist Progressive Friends in Battle Creek, Michigan.

Truth insisted on the need to include black and working women in any vision of social reform, grounding her speeches in her own experience as a black woman and former slave. She earned a reputation for oratorical power and a ready wit, as seen in the best-known speech of her career, delivered at an 1851 women's rights convention in Akron, Ohio. As reported at the time by Marius Robinson, editor of the Salem, Ohio, *Anti-Slavery Bugle*, Truth spoke proudly of her own strength and accomplishments, and, by implication, those of all women: "I have plowed and reaped and husked and chopped and mowed, and can any man do more than that? . . . And how came Jesus into the world? Through God who created him and woman who bore him. Man, where is your part?"

However, Robinson's contemporary report of this speech is far less widely known than a later account by white reformer Frances Dana Gage. In Gage's memorable retelling, Truth punctuated her speech again and again with the emphatic question, "And ain't I a woman?" Scholars have come to doubt the accuracy of Gage's account, which was published twelve years after the event in question. Gage portrayed Truth facing down a hostile crowd dominated by male skeptics of women's rights and female advocates of sharply distinct gender roles, which Painter argues was Gage's own dramatic invention. In rendering Truth's words, Gage employed a nearly unreadable dialect that reflected contemporary literary conventions about black speech far more than it did Truth's own voice. And Painter believes that Truth probably never uttered the line that has become central to her historical image.

Although her subsequent career is less widely known, Truth continued her reform activism. During the Civil War (1861–1865), she journeyed to Washington, D.C., and met President Abraham Lincoln. From 1864 to 1868, she worked with the private National Freedmen's Relief Association and the federal Freedmen's Bureau, assisting freed slaves. In the 1870s Truth participated in the American Woman Suffrage Association. She also championed a proposal to allot Kansas lands to destitute former slaves, making her last major speaking tour in a fruitless effort to rally support. When thousands of southern blacks, known as the Exodusters, actually moved to Kansas in 1879, Truth applauded them and offered her assistance. She returned from Kansas in 1880 and lived with her daughters in Battle Creek until her death.

# HARRIET
# TUBMAN
## 1820–1913

**H**arriet Ross Tubman was born on the eastern shore of Maryland around 1820, one of eleven children of Benjamin Ross and Harriet Greene. They called her Araminta, but she took her mother's name during her teenage years, demonstrating in her allegiance to her mother a defiance of the unwritten law that enslaved persons should not show any attachment to parents. When she died in 1913 she had become known as the greatest conductor of the Underground Railroad because of her exploits in leading more than three hundred enslaved Africans to freedom.

Many of her actions while still a teenager marked Harriet Tubman as a special person. Like most enslaved persons, she worked in the fields, becoming hardened by the arduous work and the exposure to the sun and elements. Once, she jumped in front of a fleeing African who was running from his slave owner. As the white man approached with an iron weight, Harriet stepped in front of him, and the weight he had in his hands, meant for the runaway, hit her in the head. She lay unconscious for several minutes. For the remainder of her life she would bear the gash in her forehead as a remembrance of the pain she suffered for trying to protect a fellow enslaved person. In addition, and perhaps worse, were the recurrent headaches, sleeping spells, and dizziness that she would experience for the remainder of her years.

Harriet married John Tubman in 1844. He was a free black man, and his freedom was to inspire her in many ways. In fact, she sought to discover the real history of her own mother, who had briefly been free because her owner had made no provisions for her upon his death, and she was free until someone else claimed ownership. This was to be a haunting thought to Harriet during her lifetime. The fact that someone could simply claim you and make you a slave, even if you had been free, disturbed her. But slavery itself created a crisis for Tubman. When her owner died in 1849, she knew that her family members could be sold deeper into the South, where slavery was even more brutal than the eastern shore. There was only one thing to do: escape. She wanted to take herself and her relatives to the north. She tried to persuade John Tubman to go along with her. He was not interested. Soon, Harriet fled without him, moving through the countryside at night, using the stars as her guide, and sleeping by day. When she reached Pennsylvania, a free state, she began to rebuild her life.

Tubman found work in Philadelphia. The menial jobs she had paid her just enough to maintain herself; but every minute she was sweeping floors, cleaning houses, or cooking, she thought about the members of her family left on the eastern shore. She saved her money in anticipation of a return trip to the South. A year after landing in Philadelphia, she made a secret trip to Baltimore and rescued her enslaved sister and her two children, bringing them safely to Philadelphia. The key black leader of Philadelphia at the time was William Still. Tubman joined with him; Thomas Garrett, the Quaker of Wilmington, Delaware; and other activists to create a loose network of abolitionists who supported fugitives as they traveled from the South to the north. As a conductor, a leader of enslaved Africans, Tubman is monumental. She made nineteen trips to the South from 1850 to 1860, and led more than three hundred men, women, and children to the north, including all of her family. In 1857 Harriet Tubman rescued her aging parents, fulfilling the mission she had set for herself as a teenager.

Tubman may have been the most remarkable individual in African history in this country. She often used all types of psychology to keep her followers inspired and courageous. Those who grew weary and wanted to argue about the route, about the weather, about the possibility of capture, would be told to "live north, or die here." Others who wanted to turn back had the gun placed in their faces and reportedly told, "Before I will see you a slave, I will see you dead and buried in your grave." Crying babies were given drugs. She used all types of disguises, created illusions, and led her pursuers on false chases. She never lost one person to the slave catchers. This was so despite the fact that there was a huge reward offered for her capture. She stopped settling Africans in the northern states after Congress passed the Fugitive Slave Act of 1850, which allowed runaways to be captured and returned to slavery. Harriet Tubman lived in Ontario for a few years, but eventually settled with her parents in Auburn, New York, in the late 1850s.

With a reputation as great as any African of her day, Tubman became a darling of the progressive forces in the country. She was a friend to Charles Sumner, John Brown, Ralph Waldo Emerson, abolitionist Sojourner Truth, and reformer Susan B. Anthony. Tubman purchased the land for her Auburn home from New York senator William Seward, who was also a secretary of state for the government. Although she admired and appreciated John Brown, she did not join his raid because of illness. Nothing touched her so deeply as his hanging for the raid on Harpers Ferry, Virginia. She believed strongly that people had to act to make life better for all. In 1860 she publicly led a crowd to rescue an African who was being returned to the South from Troy, New York.

Harriet Tubman was so violently opposed to enslavement that she would do anything to see the system overturned. Thus, during the Civil War, the government asked her to serve as a liaison between newly freed Africans and the United States army. Her job was to assist them in attaining self-sufficiency. She was encouraged to do anything necessary to assist the Union troops. She nursed the wounded, trained scouts and spies, and led a raid against Confederate troops. When the war was over, she received commendation from officers, but she received no pay. She returned to Auburn after the war to work and care for her parents. Although she was illiterate and poor, she went on the lecture circuit to raise money for the education of younger African Americans. She collected clothing for the poor former slaves, helped Africans who were too old for manual labor, and gave of herself to save children and adults when she had the resources.

Harriet Tubman married a second time, in 1869, to Nelson Davis, a Union Army veteran and former slave. During the same year, her friend Sarah Bradford published a brief biography of her. Bradford donated some of the money to Harriet's upkeep. The money was never enough, and prominent friends and acquaintances, some quite high in the government, tried to persuade the government to grant her a pension for her wartime services. This failed, but they did succeed in gaining her access to a small veteran's pension as the widow of Davis. Auburn's African Methodist Episcopal Zion Church opened the Harriet Tubman Home for Aged and Indigent Colored People in 1908, as a tribute to Tubman while she was still alive. Nevertheless, when Tubman died in 1913, she was penniless. Yet no greater hero of the African American people had ever lived, and no person any more selfless ever graced American history.

# KWAME
# TURE
1941–1998

**O**ne of the greatest Pan-Africans was born in Trinidad in 1941. There was little in the early life of Stokely Carmichael, who later changed his name to Kwame Ture, to indicate that he would grow up to be the African nationalist and Pan-African activist that he became during his lifetime. Ture's family came to Bronx, New York, when he was eleven years old. Although he had been an intelligent child, interested in history and scientific studies, there was nothing about him that distinguished him from other smart black children. He graduated from Bronx High School of Science. After high school his parents enrolled him in Howard University in Washington, D.C. At Howard University, he met and interacted with young African people from all over the world and soon began to formulate his own ideas about interracial activity. It was at Howard where some of the social ideas he had been exposed to as a high school student in New York were turned into more practical lessons. For cxample, he became a leader of demonstrations against racism while at Howard.

As a student of philosophy, Ture believed that the purpose of study was to make the world better for the poor and discriminated-against African people. Thus, he participated in the Congress of Racial Equalities marches and demonstrations and joined a Freedom Ride in 1961. He was arrested and served seven weeks in the old Parchman Penitentiary in Mississippi because he violated the segregation laws of the state. His experience in Mississippi was his call to arms, because he had never seen anything like the overt, blatant form of racism he saw in Mississippi. Having grown up in New York City, in a much more liberal and progressive atmosphere, Ture could not believe that the attitudes of whites in the South could remain unchallenged. Thus, instead of taking a job after graduating from Howard University, he headed south to work for the Student Nonviolent Coordinating Committee (SNCC). He had found his mission in life.

In the South his main purpose was to increase the black voter registration in Lowndes County, Alabama. The aim was to show blacks that they could have a profound impact on the conditions of their own lives by registering to vote and punishing the politicians who represented racist and segregationist views. While working in the South he laid the foundation for an organization called the Lowndes County Freedom Organization. The symbol of the organization was a black panther.

In the early 1960s Ture emerged as a photogenic orator, full of enthusiasm and passion. He was able to translate the struggle for freedom in terms that young college-age people understood and appreciated. Risking his career and his life, Kwame Ture evolved as a militant fighter for justice and civil rights by engaging in more protests, demonstrations, and confrontations with segregationists in the South during 1966 than he had in the previous years.

What was different in 1966, however, was the use of the phrase "Black Power." Willie Ricks, also with SNCC, is usually credited with being the first to use the phrase in 1966. However, even before Mukasa (Willie Ricks) or Kwame Ture used the term, Adam Clayton Powell used it in a 1964 commencement speech at Howard University. It is probably from that speech, based on a term employed even earlier by Richard Wright, that the term was used in the South.

Nevertheless, Ture must be given credit for popularizing the term. He became chairman of SNCC during 1966 and when he ended his speech with a call for "Black Power" in August of that year he ignited an entire nation. The term became a rallying point in the 1960s and into the early 1970s. A split occurred among the civil rights organizations after the cry for Black Power because the more conservative groups felt that SNCC was advancing into dangerous political territory. They cautioned against agitating the white population unnecessarily by calling for Black Power. Ture took this as his rallying cry seeing it as the opportunity to push the establishment to yield more political and economic advantages. He published a book, *Black Power*, with political scientist Charles Hamilton of Columbia University in 1967. The idea behind Black Power was independent political and economic development by blacks. This was seen as a necessary element for social transformation.

In 1967 Ture went on a world tour to publicize the activities of the civil rights organizations in the United States. One of the stops on his tour was Cuba. Because he visited Cuba the state department had his passport revoked. He was told that he faced charges of sedition, but he was never prosecuted. The following year he became the prime minister for the Black Panther Party, went to work for the All-African People's Revolutionary Party in Ghana, and in 1969 Ture married South African singer Miriam Makeba and moved from Ghana to Guinea.

Stokeley Carmichael changed his name to Kwame Ture in 1978, taking the first name of Kwame Nkrumah of Ghana and the last name of Séku Turé of Guinea, the two philosopher-leaders who were his mentors. He continued to travel and speak out against all forms of oppression until his death in Guinea in 1998.

# HENRY McNEAL
# TURNER

1834–1915

**H**enry McNeal Turner was born on February 1, 1834, in Newberry Courthouse, South Carolina. He would become the greatest preacher in the African Methodist Episcopal Church since the days of its founder, Richard Allen. Before his death on May 8, 1915, in Windsor, Ontario, Canada, Turner challenged the authorities in the South, articulated a back-to-Africa philosophy, and defended the American Colonization Society. He would rival his contemporaries, Henry Highland Garnet, Frederick Douglass, and Booker T. Washington, in the imagination of the nineteenth-century African American community.

Turner was born free to a teenage mother, Sarah Turner, whose deep sense of responsibility for him, as well as the love of his maternal grandmother, Hannah Greer, had a powerful influence on him. His grandmother is said to have had a strong impact on Turner's belief in his African heritage. She told him as much as she knew about Africa and instructed him to study and learn so that he could become a leader of the African people. It is no wonder that while he was still a young man, around fifteen years of age, he had a religious conversion that made him believe that he had been called to the ministry. A few years later, at the age of nineteen, he became an evangelist for the Methodists.

Turner was twenty-four years old in 1858 when he became a member and minister of the African Methodist Episcopal Church (AME). He served as pastor for churches in Baltimore and Washington for the next few years. When the Union Army started accepting African soldiers during the Civil War, it was Turner who raised the first black regiment for the army. He was subsequently commissioned as the chaplain of the regiment. When the war was over, Turner went to Georgia to lead the African Methodist Episcopal effort in Georgia. He briefly served as worker for the Freedmen's Bureau, but he remained tied to his church evangelism. Turner found his job challenging and energizing. He became driven in his desire to establish AME churches in the state. It was through his extensive travels in Georgia after the Civil War that he became convinced that the white population would never give up its belief in white superiority. Because of the success of his missionary work, he was offered the job of directing the publishing operation of the church. By 1876 Turner's own efforts through the publishing arm of the church had made him the most popular person in the church and one of the most important black voices in the nation. Four years later he was elevated to the post of bishop, becoming the first southern African American to serve in that capacity in the church. He went on to be involved in the Republican Party politics of Georgia in 1867 as one of the writers of the state constitution. Immediately after the constitution was ratified he ran for office and won a seat in the state legislature in 1868. However, in 1869 the twenty-three black state legislators were illegally unseated by their white peers, both Democratic and Republican. Turner found a position as postmaster in Macon, Georgia, and in 1870 he was again elected to the state legislature.

When Turner arrived in Georgia after the Civil War he held opinions and beliefs that were different from the majority of the black population. For example, he was against the distribution of land to Africans. Instead he urged Africans to feel happy that they had won "freedom of labor." While Turner has come to be seen as one of the most militant antislavery partisans, he was one of the first supporters for clemency for Jefferson Davis, the former leader of the Confederate states. He also was opposed to the sale of plantations for nonpayment of taxes.

The preacher could not stem the tide of hostility toward his position. He discovered that the white southerners were extremely hostile toward Africans. This made Turner become more politically militant. He harshly spoke out against the racism that he felt in the South and soon argued that Africans should consider leaving the United States for a country such as Haiti. Active on all levels, Turner took up the idea that blacks should move to a federal government reserve in New England. He did not stop with New Mexico as the area where blacks should be settled. He believed that Africans in America should immigrate to Africa. It was his belief that African Americans would be able to have a better life by immigrating to Africa. Bishop Turner became vice president of the white-dominated American Colonization Society in 1876, a move that caused many blacks to doubt his consistency in defending Africans because the organization was considered anti-African. In view of the fact that the government had at one time supported slavery, Turner argued that it should now underwrite the cost of any program of back-to-Africa as partial reparation for slavery.

Turner, like Douglass, was a traveler. In the 1890s he traveled to Africa on four trips. He visited Liberia, Sierra Leone, British South Africa, and the Transvaal. During all of his travels he was quite outspoken on American imperialism in Cuba, the Philippines, and Hawaii. When he became editor of the *Voices of Missions*, publishing articles on civil rights, racial discrimination, and history, he was challenging the customs and laws of the United States.

Turner did not seem to have a consistent political ideology. During the early twentieth century he became identified with Booker T. Washington and not with the more progressive W. E. B. Du Bois. Turner's death in 1915 of a stroke while attending an AME gathering in Windsor, Ontario, brought to an end the life of a masterful political preacher.

# TURNER

1800–1831

**W**hen Nat Turner was born on Benjamin Turner's plantation in Southampton County, Virginia, in 1800, the fires of revolution were burning brightly in Haiti. Boukman's preachings had stirred the masses against their French overlords and the appearance of Touissant L'Ouverture would turn complaints into total revolution. In the United States, Gabriel Prosser had organized in the same year a huge revolt of the enslaved Africans against plantations around Richmond, Virginia. It is thought by some that Turner's father, whose name is unknown, may have lived free with other escaped Africans in the Great Dismal Swamp, on the borders of Virginia and North Carolina. It is also believed that Nat Turner's mother, Nancy, who had been captured in 1793 on the West Coast of Africa, felt her son was destined to deliver his people from bondage. She taught him early that he was called to do great things. He learned to write and read when no other enslaved children could do either. He identified himself as a preacher from the little he heard about religion and began to have visions that portrayed his leadership role among other Africans.

When he was twenty-one years old, Turner ran away to freedom and remained on his own for one month. While he was free, he experienced a number of visions about his mission to lead a slave revolt. When he got back to the plantation he simply waited for a symbol that would let him know when to begin.

Turner turned his visions into sacred texts from which he preached liberation to all who would hear him. He was not a

Christian preacher in the sense that he followed the strict interpretations of the Bible, nor did he believe that his religion and
that of his slave masters was the same religion; he was more an
African priest, as Boukman had been in Haiti, experiencing what
he believed to be the truth of the divine. He wanted his people to
be free, as he had been, and to see themselves on their own, like
his mother's people had been before her capture in Africa.

When the symbol of the solar eclipse occurred in February
1831, Turner believed that it meant the time had come for revolution. He recruited four other men, went over plans and then
launched the revolt after midnight on August 22. Turner's forces
moved from one plantation owner to the next during the night,
until sixty-six whites had been killed. Never in America's history
had a slave uprising against the slave owners been so initially
successful. It looked as though the revolt would create havoc in
the nation. Turner wanted to capture the capital of the area, a
small town called Jerusalem. In the Christian theology Jerusalem
stood for deliverance, but in Virginia it stood as the seat of the
white planters' control over hundreds of Africans. In Jerusalem
he would have found the arsenal that would allow the Africans
to arm themselves adequately with weapons. Nearly two hundred strong, the group became less organized and lost the element of surprise when whites quickly organized a militia and
blocked the approach to the arsenal.

Turner's army was eventually halted. Africans scattered and
many were killed. The army had only knives and sticks and could
not stand against the arms of the white militia. Nat Turner
escaped and was not immediately captured. He eluded the white
captors until October 30, when he was accidentally discovered
and reported to the white authorities. He was tried, sentenced to
death, and hanged in Jerusalem, Virginia, on November 11, 1831.
His narrative was recounted to a court-appointed attorney,
Thomas Gray. More than three hundred Africans were killed
after the uprising. Turner was decapitated and his head was held
in a laboratory at Wooster College in Ohio.

# DAVID
# WALKER
## 1785–1830

In many ways David Walker was the first black militant. He wrote *An Appeal to the Colored Citizens of the World* (1829), one of the most powerful documents ever produced by an African in the United States and became a symbol of resistance to degradation. It is believed he was born in 1785 of a white mother and an enslaved father. Taking the status of his mother, as the law in North Carolina stipulated at the time, he was born free. Of course, his free birth did not mean that he was white, and he could not be educated in the South. It appears, however, that he knew how to read and write prior to arriving in Boston.

Once in Boston, David Walker established himself as a barber. But he became increasingly angered by the system of slavery that defined Africans as inferior to whites, and he was even more struck by the hypocrisy of the "white Christian Americans," whom he called the most brutal people on the face of the earth.

No African person was as convinced as David Walker was in the 1820s that the only way Africans would be free was to free themselves. This was the beginning of the school of thought that has been called "nationalism." Walker's belief would influence the thought of the most electrifying intellectuals and political activists in African American history. He predated Henry Highland Garnet, Bishop Henry McNeal Turner, Martin Delany, Alexander Crummell, and Marcus Garvey.

*An Appeal to the Colored Citizens of the World* was the most challenging document written by an African in America until that time. It consisted of a direct call to the enslaved Africans to rise up against their masters in a violent revolt. To put it mildly, Walker was fed up with the fact that the abject conditions of the African community did not cause more revolution. He was familiar with Thomas Jefferson's *Notes on the State of Virginia* (1785), as well as the revolution in Haiti, Gabriel Prosser's 1800 conspiracy, and Denmark Vesey's 1822 attempted revolt.

In addition to being a barber, Walker had a small tailoring business in Boston. It is thought that his shop was a gathering place for those who engaged in antislavery activities. Indeed, his pamphlet was distributed as far as the Carolinas by the black Bostonian seamen. Walker's wife, Eliza, said that he was "slender and well-proportioned. His hair was loose, and his complexion was dark." It seems that Walker was a member of the Massachusetts General Colored Association, which was organized in 1826 to petition the Massachusetts government in the interests of African Americans. In addition, Walker was a representative for *Freedom's Journal* (1827–1829).

Walker's speech to the 1828 convention of the Massachusetts General Colored Association was a preview of his pamphlet. In the speech he admonished the audience to work toward self-determination and self-help. Already it was clear that Walker did not believe dependency on whites was the solution to the problems of Africans in Massachusetts. It would be seen later in *An Appeal to the Colored Citizens of the World* that he believed the same thing was true of the masses of blacks. It would be their active striking in their own interest that would make the difference.

When the *Appeal* came out in September 1829, it was one of the most politically explosive works written in America. Walker's work was pointed, historical, biblical, and prophetic. It was a call for action and an argument for the humanity of African people. Nothing could prevent the rise of African people from slavery and the inequality handed out by whites, according to Walker, more than the self-determination and self-definition of African people. If there must be violence, then there must be violence because, he believed not even God wanted Africans to be enslaved against their will.

It is no wonder that the legislatures of several southern states offered a reward for Walker's head. South Carolina and Georgia wanted Walker so intensely that they were willing to offer $10,000, if he were delivered alive, or $1,000, if dead. In the north, white abolitionists who were nonviolent in their philosophies, such as William Lloyd Garrison and Benjamin Lundy, criticized Walker for being too forceful in his rhetoric. Nine months after the publication of the *Appeal*, Walker was found dead under mysterious circumstances. Most scholars believe that he was assassinated, although it has not been possible to prove this theory.

# MADAME C. J.
# WALKER
1867–1919

**O**n December 23, 1867, Sarah Breedlove, destined to become the first African American millionaire, was born to illiterate parents, Owen and Minerva Breedlove, in Delta, Louisiana. She grew up on the Burney plantation outside of Delta. As a child she lived in abject poverty, working in the cotton fields and the tomato and bean patches on the plantation. She was a hard worker, believing that the best way to improve herself was to learn how to endure hardship. Thus, the more work she was given, the more work she did.

Sarah Breedlove was uneducated and could not read or write before she became an adult. When she was fourteen years old she married Moses McWilliams and had a daughter, A'lelia, in 1883. Two years later Sarah's husband, Moses, was killed by a white lynch mob, and she was left alone to raise her child.

Even without a formal education, Sarah proved to be an extraordinarily bright and energetic entrepreneur. She took jobs as a domestic in order to make ends meet, but soon she had saved enough money to experiment with products for black women's hair. She practiced on her friends and family. She soon developed a technique and products that were very popular among black women. Since most African American women did not have money to purchase supplies and equipment made by the large white manufacturers, Sarah invented an iron comb that could be used to straighten black hair. This comb, with its evenly spaced teeth, could be heated on the stove or in the fireplace and used immediately on a woman's hair. Having discovered that many

African American women wanted to straighten their hair as a way to manage it, Sarah saw an opportunity for entrepreneurial activity. During the period of enslavement, African women had worn their hair in various natural forms as braids, twists, or locks. In addition, Sarah invented a hair product called Wonderful Hair Grower for those who had hair loss, as well as various other products. She married a journalist and newspaperman, C. J. Walker, whose understanding and expertise in advertising and mail order helped expand her business nationwide. When she divorced C. J. Walker, she kept his name and was known professionally as Madame C. J. Walker.

Walker had a number of business firsts. She was the first businesswoman to advertise and sell products via mail order. She was also the first businesswoman to organize door-to-door agents. Moreover, the Madame C. J. Walker Hair Culturists Union of America, an organization of the agents, was a nationwide operation with rules and regulations established by Madame Walker. She later opened her own beauty school, the Walker College of Hair Culture in Indianapolis. Joining with her daughter, Madame Walker set up beauty parlors for African American women in the major cities in the United States, South America, and the Caribbean. She became a millionaire in 1914.

Although Madame C. J. Walker did not have a formal education, she was enthusiastic about using her wealth to assist in the education of African American children. She was particularly interested in the education of African American women.

Madame C. J. Walker lived in a style that made her the symbol of African American women's beauty and charm. She was elegant in her own personal manner. Furthermore, she purchased a house in Harlem that was called the Dark Tower. She also owned a huge estate called Villa Lewaro, the centerpiece of which was a thirty-four-room mansion designed by V. Woodson Tandy, the first registered African American architect. By the time of her death in 1919, the First World War had ended, and Walker had become a legend in her own time. Numerous young artists and writers were moving to Harlem to begin their careers and to launch what would become known as the Harlem Renaissance. Walker's daughter, A'lelia, who had been at her mother's side, took over the reins of the Walker empire and continued the businesses started by Madame C. J. Walker.

# BOOKER T.
# WASHINGTON

1856–1915

**B**ooker T. Washington grew up to become the most influential African American of his time. He was born in 1856 in the part of Virginia that later became West Virginia. He worked in the salt furnaces and coalmines of West Virginia. Washington walked five hundred miles to enroll at the Hampton Institute. He completed his secondary education and college at Hampton. He later taught at Hampton, but soon left to found the Tuskegee Normal and Industrial Institute in 1881.

When Washington went to Alabama to start Tuskegee, he was certain that if African Americans could be given the ability to work with their hands, utilizing skills and expertise that the South needed, they would amass the kind of economic power that would generate progress. His philosophy, termed "accommodationist," was soon attacked by African Americans who lived and worked in the north. Their intention was to gain political and economic power, not simply economic power based on industrial knowledge. Yet Washington's position did attract money for Tuskegee from whites who believed that African Americans should be trained to work for white industries without competing in the political field. When Washington went to the northern foundations, he asked them to support his school because it taught a strong work ethic.

By 1900, Washington had achieved incredible success by making Tuskegee the best-funded black educational institution in the nation. Whites loved Tuskegee and appreciated the fact that Washington did not want to challenge their political control.

The most famous speech ever given by Washington was the 1895 Atlanta Compromise address delivered at the Cotton States Exposition. In the speech Washington told whites to utilize the resources that were in their midst: the black masses. Washington wanted the African Americans to forget about agitation for equality and political justice. He gave an analogy that spoke of the South as being like the hand in the sense that "we could be as one as the hand in all things necessary and vital and as separate as the fingers in all things social."

When Booker T. Washington died in 1915, a political institution passed from the stage of African American history. Few individuals had ever been so complex in their personalities, interests, and involvements as Washington. He was honored and accepted by thousands of ordinary African Americans and many whites as the most important black person in history. On the other hand, African American intellectuals found his practical educational ideas limited and self-defeating. Yet all Americans recognized that the presence of Booker T. Washington was enormous on the social and political landscape of America.

# IDA B. WELLS-BARNETT

## 1862–1931

**I**da Bell Wells established herself as the foremost fighter against lynch mobs and went on to become one of the greatest crusading journalists for African American equality. She was born in 1862 to Jim and Elizabeth Wells in Holly Springs, Mississippi. Her seven younger siblings became her charges when she was quite young. Always displaying a nurturing attitude toward her siblings, Ida B. Wells learned early what it meant to care for others. This would become the defining characteristic of her life. She was educated at Shaw College, now called Rust College, in Holly Springs, Mississippi. She left school when her parents died during the 1878 yellow fever epidemic.

As the eldest of the siblings, she took on the responsibility for caring for her brothers and sisters. She took a job as a rural schoolteacher in Mississippi and then in Tennessee in order to sustain her siblings and herself. Remarkably, she found time to take summer courses at Fisk University in Nashville, Tennessee. She rode the train during her trips to Nashville and other cities from Memphis. In 1884 she filed a lawsuit against the railroad company for putting her off a train because she refused to sit in the Jim Crow, or segregated and inferior, section of the train. She won a five-hundred-dollar judgment from the circuit court against the railroad company but lost her case in appeal to the Tennessee State Supreme Court in 1887. Although she resolved to fight against injustice, the enemies of justice were after her. She lost her teaching job in 1891 when she wrote a critical editorial in a Mem-

309

phis newspaper accusing the school board of providing inferior education to African American students. Wells contended that the white school board of Memphis was racist in the distribution of educational resources. Knowing that African Americans were often considered inferior by whites, she pointed out the hypocrisy of white people who denied equal opportunities to blacks and then condemned blacks for not performing as well as whites.

Out of a job and determined to find work that would not make her dependent upon whites, Wells soon started a career in journalism. She was given a job as editor of the *Evening Star* and a church weekly, the *Living Way*, in Memphis. Later, in 1889, she took over the editorship of *Free Speech*. Ida B. Wells was forthright, bright, and blunt. She wrote under the alias "Iola" and sought to shake up the status quo regarding the rights of African Americans. When she wrote two articles in 1892 condemning the lynching of three black businessmen, she was severely criticized. Whites who could not compete with black businessmen often went to their stores and lynched them. Ida B. Wells found this situation particularly heinous because it meant that even when blacks succeeded in business it was considered threatening to whites. She published the first editorial on March 9, 1892, and in the essay she urged African Americans to leave the city and head for Oklahoma. Her second editorial appeared on May 21, suggesting that white women sought out black men for sex and then, when they were discovered, said that they had been raped. Soon after the editorials were printed white mobs stormed the offices of the *Free Speech* and destroyed it.

Getting out of town as quickly as she could, Wells landed in the north. She reported for two black newspapers, the *New York Age* and the *Chicago Conservator*. She was a direct source for stories on the treatment of African Americans in the South. Using her firsthand knowledge of the Jim Crow situation, Ida B. Wells spoke out eloquently against injustice, prejudice, and segregation. Most of all, she was a campaigner against lynch law and mob rule. Taking her campaign to Europe, in the tradition of the black abolitionists a couple of generations earlier, she traveled through England, Scotland, and Wales in 1893 and 1894. When she returned to the United States, she published her most comprehensive work on lynching, *A Red Record: Tabulated Statistics and Alleged Causes of Lynching in the United States.* Her argument was that lynching had an economic base and that the whites in the South feared the economic competition that would result from an educated black population.

Two important events happened in her life in 1895. The first was the publication of *A Red Record* and the second was her marriage to Ferdinand Barnett, a lawyer and editor from Chicago. She was eventually active in the raising of four children in Chicago. Still, her interest in politics did not wane and she was a key founder of the National Association of Colored Women in 1896. Her work with the Negro Fellowship League, the National Association for the Advancement of Colored People, and the Alpha Suffrage Club gave her broad recognition for activism in the African American community. When she heard about Marcus Garvey's movement, she became involved with the Universal Negro Improvement Association and African Communities League as a way to express her nationalism. Ida B. Wells-Barnett believed in self-reliance and self-determination of the black community.

Fighting for the rights of African Americans was her lifelong passion, although she did take time off to raise her children. In the latter part of her life she wrote articles condemning the racial violence in cities like East St. Louis, Illinois (1917), Chicago (1919), and Little Rock, Arkansas (1922). Many institutions and buildings have taken her name, including a housing project in Chicago named for her in 1941. In addition, the state of Tennessee placed her in the state's Hall of Fame for heroes, and in 1990 the United States Postal Service issued an Ida B. Wells-Barnett stamp.

Ida B. Wells-Barnett died on March 25, 1931, as the nation was recovering from its deepest economic depression. Though the nation had not yet dealt with the lynching of black men, Wells-Barnett had placed her stamp on the door of liberation. The conscience of the nation would never be the same.

# WHEATLEY

**B**y the time she was nineteen years old, Phillis Wheatley was already known to the leading citizens of her day as an established poet. Those who had read her works included two of the most celebrated Americans, George Washington and Benjamin Franklin. In fact, Wheatley's fame and reputation were widespread because she not only demonstrated what an African could do but also what a woman could do, being just the second woman in America to publish a book.

It is believed that Wheatley was born, probably in 1753, in Senegal or Gambia, on the western coast of Africa. She was taken from her native home and transported into slavery in 1761 and sold to John and Susanna Wheatley in Boston. Accordingly, the Wheatleys gave her the first name of the ship upon which she was transported to Boston. We do not know what her African name was, since the records do not indicate what her parents called her. The Wheatleys allowed their daughter Mary to tutor Phillis in Latin, English, and the Bible. They soon recognized that Phillis had an excellent mind and a good facility for writing. This was demonstrated when Phillis started writing poetry. Her first poem was published in the Newport *Mercury*, December 21, 1767, when she became the first black person in the Americas to have a poem published in a newspaper. For the next three years she wrote many poems for local papers and finally, in 1770, she composed an elegy for George Whitefield, the famous evangelical preacher, that was printed in America and in England. Yet when the Wheatleys attempted to publish her first complete volume of poetry in 1772,

Phillis had to be interviewed—actually examined—by a committee of leading citizens of Boston, since so many people, including publishers, did not believe that a black person could actually have written a book. They wanted to see if she was literate enough to have written the book. The conclusion was that she could have written the book, but she still could not find a Boston publisher.

Selina, the countess of Huntingdon, an Englishwoman who was friendly with George Whitefield, arranged to have Wheatley's book published in London in 1773. The book was called *Poems on Various Subjects, Religious and Moral*. The frontispiece of the original edition identified the author as "Phillis Wheatley, Negro Servant to Mr. John Wheatley of Boston." An engraving of a young black woman at a desk, ready to write, holding a pen in one hand and a book in another, is quite striking. It is believed that the work was done by Scipio Moorhead, a young, enslaved African artist.

The publication of the book was a major literary event. Wheatley went to London for the book's publication. She met many literary figures, political dignitaries, and even received Benjamin Franklin. Wheatley was celebrated for her intelligence and literary ability, and the Wheatleys soon freed her at the urging of her friends in England.

Wheatley wrote many poems for friends and several popular poems in support of the Americans during the Revolution. One poem written in October 1775, celebrated George Washington, who invited Phillis Wheatley to visit his military quarters at Cambridge, Massachusetts.

The variety of poems in Wheatley's collection is broad. She was able to write on her feelings about America, about religion, and about Africa. In the poem "To the Right Honourable William Legge, Earl of Dartmouth," she demonstrated some sentiment about her capture from the African coast:

*When seeming cruel Fate*
*Me snatched from Afric's fancied happy seat,*
*. . . Ah! What bitter pangs molest,*
*What sorrows labored in the parent's breast?*

Wheatley married a free African, John Peters, in 1778. Soon after the wedding she presented a new collection of poetry for publication, but could not find a publisher. She then became more involved in her family and was devastated by the deaths of her first two children in infancy. Her marriage was troubled, and she tried to give birth a third time when, on December 5, 1784, she died in childbirth.

By the time of her death she was poor and obscure, living in the country outside of Boston. This great singer of poems, who in her own way blazed a new path of achievement for those enslaved and broke the chains of ignorance concerning the capabilities of Africans, went to her death having accomplished a great deal.

# WALTER F.
# WHITE

## 1893–1955

**F**ew men have ever exhibited as much courage in the face of racism as Walter Francis White. He rose to become the most powerful civil rights leader of his time and the chief interpreter of the desires and opinions of the African American people for a generation. Indeed, Walter Francis White came to be acknowledged as the principal race spokesperson for nearly thirty years.

Walter White was born in 1893. He attended the public schools of Atlanta, Georgia, and was on his way to being a schoolteacher when the 1906 race riot in Atlanta changed his course. He was frightened, believing that his family's house could be set afire by whites. His job was to make certain that there was enough water to prevent the destruction of the house by fire. He vowed after the riot that he would spend his life working for political equality and social justice.

He entered Atlanta University and graduated in 1916. Joining the National Association for the Advancement of Colored People (NAACP), he became an active member and leader of the Atlanta chapter. His activism soon led to his elevation as the assistant to NAACP executive secretary James Weldon Johnson. He took seriously his job and the possibilities of investigating racist attacks on blacks, mob lynchings, and harassment of southern blacks. White became one of the organization's best researchers. His reports for the NAACP were useful for his judicial and literary work. The two novels he published, *The Fire in the Flint* (1924) and *Flight* (1926), were written with specific purposes. The novels were heavy on political messages and brought White no great literary reputation, but gave him enough clout to apply for and receive a Guggenheim Fellowship in 1926. He used the money from the fellowship to support himself while he completed the powerful book, *Rope and Faggot: A Biography of Judge Lynch* (1929).

White took over as executive secretary of the NAACP in 1931 and served until 1955. The politically astute White worked with A. Philip Randolph to force the government to establish the Fair Employment Practices Committee in 1941. Later, he demanded executive orders banning discrimination in war-related industries. He was successful in getting the government to recognize the fact that African Americans had fought in the wars and had kept their promises to make the world safer, but the American nation had not taken up the case against lynch law. Alongside W. E. B. Du Bois and Mary McLeod Bethune, he was a delegate to the founding of the United Nations in 1945. White had many achievements, but his most enduring legacy might be the hiring of the lawyer Charles Hamilton Houston, who was as enthusiastic as White in defeating legally sanctioned racism. In fact, it was the joint effort of White as leader of the NAACP and Houston as the first full-time legal counsel that eventually led to the historic *Brown* v. *Board of Education* decision in 1954.

Walter White died on March 21, 1955, in New York City.

# ROY
# WILKINS
1901–1981

**B**efore Roy Ottoway Wilkins was born, his father had been forced to flee St. Louis to avoid being lynched for refusing to follow a white man's order to get out of the road. Wilkins was reared in St. Paul, Minnesota, where he attended racially integrated schools. He became urgently aware of racial matters at the age of eighteen, when three black Minnesotans were lynched by a mob of five thousand whites. Upon enrolling in the University of Minnesota, Wilkins became active in the National Association for the Advancement of Colored People (NAACP), as well as on the campus newspaper. He would pursue both activities in Kansas City following graduation. Wilkins worked for the *Kansas City Call,* an African American newspaper, until 1931, when he became assistant executive secretary for the NAACP, a position he held while editing the organization newspaper the *Crisis* until 1949.

In 1955 Wilkins was appointed to serve as the NAACP's executive director, the organization's highest administrative post. He steered the NAACP through the civil rights movement's most turbulent era, and with Martin Luther King Jr., helped to organize the March on Washington in 1963. Throughout his career, Wilkins upheld the principle of nonviolent, legal forms of redress, which tended to alienate him from more radical black groups. Wilkins's struggles for equality and civil rights brought him many awards, and earned him the nickname "Mr. Civil Rights."

# DANIEL HALE
# WILLIAMS
1856–1931

**P**erhaps no African American ever started with so
little but in the end gave so much
to his profession and his people as
Daniel Hale Williams. He was
born on January 18, 1856, in Holl-
idaysburg, Pennsylvania, the son
of a barber. Before his death on August 4, 1931, Williams would
become the first surgeon to perform a successful open-heart
surgery in the United States.

When he was twelve years old, Daniel Hale Williams left
home and set out on his own to make his way in the world. An
inquisitive child, he was given to adventure and curiosity. He
became a worker on a lake steamer, a barber, and a handyman.
When he was in his late teens, he moved to Wisconsin and lived
with his older sister. During this time he met Henry Palmer, a
prominent doctor and the surgeon general of the state of Wisconsin. Because of Williams's inquisitiveness, dexterity as a
barber, and general eagerness to learn, Palmer became his
mentor and helped him with tuition at the Chicago Medical
School. Williams received his M.D. in 1883 and opened a medical
practice on the South Side of Chicago. Soon he became a very
popular doctor, an attending physician at the Protestant Orphan
Asylum, and a surgeon at the South Side Dispensary.

The young doctor was an intellectual as well as a practitioner.
He served as a clinical instructor at the Chicago Medical College and
as a physician with the City Railway Company. In 1889 the Illinois
Board of Health made him a member of the board and he served for
four years. Using his position on the board, Williams worked to

keep infectious diseases from overtaking the black communities. In order to control the diseases, he enforced medical standards.

The work Williams did in this area was extraordinary given that blacks were not allowed to serve on hospital staffs or to use the equipment in the hospitals. Williams was also concerned that African American women were not allowed to be nurses, so he decided to found a school that would train nurses. In 1891 he founded the Provident Hospital. It became the first black-owned hospital and attracted black and white medical officers. At the hospital, Williams made history in 1893 when he operated on James Cornish, a street tough who had been stabbed in the chest. After the external wounds were sewn up, Cornish's condition continued to deteriorate. Concluding that Cornish was bleeding internally, Williams decided to open his chest cavity and try to stop the bleeding. Finding the knife had slashed an artery and tissue around the heart, Williams used catgut thread to sew up these internal wounds. The operation was a success, and Cornish lived another twenty years.

Williams became the chief surgeon at Freedmen's Hospital in Washington, D.C., in 1894 and immediately began to reorganize the hospital. Changing the leadership of the institution and establishing a nursing program and school, Williams used all of his skills and knowledge that he had learned in Chicago to bring the Howard University facility up to the highest standards. Most of the staff members gave him high marks for bringing a new professionalism to the school, but he also had his detractors, and after a few years he returned to Chicago. Rejoining Provident Hospital, Williams opened his private practice and started to receive patients from all over Chicago. His reputation among African Americans grew, and he was seen as the most famous doctor in African American history. As a scholar and a scientist, Williams published widely in the most respected medical journals. In 1913 he was made an associate attending surgeon at one of Chicago's best hospitals, St. Luke's Hospital. Later, he was the only black doctor accepted as a charter member of the American College of Surgeons. He retired to Michigan, where he died in 1931.

# AUGUST
# WILSON
1945–

**A**ugust Wilson was born Frederick August Kittel in Pittsburgh, Pennsylvania, in 1945. The area where he was born, called "the Hill," was a low-income neighborhood. Wilson learned about racism very early. His father was a white baker who was seldom around, and his mother an African American woman who had to do odd jobs in order to support her six children. Indeed, August Wilson was relieved when his mother remarried and moved the family out of the Hill District. However, his enthusiasm was soon dashed when the family's mostly white neighbors expressed their racism in an overt, direct fashion. The incident that Wilson believes made the most difference in his life occurred when a teacher falsely accused him of plagiarism.

Young Wilson dropped out of school but went to the libraries to read African American authors such as Richard Wright and Ralph Ellison. Wilson was deeply imbued with the culture, learning on the street corners and in the community with friends like the playwright Rob Penny and others who participated in the development of African American drama productions in Pittsburgh.

Wilson first wrote poetry, influenced by the lyrical style of Dylan Thomas and the dramatic sense of Amiri Baraka. When he became involved in the Black Horizon Theatre Company in his old neighborhood, the Hill, in 1968, he discovered that drama was his natural genre. He loved the blues and found himself surrounded by the rich culture of the African American people and decided that he would capture this richness himself. He soon rejected his white father's name, Kittel, and took his black mother's maiden name, Wilson, in solidarity with the struggle for liberation.

Wilson emerged almost full-grown as an artist in the 1970s. He wrote *Black Bart and the Sacred Hills*, a musical satire, and he later finished two more plays, *Jitney* and *Ma Rainey's Black Bottom*.

Shortly after writing *Ma Rainey*, he wrote *Fences*, which won the 1987 Tony Award for Best Play. He then wrote *Joe Turner's Come and Gone* (1986), and it debuted while *Fences* was still running on Broadway. *The Piano Lesson* was written in 1987. The story is about a family that is divided over selling the piano, which has become an heirloom, or keeping it. If they sell it, they can purchase their ancestral land. *The Piano Lesson* won a Pulitzer prize.

In 1990 Wilson wrote *Two Trains Running*, a play about the difficulties of friendships during the late 1960s. Five years later he wrote *Seven Guitars*, a treatment of relationships between musicians set in Pittsburgh during 1948.

August Wilson has demonstrated unusual courage in criticizing the American artistic establishment for its racism. He was attacked by black and white defenders of the literary establishment, one attacker even claiming that he was ungrateful to the establishment since he had received the Pulitzer prize. He has declared that he will write a drama about black American life in each decade of the twentieth century. Few dramatists have ever been so driven toward demonstrating the full range of African American emotions, experiences, and possibilities as August Wilson. He remains one of the greatest African Americans.

# OPRAH
# WINFREY
1954–

**O**prah Gail Winfrey was born on a farm in Kosciusko, Mississippi, in 1954. Her paternal grandmother raised her until she was six years old. She was sent to live with her mother in Milwaukee, Wisconsin, while she was still in elementary school. She was sexually abused by male relatives and became increasingly troubled as a young girl. Because her mother, Vernita Lee, was raising two other children and trying to work as a maid to support the family, she decided to send Oprah to her father in Tennessee. Her father, Vernon, was a religious man with a strong sense of discipline. Oprah did well under his tutelage and won all kinds of academic and public speaking awards. When she was sixteen, she won a partial scholarship to the Tennessee State University in a contest sponsored by the Elks Club. It was while she was a freshman at Tennessee State that Oprah Winfrey got her first broadcast work. Victories in two beauty pageants won her a position as a news anchor at WTVF-TV in Nashville, where she became the city's first African American woman news anchor. In 1976, only a few months away from earning her bachelor's degree at Tennessee State University, Winfrey quit school and took a job as an evening coanchor at WJZ-TV in Baltimore, Maryland. She did not succeed in that position but was offered a talk show, *People Are Talking*. She cohosted the show and it became a rating success.

Eight years later Winfrey was offered a job as the host of *A.M. Chicago*. This talk show aired opposite Phil Donahue's popular morning show. It had always been beaten in the ratings by Donahue until Winfrey's appearance. In three months she surpassed Donahue in the ratings. Donahue moved his show to New York in 1985, and in the same year *A.M. Chicago* was renamed *The Oprah Winfrey Show*. A year later it was syndicated and became the highest rated talk show ever. By 2001 more than 22 million viewers watched the show in the United States, and more than 132 countries broadcast some portion of the show. It has received more than twenty-five Emmy awards, and Winfrey has been called the greatest television host in history.

There is much more to Winfrey than her hosting ability. She earned the Golden Globe and Academy Award nominations in 1985 for her portrayal of Sofia in the film *The Color Purple*. In 1986 she founded HARPO Productions, becoming only the third woman to own her own television and film studios. HARPO ("Oprah" spelled backwards) produces *The Oprah Winfrey Show* as well as dramatic miniseries, such as *The Women of Brewster Place* (1988), based on the book by Gloria Naylor, and *The Wedding* (1998), based on the book by Dorothy West.

Her political activism is seen in the fact that Winfrey testified before the United States Senate Judiciary Committee, describing the sexual abuse she suffered as a child. She supported the passage of the National Child Protection Act in 1991. President Bill Clinton signed "Oprah's Bill" in December 1993. This bill established a nationwide database of convicted child abusers. Oprah's philanthropic ventures are extensive and include donations to protect children and the establishment of educational opportunities.

# TIGER
# WOODS
## 1975–

**E**ldrick "Tiger" Woods was born in Cypress, California. His father, Earl Woods, is African American and his mother, Kutilda Punsawad, is Thai American. His father taught him at an early age how to play golf, with the intention of making him an exceptional player. Recognizing that his son had an unusual talent in golf, Earl Woods started teaching his son how to be a winner. It was not just golf that Earl Woods wanted his son to know, but how to play the game and win.

It has been widely reported that Tiger Woods could play golf before he could even read. In fact, he made two holes in one before he was six. He was a frequent guest on television shows demonstrating his precocity as a player. He had acquired a strong and commanding game by the time he was twenty-one. Woods could drive a golf ball more than three hundred yards, putt with incredible accuracy, and speak about the game in the most philosophical manner. There was always a sense of confidence and authority in his play.

Almost all golf experts saw Woods as a possible savior for the game. Over the next few years he would completely revolutionize the game and the audience. Numerous articles were written about Tiger Woods in the late 1990s praising his phenomenal ability to play golf. Some writers emphasized what they called the composure and competitiveness of the young Tiger Woods.

Tiger Woods's father had a profound impact on his sense of purpose and focus. Earl Woods had been a Green Beret in the Vietnam War and believed that the strategy for winning depended upon concentration and desire. In the opinion of Earl Woods, teaching Tiger Woods to always excel at those two qualities went along with his great physical skill. Tiger Woods attended Stanford University and during his first season won a tournament at a country club that had only recently allowed African American members.

Woods's amateur record was stupendous. He won so many national championships that he set records in many categories. He won six United States Golf Association national championships, a National College Athletic Association championship, and a record-setting three consecutive U.S. amateur championships. By the time he entered the professional ranks he had amassed an enviable record of achievements, surpassing any of his contemporaries in the number of wins on the golf course.

Tiger Woods's professional debut in 1997 was spectacular; he won two of the first seven tournaments he entered as a professional. He won the Masters Tournament—considered the most prestigious tournament in golf—in April 1997. Woods shot a record-setting 270. He won the tournament by twelve strokes, the largest margin for a win in the history of the Masters.

Tiger Woods became, by virtue of his tournament win, the first person of either African American or Asian American heritage to win the tournament. He was also the youngest Masters winner. When 1997 ended, Woods had four tournament wins, finishing in the top ten in all but one of his entries.

Woods extended his domination of the sport in succeeding years. In 1999 he had nine victories in his last thirteen tournaments, including a major championship. He appeared virtually unbeatable during the year, with the highest winnings in the history of the sport. At the end of the year he was voted the Professional Golf Association Tour Player of the Year. At twenty-four years of age he had broken and set many records and showed no signs of stopping this trend. Most experts believe that he will continue to get better in the next few years.

Although Woods is one of the most recognized personalities in the world, he lives in the small community of Isleworth,

Florida, where he enjoys his free time listening to music, collecting coins, and lifting weights for strength. He is conscious of the fact that other black golfers pioneered and paved the way for him. He cites Charles Sifford; Lee Elder, the first African American to play in the Masters; and Ted Rhodes, the first African American to play in the U.S. Open. Woods has enlarged the audience and attractiveness of the sport for many African Americans. He learned about discrimination and racism early in his life, when he was tied to a tree and taunted by white students on his first day of kindergarten. Playing under severe pressure, he often receives death threats before tournaments. Nevertheless, he has continued to add to his achievements by winning most of the major tournaments. On August 26, 2001, exactly five years after he turned professional, Woods defeated a brilliant golfer, David Furyk, to win his twenty-ninth golf tournament. A truly exceptional talent, committed to demonstrating the best possible skill as well as the irrationality of racism, Tiger Woods continues to build on his remarkable feats.

On June 16, 2002, Woods became only the sixth golfer to win the U.S. Open and the Masters in the same year—and the first in more than thirty years. After winning at a public course on Long Island, he was dubbed "the people's champ."

# CARTER G.
# WOODSON

1875–1950

**E**ach February millions of African Americans and other citizens of the United States celebrate African American History Month. Carter Godwin Woodson was the initiator of this commemoration.

Woodson was born on a farm in New Canton, Virginia, in 1875. His mother, a former enslaved person, knew how to read and write, and taught her nine children as much as she knew. However, it was Woodson's two uncles, who had been educated by the Bureau of Freedmen, Refugees, and Abandoned Lands, who inspired him to consider higher training. Moving from New Canton to Huntington, West Virginia, in 1892, Woodson worked in the coal mines in order to make a living, but he had a burning desire to have a better education. Thus, at the age of twenty he entered Frederick Douglass High School.

Woodson worked in the coal mines while attending school, completing the four-year high school curriculum in two years. A high school diploma was his ticket out of the coal mines and into the teaching profession. He began teaching at Winona, West Virginia. He was such a successful teacher that he was hired in 1901 as a teacher at his former high school, where he later became principal. Knowing that he did not have enough education to achieve the high goals he had set for himself, Woodson enrolled at Berea College in Kentucky. The college had become well-known as one of the schools in the South that would accept African American students. Berea was an integrated college set up by abolitionists in the nineteenth century, but it was perfect for Woodson because he could attend classes during summer vacation. He graduated from Berea College in 1903.

Soon after graduating from Berea, Woodson took a job with the United States War Department to teach English in the Philippines. While teaching in the Philippines, Woodson studied the Spanish language through a correspondence course from the University of Chicago. After leaving Asia, he traveled through Europe and when he got back to the United States in 1907, he enrolled at the University of Chicago where he received a B.A. degree and an M.A. degree in European History. Woodson was able to complete the two degrees in less than two years. He then matriculated in history at Harvard University, where he worked on his doctoral degree. In 1909 he started teaching at Dunbar High School in Washington, D.C. After Woodson received his Ph.D. in 1912, becoming only the second African American to earn a Harvard doctorate degree in history, he set about making history himself.

It did not take Carter G. Woodson long to found the Association for the Study of Negro Life and History in 1915. The organization Woodson started still exists, as the Association for the Study of Afro-American Life and History. According to Woodson, the association's objective was the publication of research about African Americans. Woodson also founded the *Journal of Negro History* (1916), the Associated Publishers (1921), and the *Negro History Bulletin* (1937). Woodson was a dynamic intellectual and he believed in his mission. Although he was unsuccessful in gaining wide foundation support from private sources, he built his legend on the strength of his own integrity, principle, and substance. To remain independent, Woodson did not associate his journal or organization with any college or foundation. His attempt was to rely on the support and participation of African American people.

Carter G. Woodson initiated Negro History Week in 1926 to celebrate and commemorate contributions made by African Americans. It was held during the second week in February, taking in the birthdays of Frederick Douglass, the great abolitionist, and

Abraham Lincoln. Woodson also wrote and distributed kits with photographs, charts, quizzes, and brief histories to teach people how to celebrate the week. During the 1960s the Association for the Study of African American Life and History renamed and extended Negro History Week to be African American History Month.

The intellectual and scholarly career of Woodson was extraordinary given that, with all his training and worldly experience, he could have used his talents for some other purpose but chose to spend his entire professional life devoted to researching and publicizing the history of his people. He did this without financial or moral support from the highest academic, scholarly, or philanthropic institutions in America. Yet he was prolific as a writer, authoring nineteen books on African and African American history.

Carter G. Woodson might be called the Shaka of African American history in the sense that he blazed new trails in attacking the enemies of the African American people. In Woodson's mind the racist ideas of African American inferiority were fed by the notion that there were no achievements by African Americans. He sought to shatter these ideas by demonstrating that Africans and African Americans had an extensive history. With his knowledge of Spanish, he was able to compare the conditions of Africans in Central and South America with those in North America. Furthermore, he sought to dispel the idea that the enslavement of Africans was good for African people. Indeed, in his most famous book, *The Mis-Education of the Negro*, he contends that African American education was creating a population that believed the myths of black inferiority. In Woodson's own words, "If a race has no history, if it has no worthwhile tradition, it becomes a negligible factor in the thought of the world, and it stands in danger of being exterminated."

Woodson died in 1950.

# RICHARD
# WRIGHT
1908–1960

Richard Wright was born in 1908 in Roxie, Mississippi, near Natchez. He grew up in an environment where white supremacy was the principal doctrine of all institutions. His mother was a schoolteacher and his father, a farmer. When his father abandoned the family in 1914, young Richard and his brother were moved to Memphis, where his mother took domestic jobs. No longer able to teach in Memphis or to find permanent employment, his mother moved the family to rural Arkansas.

Probably because of the tremendous burden on her, Richard's mother suffered a stroke, and he and his brother had to return to Mississippi to live with their grandmother. She was a fundamentalist in religion and did not approve of his desire to write poems and stories. She wanted him to learn to farm. Richard Wright looked for every opportunity to leave the South after that time. He did not see his future in the cotton fields of Mississippi. Consequently, as soon as he finished the ninth grade he left Mississippi, never to return for any extended period of time. In addition to his hatred of racism and the South, Wright also disdained the hypocrisy in religion.

While in Chicago, Richard Wright read the works of the most important American and European writers as a way to educate himself in literature. He also made his way through the economic pitfalls of Chicago in the late 1920s and early 1930s, when he found a job at the post office.

Once Wright had secured a job, he ventured out to meetings

of socialist organizations and found a community in the Communist Party. His early writings were poems and short stories in leftist newspapers. Using the talents he had developed by writing regularly for the Communists, Wright wrote travel guides for the Federal Writers' Project. He was committed by then to writing, and moving between Chicago and Harlem gave him a sense of the possibilities for a black writer. Some of his first stories were about racism and the stupidity of white supremacy. The novel *Lawd Today*, published posthumously in 1963, contained much of what he had written in the 1930s and 1940s.

It is generally accepted that Wright's debut into the major publishing world was the publication of *Uncle Tom's Children*, a collection of crude novellas, in 1938. He used his childhood in Mississippi, Arkansas, and Tennessee as the foundation for many of those stories.

The next few years saw Wright reach heights never before attained by African American literary figures. His next novel, *Native Son* (1940), was powerful. It is a story built on an accidental killing of a white woman by the main character, Bigger. The idea behind this work is that society is as guilty as Bigger. Wright's theme is that society had created the conditions that caused Bigger's behavior in the killing of the white woman. Bigger felt freedom for the first time in his life when he was engaged in the act of killing the woman. The editors moderated the original manuscript, believing that it would offend most white readers if published without modifications. The original version was not published until 1992, long after Wright's death. The book brought Wright immediate literary and commercial success. It was a best-seller, a Book-of-the-Month Club selection, and was staged on Broadway in a production by Orson Welles.

Either because of the success of his novel or the evolution of his thought, Wright was invited to write an article about communism. Thus, in 1944 he wrote an essay for the *Atlantic Monthly*, entitled "I Tried to Be a Communist," that publicly explained for the first time how he was disillusioned by the Communist Party. He continued to write about the condition of the American society in his novel, *Black Boy* (1945), the autobiography of his youth in the South. Like his previous works, *Black Boy* was a powerful account of life under the doctrine of white supremacy.

When Wright visited Paris in the late 1940s at the invitation of Gertrude Stein, an American writer living in Paris at the time, he was stunned by the audience he had gained in Europe. The French responded with enthusiasm to his presence and his work. He met the leading French writers, including the philosophers Jean-Paul Sartre and Simone de Beauvoir. Wright decided that he wanted to live in Paris because he did not like the idea that America saw him only as a "great black writer"; he preferred the French recognition of his talents as a great writer. He soon moved with his second wife and young daughter to Paris.

In France, Wright was active, writing three more novels. None of these books was well received in the United States. The Americans tended to see him as an expatriate who had become more French than American in his imagination. Many critics saw him as being overly intellectual, perhaps the influence of the existentialists on his literary style. His corpus while in Paris included the books *The Outsider* (1953), *Savage Holiday* (1954), and *The Long Dream* (1958); a collection of stories, *Eight Men* (1961); the nonfiction works *Black Power* (1954), *The Color Curtain* (1956), *Pagan Spain* (1957), *White Man, Listen!* (1957); and an autobiography, *American Hunger* (1977). Wright also wrote articles on colonialism in Africa. Just before his death in Paris in 1960, Wright had become an international spokesperson for Pan-Africanism and African liberation.

# MALCOLM
# X

## 1925–1965

**M**alcolm X was born Malcolm Little in Omaha, Nebraska, in 1925. Before he died in 1965 he again changed his name, to El Hajj Malik El Shabazz. He was the son of Louise and Earl Little, who was a Baptist preacher and leader of Marcus Garvey's Universal Negro Improvement Association. Malcolm, along with his siblings, was educated in Omaha and in Lansing, Michigan. Young Malcolm experienced some traumatic racist events during his early life. Klansmen burned his family's home in Lansing. Soon thereafter, Earl Little, Malcolm's father, was killed under mysterious circumstances. The white-dominated welfare agencies split up the children and eventually committed Louise Little, Malcolm's mother, to a state mental institution. This was a tragic turn of events for a family that had begun with such promise, because the father had been a strong ethical influence. Soon Malcolm was forced to live in a detention home run by a person who was hostile to African American children. The detention home authorities grew tired of Malcolm's discussions about race and racism.

Malcolm X was clearly the most authentic voice of African American transformation during the 1960s. Nothing in his life was unclear when it came to his commitment for the liberation and freedom of African Americans. He was not confused, nor did he participate in the rhetoric of indirection. A part of his strength and charisma was that he said what he meant and his audiences believed that he meant what he said. He was thirty-nine years old when he was assassinated in a Harlem auditorium as he gave a speech.

How did Malcolm X become the most revolutionary African American icon of the twentieth century? Clearly he was destined to overcome the obstacles that confronted his family and himself at an early age. When he left school in Lansing to go live with his sister Ella in Boston, he had already missed several years of close parental supervision. Consequently, the death of his father and the institutionalization of his mother left Malcolm and his siblings with little familial guidance. Thus, the big city of Boston was to be an education for him. He discovered the fast life, the nightclubs, the petty street criminals, and the dance craze called the Lindy Hop.

The period of the Second World War saw powerful forces in the African American community emerging to demand basic civil rights. Malcolm was busy learning the life of the hipsters while race riots were breaking out in major American cities. The early 1940s saw a politically attuned black leadership hoping to link the fight against fascism with the struggle against racist oppression. Malcolm wanted no part of either the world war or the rising militancy in the African American community.

By the time he was eighteen years old he had made his way to Harlem, the "Mecca of the Black World." Using the street knowledge and techniques he had learned in Boston, Malcolm supported himself with drug dealing, pimping, gambling, and petty theft. When he was arrested in 1946 for burglary, and sentenced to ten years in prison, he was rescued from a life of crime.

The conditions in prison, and particularly the lives of black men in prison, sent Malcolm to the libraries. Furthermore, he began an intensive examination of his own lifestyle with the assistance of Nation of Islam preachers. He was eager to learn African American history and culture because he felt that was the only way to understand the situation in America. He was introduced to the teachings of the Honorable Elijah Muhammad, the leader of the Nation of Islam. Muhammad, who had been born Elijah Poole, was a follower of Wallace D. Fard, the founder of the Lost and Found Nation. Malcolm found that these teachings explained to him many of the contradictions he had seen in his own life, and most importantly, they explained the behavior of the white man toward blacks. This awareness was followed with a conversion to Islam as a faith, a belief in the Koran, and an avid interest in all types of black nationalist literature.

Once he had learned the ideology and the arguments Malcolm became one of the most effective orators for the Nation of Islam in prison. Malcolm was the leading debater on the prison team that debated the Massachusetts Institute of Technology. The prisoners were granted the win over the MIT team and later Malcolm would use his ability to speak effectively as his vehicle for establishing his own persona. He came out of prison with a new attitude. He knew that he was a black man, an African, and so he could no longer carry the white man's name. He changed his name from Malcolm Little to Malcolm X, the sign of the unknown because no black person in America really knows his or her name.

Malcolm rose quickly in the Nation of Islam. He became a devoted votary of the teachings of the Honorable Elijah Muhammad and was given the charge to minister to several mosques. He was minister at the Harlem Temple, No. 7, in 1954 when the *Brown* v. *Board of Education* decision was handed down. He later preached for the Detroit and Philadelphia mosques. Already by the late 1950s, Malcolm was making a reputation for himself as the most ardent recruiter for the Nation of Islam. The organization, which had been relatively moribund prior to Malcolm's ministry, took off in membership with his preaching and lecturing.

His rise to fame came through the thoroughness of his debating techniques and the various television appearances that he made on behalf of the Nation of Islam. He also helped to set up the nationally distributed newspaper *Muhammad Speaks*, which created a sensation in the African American community. Malcolm's criticism of the American government and his pointed barbs at the black leaders who did not understand the full extent of racism and the doctrine of white supremacy earned him a place in the hearts of the black community.

Malcolm X loved the Honorable Elijah Muhammad as the person who taught him his true identity. His appreciation led him to see the Honorable Elijah as almost infallible. The teachings of the great minister made Malcolm a devotee of the highest level. He believed in the moral values and subscribed to the attitudes of the Nation of Islam. Indeed, he was responsible for creating some of those attitudes himself.

As his own reputation grew, Malcolm X was called upon to participate in more activities in the African American community. This engagement with the larger community caused him to question the Muslim ban on politics. He believed that it was necessary to be involved in the political arena in some way. By 1962 he was becoming an independent force to be reckoned with in the political and social arena. He was Pan-Africanist, nationalist, and anticolonialist. Malcolm's love for Africa, probably something he inherited from his father, although he was certainly imbued with enough cultural esteem from the Nation of Islam, meant that he would travel to the continent. And he did travel to Egypt, Sudan, Nigeria, and Ghana in 1959. The trip was important to him because it demonstrated to him how closely allied the African American people were with the African masses. Five years later, when he traveled to Saudi Arabia for the Islamic hajj to Mecca, he was prepared for the complexity of international politics and power. The 1964 trip is talked about more than the 1959 trip because of Malcolm's own declaration about seeing so many different kinds of Muslims.

The tension between the public Malcolm and the more reserved Elijah became visible when Elijah Muhammad silenced him after he remarked that the killing of President Kennedy was just a case of "the chickens coming home to roost." Widely misunderstood, Malcolm tried to make it clear that when the government of the United States fails to protect its black citizens, it cannot protect the president, either.

Rumors that Malcolm had been targeted for assassination by his own organization moved him to announce his resignation on March 8, 1964. He immediately created the Muslim Mosque, Inc., a group devoted to working for civil rights. Later that year he made his pilgrimage to Mecca and when he returned he took the name El Hajj Malik El Shabazz. Now as a practitioner of Sunni Islam, he also found the "true brotherhood" of all human beings. While still claiming to be a black nationalist, he could no longer preach that all whites were devils. In the summer of 1964 he created the Organization of Afro-American Unity. The organization was a vehicle to give Malcolm more freedom to advocate for independent black schools, centers, and programs. When he was gunned down in 1965 he was preparing to submit to the United Nations a petition that showed how extensively the United States had violated the rights of African Americans.

While Malcolm's death ended his own personal activity, since his death he has become an institutionalized icon for resistance in the African American community. More than anything or anyone else it has been the ordinary people who have elevated Malcolm to his station as one of the greatest African Americans. Rap musicians, filmmakers, bookstores, vendors, and Afrocentric scholars have all advanced the Malcolmian ethos. Its remarkable vitality is due to the selflessness of Malcolm's quest for human equality.

# A FINAL WORD

The individuals presented in *100 Greatest African Americans* represent bold innovators, artistic and intellectual geniuses, and intrepid adventurers whose missions have been to advance liberation. Fearless men and women, whose only ambition has been to live free, have created for themselves impeccable records of achievement in African American history. They have often exercised their wills in a form of gallantry that has seen them place freedom above life itself. These are not people of ordinary accomplishment, but those who have been willing to challenge the status quo, to engage the established authorities, and to risk their positions or their lives in the quest for what is right.

One quality that appears in the lives of each individual is tenacity. They have demonstrated an extraordinary ability for consistency in the quest for freedom, justice, and equality. Whatever the perils to their persons or positions, the 100 greatest have set standards for generations to come. In my desire to cite the salient characteristics of these individuals, I have concentrated on the talents, abilities, and interests that mark them as African American greats. This is not a book, for example, about African Americans who are great only in the context of business, education, the military, science, or art, but about those who have risen above the mundane concerns of everyday existence to stretch our imaginations with the possibilities. If they are in any of the common fields of human endeavor it is not so much, from what I have seen, the endeavor that defined them, but rather their spirit that created an entirely new way to view the field, whether athletics, art, or literature. They have been outstanding and remarkable examples of selfless service and devoted social purpose; these are the hallmarks of African American heroes. Indeed, to be great, as defined by these lives, is to be involved in the relentless pursuit of freedom and justice.

Throughout African American history, an endless number of individuals have engaged in the common struggle against racism and discrimination in order to bring about equality and freedom. Courage has appeared and reappeared in local and national heroes, such Daisy Bates, Bobby Seale, Fred Shuttlesworth, Cecil Moore, Al Sharpton, or Alton Maddox, who, by virtue of their bitter opposition to the exploitation of the masses, discrimination in the workplace, and injustice of the legal system, have become models of resistance. Whenever the times call for a support of human dignity or for the redress of wrongs, there will be African Americans ready to make personal commitments to the collective good of the society.

# BIBLIOGRAPHY

Adams, Barbara. *Master Teacher: John Henrik Clarke, The Early Years*. New York: A & B Books, 2000.

Adams, Russell L. *Great Negroes: Past and Present*. Chicago: Afro-Am Publishing, 1984.

Allen, Richard. *The Life Experience & Gospel Labors of Rt. Rev. Richard Allen: The Rise and Progress of the African Methodist Episcopal Church in the United States*. Philadelphia: Lee and Yeocum, 1888.

Anderson, Jervis. *A. Philip Randolph: A Biographical Portrait*. Berkeley: University of California Press, 1987.

Angell, Stephan. *Bishop Henry McNeal Turner & African American Religion in the South*. Knoxville: University of Tennessee Press, 1972.

Asante, Molefi Kete. *African American History: A Journey of Liberation*. Saddlebrook, N.J.: Peoples Publishing, 2001.

Asante, Molefi, and Mark Mattson. *Historical and Cultural Atlas of African Americans*. New York: Simon & Schuster, 1999.

Balfour, Lawrence. *The Evidence of Things Not Said: James Baldwin & The Promise of American Democracy*. Ithaca: Cornell University Press, 2001.

Bennett, Lerone. *What Manner of Man: A Biography of Martin Luther King Jr.* Chicago: Johnson Publishing, 1968.

Bolden, B. J. *Urban Rage Bronzeville: Social Commentary in the Poetry of Gwendolyn Brooks 1945–1960*. Chicago: Third World Press, 1999.

Bontemps, Arna. *Personals*. Detroit: Broadside Press, 1963.

Bowser, Pearl. *Writing Himself into History: Oscar Micheaux, His Silent Films & His Audience* . New Brunswick: Rutgers University Press, 2000.

Cannon, Poppy. *A Gentle Knight: My Husband, Walter White*. New York: Rinehart, 1966.

Chisholm, Shirley. *Unbought & Unbossed*. New York: Houghton Mifflin, 1970.

Clark, Kenneth Bancroft. *Dark Ghetto: Dilemma of Social Power*. New York: University Press of New England, 1989.

Cole, Bill. *John Coltrane*. New York: DaCapo Press, 1993.

Conyers, James L. ed. *Carter G. Woodson: A Historical Reader*. New York: Garland Press, 2000.

Curley, Edmund F. *Crispus Attucks: The First to Death*. Philadelphia: Dorrance & Company, 1973.

Cronon, Edmund David. *Black Moses: The Story of Marcus Garvey and the Universal Negro Improvement Association*. Madison: University of Wisconsin Press, 1969.

Davis, Benjamin, Jr. *Benjamin O. Davis Jr., American: An Autobiography*. Washington, D.C.: Smithsonian Institute Press, 2000.

Delany, Martin R. *Origins of Races & Color: With an Archeological Compendium of Ethiopian and Egyptian Civilization*. Baltimore: Black Classic Press, 1994.

Dunham, Katherine. *A Touch of Innocence: Memoir of Childhood*. Chicago: University of Chicago Press, 1994.

Ellington, Duke. *Music is My Mistress*. New York: DaCapo Press, 1976.

Fox, Stephan R. *The Guardian of Boston: William Monroe Trotter*. New York: Scribner, 1971.

Franklin, John Hope. *Runaway Slaves*. New York: Oxford University Press, 2000.

———. *From Slavery to Freedom: A History of African Americans*. New York: McGraw-Hill Higher Education, 1999.

George, Carol V. R. *Segregated Sabbath: Richard Allen and The Rise of Independent Black Churches 1760–1840*. New York: Oxford University Press, 1973.

Graham, Shirley. *Benjamin Banneker*. Trenton, N.J.: Africa World Press, 1995.

———. *Jean Baptiste DuSable: Founder of Chicago*. Trenton, N.J.: Africa World Press, 1995.

Gray, Fred D. *Preacher, Attorney, Politician & Lawyer for Rosa Parks*. Montgomery, Ala.: Black Belt Press, 1999.

Greenfield, Eloise. *Mary McLeod Bethune*. New York: Thomas Y. Crowell, 1973.

Hansberry, Lorraine. *To Be Young, Gifted and Black*. New York: New American Library, 1987.

Haygood, Wil. *King of the Cats: The Life and Times of Adam Clayton Powell Jr*. New York: Houghton Mifflin, 1994.

Henry, Charles. *Ralph Bunche: Model Negro or American Other*. New York: New York University Press, 1994.

Hutchinson Ofari, Earl. *Let Your Motto Be Resistance: The Life and Thought of Henry Highland Garnett*. Boston: Beacon Press, 1972.

Johnston, Brenda. *Between the Devil and the Sea: The Life of James Forten*. New York: Harcourt, 1974.

Just, Ernest Everett. *The Biology of the Cell Surface*. New York: Garland Publishing, 1988.

Karenga, Maulana. *Introduction to Black Studies*. Los Angeles: University of Sankore Press, 2001.

Keiler, Allan. *Marian Anderson: A Singer's Journey: The First Comprehensive Biography*. New York: Simon & Schuster, 2000.

Kunjufu, Jawanza, Erica Myles, and Nichelle Wilson. *Great Negroes: Past and Present*. Chicago: African American Images, 1999.

Lanning, Michael, Lee. *The African-American Soldier: From Crispus Attucks to Colin Powell*. Secaucus, N.J.: Carol Publishing Group, 1997.

Lee, Chano Kai. *For Freedom's Sake: The Life of Fannie Lou Hamer*. Urbana: University of Illinois Press, 2000.

Lewis, David L. *W. E. B. Du Bois: The Fight for Equality and the American Century 1919–1963*. New York: Henry Holt, 2000.

Locke, Alain. *The New Negro*. New York: Scribner, 1997.

Manning, Kenneth R. *Black Apollo of Science: The Life of Ernest Just*. New York: Oxford University Press, 1983.

Marshall, Herbert. *Ida Aldridge: Negro Tragedian*. Washington, D.C.: Howard University Press, 1994.

Martin, Tony, ed. *Message to the People: The Course of African Philosophy by Marcus Garvey*. Wellesley, Mass.: Majority Press, 1986.

Mason, Julian D., ed. *The Poems of Phillis Wheatley*. Chapel Hill: University of North Carolina Press, 1989.

Mays, Benjamin E. *Born to Rebel: An Autobiography*. Athens: University of Georgia Press, 1987.

McFeely, William S. *Frederick Douglass*. New York: W. W. Norton, 1991.

McMurry, Linda O. *George Washington Carver: Scientist and Symbol*. New York: Oxford University Press, 1989.

Means, Howard. *Colin Powell: Soldier Statesman/Statesman Soldier*. New York: Ballantine Books, 1993.

Millender, Dharathula H. *Crispus Attucks: Black Leader of Colonial Patriots*. New York: Simon & Schuster, 1982.

Miller, Floyd. *Ahdoolo! The Biography of Matthew A. Henson*. New York: Dutton, 1963.

Moore, Eva. *The Story of George Washington Carver*. New York: Scholastic, 1985.

Myers, Walter Dean. *The Greatest: Muhammad Ali*. New York: Scholastic, 2000.

Painter, Nell Irvin. *Sojourner Truth: A Life, A Symbol*. New York: W. W. Norton, 1996.

Patton, Sharon F. *Memory and Metaphor: The Work of Romare Bearden 1940–1987*. New York: Oxford University Press, 1991.

Petry, Ann. *Harriet Tubman: Conductor on the Underground Railroad*. New York: Harper Trophy, 1996.

Rampersad, Arnold. *Days of Grace: A Memoir of Arthur Ashe*. New York: Random House, 1994.

———. *The Collected Poems of Langston Hughes*. New York: Vintage Books, 1994.

Rowland, Della. *Martin Luther King Jr.: The Dream of Peaceful Revolution*. New York: Silver Burdett, 1990.

Sally, Columbus. *The Black 100*. Secaucus, N.J.: Citadel Press, 1999.

Sinnette, Elinor Des Verney. *Arthur Alfonso Schomburg: Black Bibliophile & Collector*. Detroit: Wayne State University Press, 1989.

Spain, Valerie. *Meet Maya Angelou*. New York: Random House, 1994.

Sterling, Philip, and Rayford Logan. *Four Took Freedom: The Lives of Harriet Tubman, Fredrick Douglass, Robert Smalls, and Blanche K. Bruce*. Garden City, N.Y.: Doubleday, 1967.

Terrell, Mary Church. *A Colored Woman in a White World*. Washngton, D.C.: Ransdell, 1940.

Thomas, J. C. *Chasin' the Train: The Music and Mystique of John Coltrane*. New York: DaCapo Press, 1976.

Trice, Linda. *Charles Drew: Pioneer of Blood Plasma*. New York: McGraw-Hill Professional Book Group, 1999.

Urquhart, Brian. *Ralph Bunche: An American Life*. New York: Norton, 1998.

Walker, David. *David Walker's Appeal, in Four Articles; Together with a Preamble to the Coloured Citizens of the World, but in Particularly and very Expressly to those of the United States*. New York: Hill and Wang, 1995.

Washington, Booker T. *Up from Slavery*. New York: Signet Classic, 2000

Wheeler, Lonnie. *I Had A Hammer: The Hank Aaron Story*. New York: HarperCollins, 1992.

Wilson, Jeremiah. *Alexander Crummell: A Study of Civilization and Discontent*. New York: New York University Press, 1989.

Williams, Juan. *Thurgood Marshall: American Revolutionary*. New York: Times Books, 2000.

Wilson, Sondra Katherine. *Along This Way: The Autobiography*. New York: DaCapo Press, 2000.

———. *In Search of Democracy: The NAACP Writings of James Weldon Johnson, Walter White and Roy Wilkens*. New York: Oxford University Press, 1999.

Woodson, Carter G. *The Mis-Education of the Negro*. Trenton, N.J.: Africa World Press, 1990.

Wright, Richard. *Native Son*. New York: HarperCollins, 1989.

X, Malcolm. *The Autobiography of Malcolm X*. Edited by Alex Haley. New York: Grove Press, 1965.